TM

References for the Rest of Us!™

BUSINESS AND GENERAL REFERENCE BOOK SERIES FROM IDG

D0509685

Do you find that traditional reference books are overloaded with technical details and advice you'll never use? Do you postpone important life decisions because you just don't want to deal with them? Then our ...*For Dummies*™ business and general reference book series is for you.

...*For Dummies* business and general reference books are written for those frustrated and hard-working souls who know they aren't dumb, but find that the myriad of personal and business issues and the accompanying horror stories make them feel helpless. ...*For Dummies* books use a lighthearted approach, a down-to-earth style, and even cartoons and humorous icons to diffuse fears and build confidence. Lighthearted but not lightweight, these books are perfect survival guides to solve your everyday personal and business problems.

Already, millions of satisfied readers agree. They have made ...*For Dummies* the #1 introductory level computer book series and a best-selling business book series. They have written asking for more. So, if you're looking for the best and easiest way to learn about business and other general reference topics, look to ...*For Dummies* to give you a helping hand.

IDG BOOKS WORLDWIDE
TM

5/97

COLLEGE
PLANNING
FOR
DUMMIES™
2ND EDITION

COLLEGE PLANNING FOR DUMMIES™
2ND EDITION

by Pat Ordovensky

IDG Books Worldwide, Inc.
An International Data Group Company

Foster City, CA ♦ Chicago, IL ♦ Indianapolis, IN ♦ Southlake, TX

College Planning For Dummies™, 2nd Edition

Published by
IDG Books Worldwide, Inc.
An International Data Group Company
919 E. Hillsdale Blvd.
Suite 400
Foster City, CA 94404
www.idgbooks.com (IDG Books Worldwide Web site)
www.dummies.com (Dummies Press Web site)

Library of Congress Catalog Card No.: 97-72423

ISBN: 0-7645-5048-9

Printed in the United States of America

10 9 8 7 6 5 4 3 2

2E/RW/RQ/ZX/IN

Distributed in the United States by IDG Books Worldwide, Inc.

Distributed by Macmillan Canada for Canada; by Transworld Publishers Limited in the United Kingdom; by IDG Norge Books for Norway; by IDG Sweden Books for Sweden; by Woodslane Pty. Ltd. for Australia; by Woodslane Enterprises Ltd. for New Zealand; by Longman Singapore Publishers Ltd. for Singapore, Malaysia, Thailand, and Indonesia; by Simron Pty. Ltd. for South Africa; by Toppan Company Ltd. for Japan; by Distribuidora Cuspide for Argentina; by Livraria Cultura for Brazil; by Ediciencia S.A. for Ecuador; by Addison-Wesley Publishing Company for Korea; by Ediciones ZETA S.C.R. Ltda. for Peru; by WS Computer Publishing Corporation, Inc., for the Philippines; by Unalis Corporation for Taiwan; by Contemporanea de Ediciones for Venezuela; by Computer Book & Magazine Store for Puerto Rico; by Express Computer Distributors for the Caribbean and West Indies. Authorized Sales Agent: Anthony Rudkin Associates for the Middle East and North Africa.

For general information on IDG Books Worldwide's books in the U.S., please call our Consumer Customer Service department at 800-762-2974. For reseller information, including discounts and premium sales, please call our Reseller Customer Service department at 800-434-3422.

For information on where to purchase IDG Books Worldwide's books outside the U.S., please contact our International Sales department at 415-655-3200 or fax 415-655-3295.

For information on foreign language translations, please contact our Foreign & Subsidiary Rights department at 415-655-3021 or fax 415-655-3281.

For sales inquiries and special prices for bulk quantities, please contact our Sales department at 415-655-3200 or write to the address above.

For information on using IDG Books Worldwide's books in the classroom or for ordering examination copies, please contact our Educational Sales department at 800-434-2086 or fax 817-251-8174.

For press review copies, author interviews, or other publicity information, please contact our Public Relations department at 415-655-3000 or fax 415-655-3299.

For authorization to photocopy items for corporate, personal, or educational use, please contact Copyright Clearance Center, 222 Rosewood Drive, Danvers, MA 01923, or fax 508-750-4470.

is a trademark under exclusive license to IDG Books Worldwide, Inc., from International Data Group, Inc.

About the Author

Pat Ordovensky has been dealing with college officials, and picking their brains about how they do their jobs, since he was a college student. He spent those student days in an idyllic rural environment called Ohio University (not to be confused with Ohio State) where he dealt with deans and presidents as editor of a newspaper called the *Ohio University Post*. Both the university and the *Post* have become stronger institutions since he left. (He says his kids are "Class Z legacies." When the alumni office asks for money, he gives the minimum necessary to get his name on the donors' list.)

The years between Ohio University and 1980 are a dark period in Ordovensky's career. All he will say about that time is that he's a "recovering editor."

Ordovensky became a serious student of the college admission and financial aid processes during the 13 years (1980-92) he was an education writer for *USA Today* and its sibling organization, Gannett News Service. During those years, he interviewed hundreds of admission and financial aid officials, attended their conventions, learned their language, and sat in on their committee deliberations. In 1988, he founded *USA Today's* annual College Admission/Financial Aid Hotline. For three days every October, more than 4,000 students and parents get questions answered by hotline experts who volunteer to answer the phones.

Ordovensky says a highlight of his career came in 1992 when the College Board invited him to a convention of admission officials — from Harvard's Dean Richard Fitzsimmons down — and asked him to speak at the concluding session about what he learned from the meetings. He recalls that speech with the words, "You think this book is irreverent?" Since 1992, Ordovensky has been a freelance writer based in Sarasota, Florida. He still coordinates *USA Today's* annual hotline and the All-USA Academic Team programs that honor outstanding college and high school students. He has written three other books on getting into college and paying for it: *Opening College Doors* (co-authored with Robert Thornton), *USA Today's Getting Into College,* and *USA Today's Financial Aid for College.*

He insists some of his best friends are college admission officials even though he makes fun of the way they talk.

ABOUT IDG BOOKS WORLDWIDE

Welcome to the world of IDG Books Worldwide.

IDG Books Worldwide, Inc., is a subsidiary of International Data Group, the world's largest publisher of computer-related information and the leading global provider of information services on information technology. IDG was founded more than 25 years ago and now employs more than 8,500 people worldwide. IDG publishes more than 275 computer publications in over 75 countries (see listing below). More than 60 million people read one or more IDG publications each month.

Launched in 1990, IDG Books Worldwide is today the #1 publisher of best-selling computer books in the United States. We are proud to have received eight awards from the Computer Press Association in recognition of editorial excellence and three from *Computer Currents'* First Annual Readers' Choice Awards. Our best-selling *...For Dummies*® series has more than 30 million copies in print with translations in 30 languages. IDG Books Worldwide, through a joint venture with IDG's Hi-Tech Beijing, became the first U.S. publisher to publish a computer book in the People's Republic of China. In record time, IDG Books Worldwide has become the first choice for millions of readers around the world who want to learn how to better manage their businesses.

Our mission is simple: Every one of our books is designed to bring extra value and skill-building instructions to the reader. Our books are written by experts who understand and care about our readers. The knowledge base of our editorial staff comes from years of experience in publishing, education, and journalism — experience we use to produce books for the '90s. In short, we care about books, so we attract the best people. We devote special attention to details such as audience, interior design, use of icons, and illustrations. And because we use an efficient process of authoring, editing, and desktop publishing our books electronically, we can spend more time ensuring superior content and spend less time on the technicalities of making books.

You can count on our commitment to deliver high-quality books at competitive prices on topics you want to read about. At IDG Books Worldwide, we continue in the IDG tradition of delivering quality for more than 25 years. You'll find no better book on a subject than one from IDG Books Worldwide.

IDG BOOKS WORLDWIDE

John Kilcullen
John Kilcullen
CEO
IDG Books Worldwide, Inc.

Steven Berkowitz
Steven Berkowitz
President and Publisher
IDG Books Worldwide, Inc.

VIII WINNER

Eighth Annual Computer Press Awards ≥ 1992

IX WINNER

Ninth Annual Computer Press Awards ≥ 1993

X WINNER

Tenth Annual Computer Press Awards ≥ 1994

XI WINNER

Eleventh Annual Computer Press Awards ≥ 1995

Dedication

To Taryn, Daniel, Hannah, Kylie, and Mary Joy: The next generation that needs this book's advice. May it serve them well.

Author's Acknowledgments

Thousands of people, whether they know it or not, helped me write this book. Carol Halstead is one. Carol is a New York City public relations person whose clients are colleges. Over lunch one day in 1988, she came up with the radical idea of inviting college admission and financial aid experts into a little room, equipping the room with phones, and publishing the phones' toll-free numbers in a national newspaper. It was such a good idea that it worked. Every October since then, more than 100 experts gather at *USA Today*'s Virginia headquarters to answer questions from callers across the land on the College Admission/Financial Aid Hotline. From those experts, I learned much of the stuff I share with you in these pages. And the 4,000-plus who call each year also helped. Without their questions, there would be no answers.

Special thanks must go to the college officials who, before and since the hotline began, have allowed me as an education writer to visit their offices, talk to their staffs, and listen while they make decisions. They include Lee Stetson at Penn, Cliff Sjogren (then at Michigan), Ted O'Neill at the University of Chicago, Ron Pomona, and others I've probably forgotten. The ever-candid Barry McCarty at Lafayette College has taught me more than anyone else about the nuances of giving away money. And Rob Thornton, a vice president at Teikyo Post University with whom I collaborated on an earlier book, gave me valuable insight into the mind of a college admission officer — which he once was.

Then there's Kathy Welton, a high-level something at IDG Books, who read about the *USA Today* hotline and asked the obvious question: "If 4,000 people a year call with questions, how many will buy a book with answers?" She's about to find out.

Now to keep my editors happy, I will conclude this expression of gratitude with a list. IDG editors love lists. They enjoy putting little check marks beside each item in a list because they think check marks make lists more attractive. If you like the check marks, you and I both thank IDG editors.

And I also sincerely thank (check marks, please):

✔ Richard Smolka, a professor emeritus at American University, who years ago taught me the art of asking irreverent questions

✔ The late George Starr Lasher, a professor emeritus at Ohio University, who years ago taught me the art of communicating in concise written English. (Sadly for all of us, Smolka's and Lasher's forms are rapidly disappearing.)

✔ Bob Dubill, executive editor at *USA Today,* who never met a good idea he didn't like and, once he meets one, won't rest until he makes it happen.

✔ Jim Walters and Eleanor Morris at the University of North Carolina-Chapel Hill, Robin Famiglietti at Eckerd College, Ed Irish at William & Mary, Nancy Church at Sweet Briar, Charlie Deacon at Georgetown, Fred Hargadon at Princeton, Gary Ripple at Lafayette, John Klockentager at Buena Vista College, Dick Steele at Bowdoin, Worth David formerly of Yale, Bill Conley of Case Western Reserve, and Colonel Pierce Rushton at West Point, all of whom added to my knowledge over the years and should have been mentioned earlier.

✔ Jane Farley Ordovensky, a professor at University of Pacific and one of my five kids, who asks me irreverent questions.

And finally I must thank (stop the check marks now) my wife, Mary Ann, for happily forgetting the idea that when we moved to Florida I would work less and play more.

Publisher's Acknowledgments

We're proud of this book; please register your comments through our IDG Books Worldwide Online Registration Form located at: http://my2cents.dummies.com.

Some of the people who helped bring this book to market include the following:

Acquisitions, Development, and Editorial

Project Editor: Kelly Ewing

Acquisitions Editor: Mark Butler

Copy Editor: Michael Bolinger

Technical Editor: Ted O'Neill, University of Chicago

Editorial Manager: Seta K. Frantz

Editorial Assistant: Donna Love

Production

Project Coordinator: Regina D. Snyder

Layout and Graphics: Linda M. Boyer, Dominique DeFelice, Maridee V. Ennis, Angela F. Hunckler, Todd Klemme, Brent Savage, Deirdre Smith

Proofreaders: Henry Lazarek, Carrie Voorhis, Christine D. Berman, Michelle Croninger, Joel K. Draper, Rachel Garvey, Robert Springer, Karen York

Indexer: Steve Rath

Special Help: Colleen Rainsberger, Senior Project Editor

General and Administrative

IDG Books Worldwide, Inc.: John Kilcullen, CEO; Steven Berkowitz, President and Publisher

IDG Books Technology Publishing: Brenda McLaughlin, Senior Vice President and Group Publisher

Dummies Technology Press and Dummies Editorial: Diane Graves Steele, Vice President and Associate Publisher; Kristin A. Cocks, Editorial Director; Mary Bednarek, Acquisitions and Product Development Director

Dummies Trade Press: Kathleen A. Welton, Vice President and Publisher; Kevin Thornton, Acquisitions Manager

IDG Books Production for Dummies Press: Beth Jenkins, Production Director; Cindy L. Phipps, Manager of Project Coordination, Production Proofreading, and Indexing; Kathie S. Schutte, Supervisor of Page Layout; Shelley Lea, Supervisor of Graphics and Design; Debbie J. Gates, Production Systems Specialist; Robert Springer, Supervisor of Proofreading; Debbie Stailey, Special Projects Coordinator; Tony Augsburger, Supervisor of Reprints and Bluelines; Leslie Popplewell, Media Archive Coordinator

Dummies Packaging and Book Design: Patti Crane, Packaging Specialist; Lance Kayser, Packaging Assistant; Kavish + Kavish, Cover Design

♦

The publisher would like to give special thanks to Patrick J. McGovern, without whom this book would not have been possible.

♦

Contents at a Glance

Cartoons at a Glance

By Rich Tennant

page 9

page 113

page 41

page 233

page 155

page 267

Fax: 508-546-7747 • E-mail: the5wave@tiac.net

Table of Contents

Introduction

*W*elcome to *College Planning For Dummies,* 2nd Edition.

Getting into college — and finding the money to pay for it — is not a mystery, although some people like to make it seem mysterious. This book helps you understand exactly what you need to know so that you can play the game with confidence. It explains how you can find the college that's the best fit for you — or the student of your choice — convince the college that it wants you, and be able to afford it.

There's no mystery to it. No magic formula. Just a lot of what our grandparents used to call common sense.

About This Book

This book is organized so that you can pick it up and start reading anywhere. It will make sense no matter where you start. It's a reference book. It has 24 chapters, and each one discusses a specific part of the college planning process. If you'd like to read about filling out an application or applying for financial aid, look up the topic in the index, find the page for that chapter, and start reading. Each chapter covers one part of the process and is loaded with valuable nuggets. The chapter on visiting a college campus, for example, offers plain advice on:

- Setting up the visit
- The admission office interview
- The financial aid interview
- Getting information from students
- Staying overnight
- Your parents' role
- What to do when you get home

There's nothing to memorize. Read what you need, mark it for future reference, and get on with your life. Feel free to use that yellow highlighter — or whatever color you like — to identify the most valuable information and make it leap out in the future. This book doesn't mind being marked up. That's why it's here.

How to Use This Book

A novel, it's not. Just because you (or someone you know) paid good money for this book, don't feel obligated to read it from beginning to end. If you'd like to do it that way, fine. But it's just not necessary. Look for the parts that interest you — the areas of college planning where you're confused.

Check the table of contents for general titles or the index for specific topics that address your own areas of concern. Once you start reading, you'll soon realize that planning for college is a messy process, but you can figure it out.

I've said it before, and I'll say it again. Getting into college is no mystery. After 15 years of watching college officials work and listening to them explain in detail how they do their jobs, I've discovered that the process is actually very simple. I'm sharing that information with the person who needs it most: you.

Who Are You?

The word you appears in this book more often than any other word. (And I'm sure some wise guy will have a computer program count the yous to see whether I'm right.) This book is written for you and addressed to you. And you, in every case, are the student planning for college.

Of course, people other than students should, and no doubt will, use this book. Some of these people are mentioned in the next section. But the reason they're reading it is to help the student. So I'm asking them to remember that you are the person whose future is on the line, the student trying to decide where to spend four or more valuable years.

Who Should Read This Book?

This book is not just for the high school junior gearing up to take the SAT. It's for every student, of any age, who may one day go to college. And it's for any relative, or friend of such a student, who may want to help.

Fourth-graders

Yes, I said fourth-graders. The earlier you start thinking about college and planning for it, the easier it will be when the time comes. Suppose that you're a junior in high school right now. Think about this: If you knew in fourth grade what you know now about, say, how important an A in math is, you might have adjusted your fourth-grade attitude toward math.

Eighth-graders

Eighth grade is essentially a turning point. It's when you start making decisions that show up on your college application. That application is the picture of everything you've done in high school. And in eighth grade, you must decide what courses you'll take when you enter high school. You'll have an edge on all your friends.

High school students

High school students get the most from this book. This book helps guide you on the journey of finding a college, applying to it, and paying for it.

Mom and/or Dad

Talk about horror stories. I've heard too many terrible tales about parents and kids getting into shouting matches over choosing a college. The information in this book is for students and parents. So when crucial decisions are to be made, *College Planning For Dummies,* 2nd Edition helps make sure that all of you are on the same page.

If you're a student, make sure that all the adults — parents and others — who try to influence your college decisions take a look at this book. If you're a parent, hey, don't tell your kid what to do. Just hand your daughter or son this book and say, "Read this."

Grandparents

If you're a parent, you've probably wondered why your own mother never spent as much on you as she does on your kids. You're not alone. A department store clerk in a children's wear section that had a rack full of $165 jackets for two-year-olds was once asked who would spend $165 on a toddler's jacket. She replied, "Grandparents."

Yes, grandparents can be the most generous of human beings. And if they'd like to direct some of that generosity toward their grandchildren's education, this book offers advice on how it can best be done.

Adults thinking about college

If you're past the traditional college age but thinking about entering college, you've got lots of company. The over-25 crowd is the fastest-growing segment of the student population. There is no reason why you shouldn't plan just like the younger folks. Most of the advice in this book applies to students of all ages. The differences are even marked with an icon.

Anyone accepted to college

Congratulations! If you've been accepted by a college, prestigious or otherwise, you have figured out the process. Or at least you've successfully coped with it. By now you probably know everything this book says. But you're probably wondering what to do next. If so, check out Chapter 16.

Who Should Not Read This Book

It's not good business for authors to recommend that people not read their published advice. But face it, in this case, some people out there just don't need this book.

Anyone with a Ph.D.

If you've inhabited a college campus long enough to put Ph.D. after your name, you probably know more about how things are done than the rookies in the admission office who are doing them. Put this book down and move on to the important stuff.

College admission officers

Some of my best friends are college admission officers. Because I enjoy their company, I learned to speak their language. But they won't like this book because it's written in English. It even offers translations from their jargon, so you'll know what they're talking about. It will be tough for them to handle a book this size in plain, simple words. So it's best they not try. Besides, if they read this book, then they'll know everything you know.

How This Book Is Organized

This book has six major parts, each of which consists of chapters. Each chapter covers a certain topic and is split into sections that look at specific issues within the topic. That's how it's organized. How you read it is up to you. Pick a part, a chapter, a section, whatever, and just start reading. Any related information is cross-referenced in the text.

If you're just starting your search, confronting the vast sea of 3,500 colleges, and you don't know where to start, check out Chapters 1 and 2.

If you know where you're applying, but you're in a tizzy about making the best impression at the admission office, go to Chapters 9 and 10.

If you've heard horror stories from friends about the trauma of applying for financial aid, and you're ready to chuck the process because you can't figure it out, this book is here to help. Read Part IV, and you'll realize that your friends are telling horror stories because they didn't read this book.

Part I: Getting Ready

This part tells you what you need to know to start planning for college. And it looks at what you can do to become a more attractive college candidate when the time comes. The chapters in this part help you deal with the mass of available information and sort what you can use from what you don't need.

Part II: Finding the Right Colleges

How do you narrow your choice to three, four, or five colleges where you can thrive as a student and to which you'll apply? This part takes you on a stroll through the process from your early high school years until your decision is made.

Part III: Getting In

This part gives you the word on what colleges want in their applicants and how they score your application. It also includes advice on how you can make yourself as presentable as possible.

Part IV: Paying for College

These chapters offer plain, simple talk on how you can get your share of the billions of dollars available each year to help students pay college bills. It's financial aid made easy.

Part V: The Rest of the Story

After you've applied and the colleges have made their decisions, there is still work to be done. This part shows you how to do it. And it tells the rest of the story for students from abroad.

Part VI: The Part of Tens

It's now a tradition in these ...*For Dummies* books that the last part gives you lists. For some reason, perhaps the David Letterman influence, they're all supposed to be lists of ten. They're important, useful, and some interesting reading that didn't quite fit anywhere else. No extra charge.

Icons Used in This Book

If you're past the traditional college age, then make sure that you check out the paragraphs marked with this icon; they contain information especiallly for you.

You'll hear a lot of academic jargon as you deal with college officials. This icon identifies places where jargon is translated into English.

This icon highlights information that college officials assume you don't know. It's how they make decisions.

When you see this icon, read the text carefully. It's something that could blow up your application for admission or financial aid or something that could damage your college experience.

This icon indicates some good advice to remember. Reach for your highlighter.

 This icon marks something to stick somewhere near the front of your memory.

 This icon highlights the usual college myths and tall stories that have been going around for years and are not true.

 This icon highlights the true story behind the myth that you should know and will help you get into college.

 This icon highlights the bits and pieces of valuable information and insights for getting into college.

Where to Go from Here

Now you're ready to take on the questions, concerns, fears, and hype of getting into college. This book equips you with the right stuff. So turn to the topic that interests you most and as you read, mark it up to your delight. The more ink and highlighter on these pages, the more successful you'll be.

Part I
Getting Ready

The 5th Wave — By Rich Tennant

"Those tests I took in high school? I thought they all meant diddlysquat. Apparently I was right."

In this part . . .

*I*f you're ready to begin looking for a college, start reading here. This part assumes that you know nothing about colleges, except that a lot of them are out there and you want to attend one. The chapters in this part explain how to find information and how to sort the stuff that you need from what you don't need.

Chapter 2 helps you start to think about decisions that you can make as you launch the process. It discusses the steps you can take to become a more attractive college applicant and to be eligible for more financial aid. It also offers advice on how to take the steps and make the decisions.

Chapter 1
What You Need to Know

In This Chapter
▶ What's a college?
▶ How many types of colleges exist?
▶ Who else is looking for a college?
▶ Where is the first stop for information?
▶ Why don't you need to worry about money?

*Y*ou've heard the stories about getting into college, and you're not sure you're ready to try. Reams of paper to be filled out. Palm-sweating tests to be taken. Essays to be written trying to make you sound impressive. Campuses to be visited. Interviews to be held. Plus the trauma of baring your soul on a financial aid application.

And before any of that, somehow you must find a few colleges that you think you'll like. Where do you look? In directories two inches thick? These books are filled with 2,000 pages of fine print. So how do you know where to start looking? In that collection of brochures in your high school counseling center? How can you tell if you're going to like a college from a brochure? And what about the colleges that haven't sent any brochures to your school?

Suppose that you're further along in the process and you know a few colleges you may want to attend. How do you know if you can get in? Are you going to be able to afford tuition? Your mind is starting to boggle already.

Friends who have gone through the college-finding process tell you how stressful it is. You believe them. And, you wonder, can going to college really be worth all the hassle?

Relax. You can avoid the stress. If you take your college-finding process one little step at a time, your search for a college will seem like the fairly easy process that it really is.

The first thing to remember is that you're the buyer. You want something — an education and four years of personal growth — that colleges are selling. And overall, more places in college freshman classes are available than the number of people like you looking for these places. College is a buyers' market.

I repeat that statement many times in this book because it's important. College is a buyers' market, which means the goods being sold (places in college) outnumber the buyers (you). Remembering that fact, as you can see in Part IV, can save you money.

Feel better now? You've taken the first step. You've discovered that you're in demand. You are wanted by some college somewhere, probably by more than one. Now if you take each of the remaining steps this way, hey, this process can turn into fun. You may even look forward to this task of finding a college.

What If You're Older

Yes, older students, you're wanted, too. You're among the buyers in that buyers' market.

The traditional college age range of 18 to 24 is rapidly disappearing. More older students are appearing on campuses every year. At many colleges, the older students are in demand more than younger students because of the maturity and stability they bring to the classroom and to campus life.

The Many Kinds of Colleges

A college is an institution in business to award degrees. Colleges give these degrees to people who successfully complete a prescribed series of courses, seminars, term papers, and other academic stuff. Some colleges think they're in business for other reasons, like winning grants for research. Those schools reward their professors not for how well they teach, but for how many grants they earn. But that's not a problem for you right now.

Degrees are being awarded this year at about 3,500 institutions across the United States. Each of these institutions legitimately can be called a college. But in that vast field of institutions are colleges of many sizes, shapes, philosophies, and missions.

Almost half of the 3,500 colleges offer four-year bachelor degrees. Most of the remaining colleges offer associate degrees, which can be earned in two years. A few, mainly medical and law schools, give only advanced degrees. Some institutions call themselves by names other than colleges, such as:

- ✔ **Universities:** These schools are the biggies, as in Ohio State University, and are a collection of individual colleges, such as the College of Engineering, the College of Arts and Sciences, and the College of Agriculture. A university usually has a graduate school offering advanced degrees. A college generally does not.

- ✔ **Institutes of Technology:** These schools are primarily engineering colleges. Most often, such a school is identified simply by the word Tech. For example, the Georgia Institute of Technology is known nationally as Georgia Tech.

- ✔ **Community colleges and technical schools:** Both of these terms identify a college that offers a two-year academic program and awards an associate degree.

The whole universe of colleges and the people they employ like to be known as *higher education*. Their bible, read each week by almost everyone who gets a college paycheck, is a newspaper called *The Chronicle of Higher Education*. Don't bother subscribing to *The Chronicle*, unless you want to read about the latest squabbles among history professors. But higher education is a little stuffy for most people. If colleges are higher, does that make elementary and high schools lower education? The term higher education is typical of the jargon that you encounter as you deal with higher educators. When you see the term higher education it means colleges.

Regardless of the name an institution uses, this book calls them all colleges, which is what they all are. Occasionally, I call them schools, which is also what they are. The following sections describe the differences between schools.

Public versus private

About 500 of the 1,500 four-year colleges are *public*, which means these schools are operated and subsidized by the states in which they're located. Almost all the rest are private. *Private* schools rely on endowments, tuition, and fund-raising campaigns for their money.

The big difference for you is the cost. Private schools, because they have no government subsidies, are more expensive. Any college you see with a tuition of $20,000-plus is a private school that counts on bill-paying customers for a large chunk of its operating income. Most large universities are public. Most small liberal arts colleges are private.

The average cost of tuition and room and board at a private college in 1997 was $18,184. At a public college, the average cost was $7,118. But those low rates at public schools go only to residents of their states, the taxpayers who provide the subsidy. All but a very few state colleges levy a surcharge to out-of-staters that pulls their costs up to private-school levels. (I talk about finding the money to pay these bills in Chapters 11 through 15.)

Private colleges, especially those in the high price range, usually have much more money to give away in financial aid than state-supported schools. Some prestigious private schools budget 30 percent of their income for what most of you know as scholarships. Many scholarships are awarded for academic talent rather than financial need.

Remember, the preceding numbers are averages. That means about half the students going to private colleges are paying less than $18,184. And even the averages need not be as high as they seem. Of the $7,118 average cost of a public college, more than $4,000 is in room and board paid by students who live on campus. A student living at home pays an average tuition of $2,966 at a public college, $12,823 at a private school.

Picky versus unpicky

Some colleges are very fussy about the students they accept. Others open their doors to anyone with a high school diploma or its equivalent. The fussy schools can be that way because their reputation or their popularity among high school seniors brings these schools many more applicants than they have places.

In accepting students, all colleges fall into one of three categories:

- **Open admission:** These schools take any high school graduate until all openings are filled. High school dropouts who get a GED usually qualify as well. Almost all two-year colleges have open admissions. Some public colleges are required by state law to take any graduate of a high school in their state, if they have the space.

- **Rolling admission:** These schools consider applications as they arrive and accept or reject them until all slots are filled. Some rolling admission schools are sold out before their published application deadlines. If a college with rolling admission says its deadline is March 1, a wise student is going to apply before February 1. (You can find out much more about how and when to apply in Chapter 10.)

- **The May 1 schools (also known as the Ivy League Model):** These schools accept their entire freshman class — and notify those who don't make the class — at the same time, usually in late March or early April. They give the winners until May 1 to decide whether they're going to enroll. The eight Ivy League colleges (Brown, Columbia, Cornell, Dartmouth, Harvard, Penn, Princeton, and Yale) agree each year to notify their applicants on the same day. That's so one school can't get an edge over the others in luring a student they all want just because one school's acceptance letter arrived first in the mail.

You can tell a college's admission policy from its listing in any major directory. Schools with open admissions or rolling admissions usually say so specifically. If a school's listing includes a date when applicants are notified, that school is in the selective May 1 category.

Single-sex colleges

Single-sex colleges are dwindling in number, but they're still around. Students who feel they may be more comfortable on a campus where they're not distracted by the other sex still have that option. Women seem to like the single-sex idea better than men. Only five all-male campuses remain in the country, but at least 60 colleges are exclusively female.

All single-sex colleges are private. The last two public single-sex colleges, The Citadel in South Carolina and the Virginia Military Institute, recently lost legal battles. Both schools had to enroll women because the courts ruled that public money must be spent equally on each gender. The single-sex campuses that remain are private and thus are not affected by laws insisting that they integrate.

The best-known colleges that serve only females are Smith, Mount Holyoke, and Wellesley in Massachusetts, Bryn Mawr outside Philadelphia, and Mills in Oakland, California. Radcliffe and Barnard also are all female, but these two colleges are components of fully integrated Harvard and Columbia Universities. Radcliffe and Barnard are independent institutions operating as parts of their parent univerisities. A student is admitted to Radcliffe, not Harvard, and Barnard, not Columbia.

Men looking for a woman-free environment can try places like Hampden-Sydney in Virginia, Wabash College in Indiana, and St. John's University in Minnesota.

Religion-affiliated colleges

More than half of the 1,000 or so private four-year colleges have links to a religious denomination. In most cases, the sponsoring denomination's role is limited to appointing trustees and providing money. Some religions, notably the Catholics, supply clergy for faculties. At a few colleges, usually those tied to a fundamentalist Christian denomination, religious life pervades the campus, and church or chapel attendance is required. Among the best-known church-sponsored colleges are Notre Dame (Catholic), Baylor (Baptist), Brigham Young (Mormon), and Southern Methodist.

Almost without exception, colleges tied to a religion welcome students who don't subscribe to their faith. Remember, college is a buyers' market. Atheist money is just as good as Baptist money. At Notre Dame, which uses priests as professors and offers courses in Catholic doctrine, the large number of non-Catholic students are free to pursue any type of non-Catholicism they desire.

Tuition-free colleges

Believe it or not, some colleges offer tuition-free education. You don't pay in dollars, you pay in time.

Five are the service academies run by the federal government. These academies train officers for the Army, Navy, Air Force, Coast Guard, and Merchant Marine. Not only are they cost-free, the government pays you a salary to attend because you're officially a member of the military. You get a college degree and then pay with a few years of your life in the service of your country.

Other tuition-free schools ask for the time while you're a student. You're required to work without pay — waiting tables, mowing lawns, answering phones — in exchange for four no-cost years and a degree. Prime examples are College of the Ozarks in Missouri and Berea College in Kentucky. Both give high priorities in admission to students of meager means.

One brilliant exception that doesn't fall into either of the preceding categories is Cooper Union in the heart of Manhattan's Lower East Side. Tuition is free, but living in New York can cost as much as a year at Yale. Cooper Union offers majors only in engineering, art, and architecture. The school is so popular that it accepts only one out of every ten applicants.

Specialty colleges

A couple hundred four-year colleges offer only one major, award only one degree, and train students for just one role in life. Most specialty colleges can be recognized by their names. Seminaries are one example. The Cincinnati College of Mortuary Science is another. So is the Deaconess College of Nursing.

Proprietary colleges

Most colleges, even those where a year's tab runs over $25,000, aren't in business to make money. They are nonprofit institutions. But a few, small, degree-granting schools scattered around the country do have a profit motive. They operate on the hope that educating you can make a buck for their owners. The major college directories describe these schools as proprietary schools.

Most proprietary colleges are legitimate institutions, usually specializing in engineering, technology-related fields, or trades such as cosmetology. But some are fly-by-night operations that have been known to take your money and run before you receive a bachelor of science. If you're looking at a proprietary school, be sure to check it out with your local Better Business Bureau or consumer protection agency. Ask whether any complaints have been filed against the school. A good bet: If the school is listed in a major college directory, it likely has survived some serious scrutiny.

Two-year colleges

All the categories I've mentioned so far are for colleges that keep you around for four years (or more, if you have a tough time getting the classes you need to graduate). The largest bloc of all colleges — more than 1,400 — is the one that gets the schooling done in two years.

Two-year colleges, most commonly known these days as community colleges, are the fastest growing segment of education at any level. Their 6.4 million students are roughly equally split in two: those planting some education roots who expect to move on to a four-year degree, and those learning a skill such as dental hygiene or computer repair.

The two-year college is an attractive option for students who don't want to leave home, who like to deal with professors whose minds aren't somewhere else, or who don't want to spend big bucks at a four-year college. Average annual tuition at a two-year college in 1997 was $1,394.

And a two-year college is an ideal reentry route for adults considering college who are intimidated by the thought of mingling with all those kids. (One-third of the students on two-year campuses are over 30.) By attending a two-year college, an adult can step into the waters gingerly, starting with one or two courses, while living at home and continuing to work.

Here comes some education jargon. Many community colleges have articulation agreements with four-year colleges in their area. Such an agreement is a good thing to have if you're a two-year college student. An *articulation agreement* means that the four-year college is going to accept any graduate of the two-year school with no questions asked. If you find a school with an articulation agreement, you can move on for a bachelor's degree without the hassle of filling out forms and writing application essays.

In the old days, community colleges — usually called junior colleges then — were the college of last resort for students who were unable to make it anywhere else. That stigma is fading fast. Today, the community college is often the college of first resort.

Colleges in other countries

Most Americans who study at universities abroad do so under the auspices of U.S. colleges — as part of their U.S. college curriculum. About 1,500 cooperative programs allow students to take courses at colleges in other lands and get credit at their schools back home. These opportunities typically are for upperclassmen — juniors and seniors who have compiled impressive records during their first two years at a U.S. college. Ask the colleges whether they offer these programs and what their requirements are if you're interested in taking advantage of the opportunity.

Some adventurous students, however, strike out on their own and look for a college in another country with no help from a U.S. school. If you're inclined in that direction, some books can offer you advice. But remember that colleges operate in the language of their country. If you're looking at a university in the Netherlands, and you speak no Dutch, you aren't likely to go far as a student, and you probably won't be admitted.

The best source of information on worldwide colleges is the *International Handbook of Universities,* published by the Paris-based International Association of Universities. This guide contains descriptions of 4,000 schools in 169 countries, including a brief history, list of majors, and language of instruction. The text is updated every two years. The *Handbook* can be found in the reference section of many U.S. libraries, or you can order the *Handbook* from the following U.S. distributor: Stockton Press, 15 E. 26th St., New York, NY, 10010.

Who's Looking?

How's 2.5 million for a number? That's how many people are joining you on this trip to search for the right college. Each year 2.5 million students enroll in a college for the first time. So you have a lot of company. Even you adults aren't alone. About 50,000 of this year's first-time college students will be 25 or older.

But here's another number to ponder: 20,664. That's the number of valedictorians produced each year by the nation's 20,664 high schools. That's enough valedictorians to fill the freshman classes at the eight Ivy League colleges, plus Stanford, Rice, and Notre Dame, and 3,500 valedictorians are still left over.

Of course, those colleges aren't going to fill their classes with valedictorians. Those schools are looking for a lot more than a high grade-point average. (Everything that the schools are looking for is spelled out in Chapter 9.) And some of the valedictorians are probably applying to colleges that are not on the preceding list. So while you have company, you also have competition. And that's what makes life fun, right?

Where to Go First — Information Sources

Okay, where do you start? Information about colleges seems to be everywhere: books, catalogs, videos, brochures, stuff that shows up in your mailbox, brightly colored programs in your high school counseling office computer. How do you make sense of all this? You can use several sources of information.

Directories

The heaviest sources (three pounds or more), and maybe the most valuable to start your search, are those thick books with small print in high school counseling offices and public libraries. These books are the major directories (at least six are on the market today) that try to provide a comprehensive description of every four-year college in the United States. Some directories even include a few two-year colleges. But don't start randomly leafing through them looking for a college that appeals to you. Wait until you read Chapter 2 so that you can be more organized.

The directories can tell you a college's size, location, admission requirements, majors, percentage of students who graduate with certain degrees, plus the number of professors, books in the library, and computer terminals. The directories also contain plenty more information that you'll probably never need to know. You can decide what you need to know after you decide what's important to you.

The toughest tickets

Do you want to join the selective crowd, the students flocking to apply to the colleges that are the toughest to crack? Or do you want to avoid them? Either way, the following table reveals the toughest colleges to get into.

These are the colleges that accepted the smallest percentage of their applicants for their 1996-97 freshman classes. That means these colleges had the most students applying in relation to the number of students that they needed.

College	Location	Applying	Accepted	Percent
College of the Ozarks ($0)	Point Lookout, MO	2,825	330	11.7
Harvard (Ivy)	Cambridge, MA	17,852	2,150	12.0
Cooper Union ($0)	New York, NY	2,244	281	12.5
Princeton (Ivy)	Princeton, NJ	14,311	2,013	14.1
Stanford	Palo Alto, CA	15,485	2,908	18.8
Amherst	Amherst, MA	4,836	943	19.5
Yale (Ivy)	New Haven, CT	12,620	2,522	20.0
Brown (Ivy)	Providence, RI	13,904	2,952	21.2
Dartmouth (Ivy)	Hanover, NH	10,004	2,163	21.6
Georgetown (C)	Washington, DC	12,832	2,860	22.3
Columbia (Ivy)	New York, NY	8,714	2,045	23.5
Williams	Williamstown, MA	4,996	1,300	26.0
MIT	Cambridge, MA	7,958	2,113	26.6
Calif. Inst. Of Technology	Pasadena, CA	1,895	512	27.0
Bowdoin	Brunswick, ME	4,122	1,256	30.5
Duke	Durham, NC	13,483	4,137	30.7
Washington & Lee	Lexington, VA	3,446	1,074	31.2
Penn (Ivy)	Philadelphia, PA	15,074	4,981	33.0
Berea ($0)	Berea, KY	1,693	569	33.6
Pomona	Claremont, CA	3,586	1,220	34.0
Swarthmore	Swarthmore, PA	3,512	1,200	34.2
Cornell (Ivy)	Ithaca, NY	20,603	7,050	34.2

$0 = Tuition-free college

C = Affiliated with Catholic Church

Ivy = One of eight colleges that band together as the Ivy League.

All the major directories available at most bookstores and libraries contain the same information. Each directory merely has a little different package. Some directories are just recitation of facts. Other directories allow the colleges to write a few paragraphs describing themselves. Be aware, however, that each directory is just as good as the information submitted by the colleges and the information is as up-to-date as the last time each college updated its own listing. No directory has all the information for all the colleges because some schools decline to report items such as admission rate, SAT scores, ethnic breakdown of the student body, and so on. After offering you all those caveats, here is a list of the major mainstream directories:

- ✔ *ARCO, The Right College,* a Prentice Hall publication, contains the same information about all the colleges as the other directories but ranks the competitiveness of each college on a six-step scale — from most competitive to noncompetitive. This scale measures competitiveness on the percentage of applicants accepted and freshman SAT scores.

- ✔ *Barron's Profile of American Colleges,* from the Barron's publishing house, also has all the data that colleges report on questionnaires and uses a six-step scale to compare competitiveness. In weighing competitiveness, the Barron's scale considers acceptance rates, SAT scores, and freshmen's class rank in high school.

- ✔ *Lovejoy's College Guide,* is the Macmillan publishing company's entry in the big-directory battle. This publication has all the same information as all the other directories.

- ✔ *Cass & Birnbaum's Guide to American Colleges,* from HarperCollins, offers the most user-friendly typography of the bunch. In the front of the book is a large-type index of colleges, by state, that you can use as a check list for size, location, and other factors that you consider important.

- ✔ *The College Blue Book,* from Macmillan. This one is a five-volume set that you can find in library reference sections but not many bookstores. Each volume deals with a different aspect of college.

Not much differentiates any of the preceding books except their choice of type fonts. In any given year, one directory can be more current than the others depending on how many colleges returned their questionnaires. And don't be too impressed by those competitiveness ratings because they can differ dramatically from book to book. For example, Wake Forest University in North Carolina is listed as most competitive by *Barron's* but just highly competitive by *ARCO*. Butler University in Indianapolis is very competitive in *Barron's* but only competitive in *ARCO*.

For an irreverent look at colleges, as seen from the students' perspective, you can try

- *Insider's Guide to the Colleges,* by the *Yale Daily News.* The Yalies tap a nationwide student network to try to keep themselves up to date.
- *Fiske Guide to Colleges,* by Edwin B. Fiske, former education writer for the *New York Times.* Fiske sends questionnaires to students, as well as college officials, and incorporates the customers' views on each college he lists.

When you look through these directories, be aware that some information may not be accurate. Nobody's trying to mislead you, but some stuff can be out of date. The directories get their information on questionnaires they send to the colleges. Sometimes colleges get a little lazy, or busy with other things, and overlook the questionnaire. So old numbers have a way of being repeated.

A dean at a large Midwestern college once complained about a newspaper story that said his school had 6,000 students. The enrollment really was about 10,000 students. But sure enough, that year's edition of a major directory listed his school's enrollment at 6,000. Nobody on campus had bothered to update the number on a questionnaire.

If you use the directories as a starting point, be sure to double-check the data that's important to you as you get further into your search.

Computer programs

Some directory publishers have developed software that offers the same information found in those 2,000 pages of fine print. That's good news and bad news. The good news is that these programs help you find what you want easier and faster. (Pressing keys or clicking a mouse is easier than turning pages.) And the program instantly screens out colleges that don't meet the criteria you've established. The bad news is that this software is expensive. At about $400 a pop, such software is out of the range of the typical family budget. The two most comprehensive programs are produced by The College Board and Peterson's. Samples of the software can be found, and some basic college searches conducted, at The College Board and Peterson's Web sites (www.collegeboard.org and www.petersons.com).

You may be able to borrow a program, though. The software is marketed mainly to schools and libraries. (The software is not for sale at your neighborhood software store.) If you're lucky, your school or library — or one near you — has such a program and a computer on which you can use the program. Computer programs have the same intrinsic drawback as the directories. The information they contain is the information colleges choose to submit.

College literature

Don't overlook those shelves in your counseling office and local library that contain promotional literature sent by colleges. But remember when you pick up these brochures that their reason for being is recruiting. The pretty pictures of smiling students on landscaped lawns are designed to lure you and your tuition money. Most literature gives you some hard information about the college in a package more attractive than a three-pound directory.

Multimedia

A few companies have sprung up in recent years offering a look at colleges on videos, CD-ROMs, and other forms of '90s technology. Some companies ask you to pay for the product. Others give the product away, earning their bucks from colleges who use them as marketing tools. You likely can find some brochures advertising these products in your high school counseling office. What you get is a high-tech version of the college brochure. You see the same beautiful campus scenes, perhaps even read the same words. The big difference is that you find live students, professors, and admission officers talking to you.

The Internet

For the adept surfer, the Net can be a valuable source of college information. Chat rooms, bulletin boards, newsgroups, and e-mail are new tools to talk to students, professors, admission officers, recent graduates, and others with firsthand knowledge of specific colleges. Some students are showing up at college fairs primed with information they've obtained solely through Internet conversations.

For the not-so-adept, the Net provides easy access to hundreds of college-planning Web sites as diverse as the Internet itself. Some information is useful. Some is a waste of time. Some is the same information you can find in colleges' brochures and videos.

COLLEGE REALITY

You can always find space — somewhere

Even if you start very late looking for a college — say a month before your high school graduation — several hundred colleges still have space for you.

That's the clearest indication that college is a buyer's market, that the number of places in freshman classes exceeds the number of students applying.

Every April since 1988, the National Association for College Admission Counseling polls the nation's four-year colleges asking about vacancies for the coming fall. Every April, many say that they still have space.

In April 1996, 490 four-year colleges reported freshman vacancies. In 1995, the number was 635. The 1996 total includes 381 that had openings in all academic areas and 109 that could take students in some areas.

More good news for procrastinators: 463 four-year colleges had not filled their on-campus

housing by April 1996. And 495 still had some financial aid dollars left to give away.

You aren't going to find any high-prestige selective colleges on the list. The Harvards, Stanfords, and Yales that get five times as many applications as they need have no problem filling freshman classes. (See the list of selective colleges, in the sidebar "The toughest tickets," earlier in this chapter.) Most vacancies are at colleges you never heard of unless you happen to live nearby.

NACAC sends the vacancy list each May to its members, half of whom are high school counselors. (The other half are college admission officers.) If you still haven't found a college by May and your counselor doesn't have the vacancy list, you can get a copy by writing to: NACAC, 1631 Prince St., Alexandria, VA, 22314-2818.

Check out the Internet search engine called Yahoo! (www.yahoo.com). Enter the keywords college entrance for a search, and you get a long list of informational sites that can be accessed with a click. On the Yahoo! search page, you're also a click away from the Web sites of 292 college admission offices and 163 financial aid offices.

Counselors

Good high school counselors know as much about the college admission process as college admission officers themselves. The good counselors go to admission officers' conventions, share the gossip, and speak the jargon. When they recommend that three of their students apply to Dartmouth, these counselors are reasonably sure all three students will be accepted because these counselors know how Dartmouth makes decisions. Poor high school counselors know as much about the admission process as you. Maybe less.

Older students whose high school years are in the past don't have access to high school counselors. That could be a blessing because the older students don't face the risk of being misinformed by a poor counselor spewing bad advice. An older student seeking counseling should drop into the admission office of a local college (four-year or two-year) to chat about the kind of campus on which the student could be successful. But don't drop in cold. Call for an appointment.

If you're lucky and you have a good counselor, rely heavily on her or his wisdom. This counselor can accurately steer you to colleges that are likely to be a good fit for you. The final decision, of course, is yours.

If you're unlucky, as many high school students are, use your counselor only for essential tasks, like filling out the counselor's evaluation on your college application. And, hey, you're not all that unlucky. After all, you've got this book.

Teachers

All teachers have been to college. And they talk to other teachers who have been to other colleges. They have a pretty good idea of what types of students fit well, academically and socially, at which colleges.

If you're a typical student, you have two or three teachers you highly respect, who know you as more than just a kid in a seat. Don't be shy about asking them for advice. Good teachers are wise people. The ones who know you well can point you in some good directions.

Friends

You probably already know this advice. Older friends, even siblings, who have gone through the process you're starting, are the only people who can offer firsthand knowledge of how it works from the student's perspective. Ask your siblings or friends who've gone to college to tell you about the college-life reality that isn't part of the glossy brochure. If you have friends you trust who are in college, trust their advice now.

Money Isn't Important — Yet

Did you notice that none of the preceding information sources mentions money? That's not an oversight. When you start your search for the right colleges, money should not even be close to the front of your mind.

Don't rule out any college, not even those $25,000-plus places, because you think you can't afford the cost. The fact is, when you start your search, you don't know how much any school will cost you. And you have no idea how much financial aid you'll be offered to reduce a college's published price tag.

Here's another number to remember: 65 percent of the nation's 1996-97 freshmen, at colleges from Harvard to Frostburg State, did not pay the full sticker price. Two of every three freshmen got some kind of help from the college at which they enrolled.

The amount of help you receive, especially at high-priced private schools, depends largely on how much a college wants you on its campus.

But still, you're going to need some money. It's unlikely that you're going to get a free ride anywhere, unless you're adept at throwing balls through hoops from beyond the three-point line. Your two main money sources will be whatever you and your parents can pay plus the aid package from your college. But you can supplement those sources with outside private scholarships. Millions are given away each year by clubs, churches, corporations, and others. The money doesn't come to you, you have to look for the money. Details on how to find money for college are in Part IV.

Chapter 2

Setting the Stage

● ●

In This Chapter

▶ Thinking about college before high school

▶ Thinking about college while in high school

▶ Making yourself attractive to colleges

▶ Answering the most important questions in your college decision

▶ Knowing the early steps to getting more college money

● ●

*W*hen you start to think about college, two questions probably pop into your mind:

✔ Where do I want to go to college?

✔ How do I know that college will want me?

You may also wonder about a third question:

✔ Can I afford the college of my choice?

Finding college money has so many ramifications, and the money can be found in so many places, that this book devotes several chapters to the subject of getting money for college. But this is not one of those chapters. Here, this chapter looks at you, the student, and just at you.

College Is Four Years, Not Your Whole Life

Where you go to college is a decision that only you can make. You may get a lot of advice, some of it good, some of it bad, some of it absolutely awful. This book tries to help you sort all that advice out and recognize good advice from the other kind. But after considering all the advice, the final decision must be yours.

Occasionally, college is compared to marriage. College is a commitment to spend a portion of your life with someone. A lot of your friends let you know whether they like, or don't like, a person you are dating. When the time comes to think about marriage, your friends' opinions are not the most important item in your mind. That's the way friends' opinions should be with college. You're making a commitment for part of your life. After you research every aspect that you can about your college choices, only you can make the commitment.

No one right college is out there waiting for you; dozens of colleges may be just waiting for you to look at them. When you start to look seriously, you'll probably find several that you think could be right for you. Then you'll decide which three, or four, or five of them to favor with an application.

How do you know that the colleges of your choice will think that you're a student they would like to have? That's also a question only you can answer. If you know what colleges want (and you will if you read Chapter 9), you can make yourself someone they want. Again you may get a lot of advice, but only you can make yourself attractive to colleges.

Like all good planners, you need to look ahead and start the college selection process as early as you can. If you have given some serious thought to both tasks discussed here — finding a college and making yourself desirable — when crunch time comes, your application process will be a downhill slide. Easy, swift. Trauma and stress will be for the other guys.

Planning may sound boring, but it's better than having no plan at all.

Read This Book in Fourth Grade

How many fourth graders buy a book on college planning? Your guess is probably right: zilch. To get into Harvard is not high on a nine-year-old's priority list, unless you're Doogie Howser reincarnated.

But the best plan for anything is the plan that starts earliest. The more time you have to walk somewhere, the easier each step is. Fourth grade is a good time to start to plan for college, because in fourth grade you're at the age when you start to think about what's important to you and make decisions based on those thoughts.

When you get to high school, the important stuff of fourth grade is forgotten. You have more mature priorities, and getting into college ranks right up at the top of the infamous priority list. You know that a college will look at your entire high school record, from ninth grade on, and you know that you can do nothing to change the record that you've already put together.

But what if you knew in fourth grade what you now know in high school? Aha, things might have been different. You'd know, for example, that a college would like you to have high grades in the toughest math and science courses. You'd be prepared to handle Advanced Placement math and science, but now you're just not ready for those courses. You shrugged off math and science all those years because that stuff didn't interest you, or your teacher made those subjects boring.

If you had known in fourth grade how important those courses are, you would have paid more attention. You would have mastered math and science in the elementary grades (you know that you could have done it if you tried) so that you would have a firm foundation to coast through the tough high school AP and honors courses with all *A*s.

Then there's the trombone. You started taking trombone lessons last year, and now you really enjoy playing the trombone. You're in the high school band and orchestra, and you become a better trombonist each week. The trombone will look good on your college application, but it would look even better if you were more experienced. And you know, you could have been. You had a chance to start playing an instrument in fourth grade, but you didn't because lessons took away time that you needed for important things. If only you knew then what you know now.

Okay, so your nine-year-old brother doesn't care about reading this book. Be nice and share its advice with him.

If You're Not in Fourth Grade, Just Read Faster

If fourth grade is in your past, no need to despair. Regardless of when you start to think about college, at whatever stage of life you want to make yourself an attractive college applicant, a few simple facts can guide your decisions.

 A college looks first at your high school record. A college wants your record to show that you took the toughest available courses and that you received top grades, preferably *A*s, in those courses. If you plan early to produce that record and lay the foundation you need to do well in tough courses, your task will be much easier when you get to the AP math class.

If You're Out of High School

If your high school diploma gathers dust in a closet, you still have no reason to fret. Anything you do at this point will not change your high school record, but you can still make yourself an attractive college candidate.

Most colleges enthusiastically welcome older students for two reasons that are totally unrelated to each other. Reason one: Colleges can't find enough 18-year-old high school graduates to fill their freshman classes. Reason two: Older, mature students usually are better students. James Walters, Director of Undergraduate Admissions at the University of North Carolina-Chapel Hill, says his records show adults are "remarkably successful" at college compared to their younger colleagues. As Walters puts it: "They're a heckuva good bet."

Because most admission officers feel the same way as Walters, older students get favorable consideration when they apply because of their age. Many admission officers consider your *life experience,* the education you have acquired just by your survival in the world, as a supplement or even an alternative to your high school record. Some picky colleges, though, give no break at all to older students. Those that do tell you so, if you ask.

Here's a number for you: 1.6 million. That's the total of current college students who have passed their 40th birthday. If you're an older student, chances are excellent that you won't be the only one at your school.

Steps to Take Early On

If you want to think about what's important before it really becomes important, I suggest steps you can ponder as you approach those crucial high school years. Many steps are also good advice for high school students as they approach the crucial application time. Of course, every single step is not a good idea for everyone. Pick and choose the ones that suit you.

Stay awake in fourth-grade math

You want good grades in high school math. To get good grades is difficult enough if you're well prepared. But if you're unprepared for algebra and geometry because you slept through fourth-grade fractions — or ignored them as boring and unimportant — your chances to do well in these subjects are remote. You should make sure that you have a thorough grounding in math — if you missed it in fourth grade, go back and study it again.

If you slept through fourth-grade math, you can torpedo your chances of getting into a selective college.

Unplug the TV

If pulling the plug is too hard, just turn your television off. If the rest of the family complains, let them have their way, but go somewhere where you can't hear the TV. You don't need to swear off TV forever, just a couple hours a day.

For those TV-free two hours, do something that requires putting your mind in gear. You can do homework, if your school still requires it. You can read something — a magazine, baseball box scores, or stuff in your CD-ROM encyclopedia that you need for a term paper. You can write something — maybe the term paper or a diary entry. (See the "Keep a diary" section, later in this chapter.)

You can accomplish several good things this way. You can keep your mind from getting rusty. (And you need a well-tuned mind for the challenges ahead.) You can practice skills (reading, writing, thinking) that serve you well in those tough high school courses and in the tests and essays you must endure to get into college.

You can do all of these activities with the TV on, of course. But the experience is not the same. TV has a way of quickly numbing all minds within the sound of its speakers. As soon as Seinfeld lures you into his show with a bad joke, your mind is back in neutral. So just do it. Unplug the TV.

Take the toughest courses

Take the toughest courses — the earlier the better. When you're trying to impress a college admission officer, you'll want your record to show that you met every academic challenge you faced. When you have choices earlier in life, choose the road that's hardest to travel. You'll thank yourself later.

Learn to play the tuba

If you can't stand tuba music, move on to another section of this book. Or think about the flute. Wherever your musical interest goes, follow it.

Playing a musical instrument is a talent that many colleges consider special. And applicants with special talents get special consideration, above and beyond those who do nothing in school but get good grades.

The most special instrument of all is the tuba, because not many students play it. Again, it's the law of supply and demand. Every college band needs a tuba, often more than one. Frantic band directors have been known to plead with their admission offices to find a tuba player because the only one in school is graduating. If you play the tuba well, you may be recruited as heavily as an adept tight end.

At the very worst, your tuba gives you extra points on your application score. A flute or trombone also adds points, but not as many because flutes and trombones are more plentiful.

If you have an inclination toward making music, don't repress it. Find the person who gives fourth-grade tuba (or flute, or trombone, or violin, or whatever) lessons. And practice well.

Become fluent in Russian

Another talent often considered special is fluency in a foreign language. As with musical talent, supply and demand is at work. Although applicants who speak French or Spanish get extra points, they don't get as many as those who speak Farsi or Swahili. The key, however, is fluency. An accomplished French speaker is a more attractive college applicant than one who hasn't mastered a lesser known language.

Russian, if your school offers courses in this language, is a good language to learn. Russian speakers are scarce enough that they're treated very kindly in admission offices. And some well-paying jobs are out there for Russian-English interpreters.

If you have an interest in speaking other tongues, pursue it diligently. A second language helps your college application, even if the language is French.

Keep a diary

Keeping a diary is silly, you say? Who would ever want to read what you do every day in your dull life? You'll be surprised. You will.

A diary can do several things to ease the stress when college time comes. The most basic service of a diary is keeping your mind alert. For the time you spend entering each day's report, even if it's just five minutes, your mind is in gear and in less danger of sputtering when you need to work this divine muscle.

Your diary is a record of your life. The time will come when you will thank your diary for being there. When you must list on a college application all your activities and the roles you played in them, your memory will certainly overlook a few. But you don't have to trust your memory alone, because your written record doesn't forget.

For your diary to make its most important contribution, you must help. When you write in your diary, use whole sentences. Make sure that each has a subject and verb. Resist the temptation to just scribble down your stream-of-consciousness thoughts.

By keeping a diary you gain daily practice in writing coherently about yourself. And that's precisely the skill you need when the time to write that all important application essay is upon you — the one part of the process that for many is the most stressful.

College admission officers read your essay to learn something about you and to see how well you write. For most students, the essay is stressful because it's a new experience. Students aren't used to writing about themselves. But for you, the essay will be easy. You will have written about yourself every day.

Your diary can remind you of meaningful experiences that you can use as an essay topic — and they're experiences about which you've already written. Quite possibly, a diary entry could be the first paragraph in your application essay.

Believe me, your essay will be finished, in whole, complete sentences, while your friends are still biting their nails and scratching their heads. (Read more about the essay in Chapter 10.)

See whether the homeless shelter needs help

Your college application is a snapshot — actually more like a full-color portrait — of four years of your life. That portrait includes your life outside school. The application asks you to report your activities in the community and your contributions to them.

Your contributions are more important than the activities themselves. Colleges want to see you doing something, not just joining organizations. A long list of activities is not as impressive as a short list with clear evidence that you have made a contribution. One clear example of contributing is staying with an activity over a period of time.

So find something you like doing as early in life as you can. Volunteering at a homeless shelter is one example, but hardly the only one. Any good cause in your town probably welcomes enthusiastic help.

Make sure that you choose work that you enjoy enough to stay with it through the years. Keep a record — in your diary — of all the things you do, all the contributions you make. Later, you won't have trouble remembering them.

So much for your younger days. Later in this chapter, when I get around to the distasteful word money, I have tips on fourth-grade activities that can help your search for cash. But for now, stick with making yourself presentable.

Your First Decisions

Somewhere around your freshman or sophomore year, you need to start thinking about college in specifics, about where you might want to go and why. If your sophomore year already is history, don't worry. Just think faster.

The first thing you need to do is make a list of colleges that might be right for you. I show you how in Chapter 4, where you can start to look at the college-finding process. But you can't very well make a list until you know what you want to put on it. And you may be mulling over some of those list items for months ahead of time. No decisions are needed. Just mull. See which way your feelings make you lean.

Do you want to leave home?

Deciding whether you want to leave home is one of the first decisions you need to make. Are you ready to flee the nest and try flying on your own? Do you look forward to college as, among other things, your first experience with independent living, a chance to explore life free of your hovering family?

Or are you not yet ready to make the break? Are you more comfortable entering college from the security of your home? Is dealing with college life challenge enough that you don't need other major disruptions? Do you want to save the expense of room and board by starting college from home?

Think about where you want to live as you begin college and think about some other things as well. If you're ready to leave, how far do you want to go? Do you want to come home every weekend? Do you want to be close enough to stay in touch with friends?

Does traveling across the country appeal to you? Can you get by if you see your family only at Thanksgiving, Christmas, and spring break? Can you handle a climate change? If you now live in the South, can you cope with three months of snow?

Mull these questions over every now and then, while you have the TV unplugged. Get a sense of how strongly you feel about each answer. When the time comes to make your decisions, you'll be ready.

Large or small campus?

The University of Nebraska has 20,000 students. Nebraska Wesleyan University has 1,400 students. The only things they have in common are that they offer an excellent education, and they're located in Lincoln, Nebraska. Each is the right school for some students, but neither is right for all students.

Some students thrive in the big sea. They enjoy the wide variety of social, cultural, and other activities that comes with a large university. They're willing to sacrifice some individual attention (sometimes they'll just be numbers in huge classes) in exchange for a giant school's opportunities.

Other students have the opposite reaction. They like the small college atmosphere, where everyone seems to know everyone else, where real professors teach courses and know students' names. They'd feel like they were drowning if they were dropped in an ocean of 20,000 students.

Do you have strong feelings one way or the other? Or is the size of a college not an issue for you? It's something to think about.

Big city or little town?

By the way, the size of a college is not necessarily related to the size of its town. You can find tiny schools in large urban areas and king-size campuses in such remote outposts as Fayetteville, Arkansas (University of Arkansas), and State College, Pennsylvania (Penn State). A college's location is another variable for your list.

Do you want to avoid, or be in, a big city? Do you like the rural life, where a shopping mall is a major journey? Do you lean toward a campus in the suburbs with big city amenities a short drive away? How about a quaint small town where the college and community live as equal partners? Or do you care? Think about the type of community in which you want your college to be located.

Your major

Do you have an idea of what you want to study in college? If not, it's something else for the Mull List (see the Appendix). But don't lose any sleep over such decisions. Even if you show up as a college freshman without a major, you'll have lots of company. Most students don't decide how to focus their college years until after they arrive. And many schools, recognizing this widespread indecision, don't require a choice of major until a student's second or third year.

If you have strong leanings toward a certain field, think about how strong those feelings are. Will you be ready, when the time comes, to narrow your search to colleges with your chosen major? If you're not totally sure, stay flexible. Wait until you're 100 percent certain before nailing down your decision.

Where do you want to live?

Do you feel strongly about being a part of campus life? Are you looking forward to living in a dorm? If so, are you fussy about a single-sex or coed dorm?

Do you want to attend a school where most students live on campus? Or do you care whether most of them commute from home each day? A majority of colleges can be classified either as residential or commuter, with at least two-thirds of their students in one of the two categories. But some colleges strike an even balance between on-campus and live-at-home students. Is that important?

With whom do you want to live?

How about your peers? Are you more comfortable with grungy or are you a neat freak? Is the party scene a big thing for you? Do you crave life in a fraternity or sorority? Do you want to be on a campus where your sex dominates? Or where you're outnumbered by the opposite sex?

Is ethnic diversity important? If you're African-American, do you prefer a predominantly black campus? How about geographic diversity? Some colleges get more than 90 percent of their students from their own states.

Don't worry about finding answers to these questions. All you're doing now is wondering whether you want to answer them. These are the kinds of questions that make mulling fun.

Why are you going to college?

Here's the last question, for now — the one at the heart of why you're as[king] yourself all those other questions. Do you know why you want to go to college? Be sure to answer this one.

Do you want to go to college because your friends are going? Because your parents expect you to? Because you can make more money with a degree? Because you want to train yourself for a career? Or do you want to go to college because you don't know as much as you think you should know? Because college is an easy way to cut the ties to your parents' nest? Because you can't think of anything else to do after high school?

Your answer may be some, or all, of the preceding. And your answer will probably change as you continue to ask through the years. So think about why you want to go to college often. And answer this question again and again. Your answer will help immensely in your search. And it's a question you likely will have to answer aloud at your interview in a college admissions office.

Money Is Not Important — Yet

Okay. Here it is. The nasty word. Money.

In that long list of things to think about, I didn't mention money. That's because you don't need to think about money. Not yet. At least not while you're mulling over decisions you'll have to make soon.

The cost of a college, of course, is a key factor in determining where you go. You won't enroll in a college if you can't pay its bills. But money is not something to think about when you compare colleges this early in the game, because you really don't know how much each college will cost.

Sure, you can look at the price tags in the college directories. Harvard charges $28,896 a year for tuition and room and board. At Stanford, the tab is $27,827. If you're reading this in fourth grade, even modest inflation could push the price over $100,000 a year by the time you're ready for college. But you have no idea — yet — how much of that tab (whether you get into Harvard or Stanford) you'll be paying.

You have no idea — yet — how much your price will be reduced by financial aid.

...memory bank. In September 1996, two-thirds of all
...e United States were not paying their school's full
...

...phasis. Two of every three freshmen — from Yale to
... — were not paying the price advertised in directories.
...ing financial aid.

...cipients are not just the poor. At high-priced private colleges, which
...ve away millions of their own dollars to help students pay bills, some aid
flows to students whose families earn six-figure incomes. And no one bends
the rules to get this money.

You can get an estimate of your financial aid eligibility by reading Chapter 12.
But that's just an estimate. All financial aid, especially at private schools, is
flexible, if not negotiable. If you play the tuba, you could get more aid than
your friend who doesn't. (Financial aid is explained in detail in Chapters 11
through 15. You can also refer to *College Financial Aid For Dummies* [IDG
Books Worldwide, Inc.] by Dr. Herm Davis and Joyce Lain Kennedy.)

Still, you will need to spend money to go to college, you just don't know how
much. So your concern right now should not be how expensive College X is
compared to College Y. Wait until you have some real numbers for comparison. Your financial concern, as you move through high school, should be
finding the money to spend no matter where you decide to go.

Early Steps to Get More College Money

As you set the stage to become an attractive college applicant, you can do
several things to set the stage for paying the bills. If you plan with care, you
can make sure that you not only maximize your own resources, but that
you'll be eligible for all the money the rules say you deserve when the time
comes to distribute financial aid.

Find a work-free income source

Many people out there are willing to pay you good U.S. dollars and won't ask
you for even a few minutes of work. They go by lots of different names, but
quite a few call themselves bankers. These people want to borrow your
money for a while, and they pay you to let them have it. They'll take $1 a
week if that's all you can afford.

This profitable activity, lending money to bankers, is usually called savings. That's a dull, boring word, and it's why most people don't save. Polls regularly show that most people would rather spend the money they have than, yechh, save it. Saving is not much fun.

So I'm not suggesting you save money. I'm encouraging you to find a new, work-free source of income. Lend some money to a banker, or a mutual fund, or someone every week, every month, or whatever suits your budget. When the banker pays you for using your money, let him keep that money, too. Then he'll pay you not only for using your money, but also for using the money that he paid you earlier. This is the magic of compounding. Compounding is how rich people get even richer. They lend money to bankers.

Tell Grandma what to do with her birthday presents

You may have heard about tax shelters. Tax shelters are where rich people put their money because, through loopholes in the law, they legitimately can avoid paying taxes on this money. Anyone thinking about going to college should be aware of the provision in the financial aid rules that I'll call the Grandma Shelter.

The shelter actually is available to any friend or relative who is not in your immediate family. Grandma is used here because she's handy and she's often very generous with her grandkids.

When you apply for financial aid, you'll be asked to bare your financial soul. If you're a dependent of your parents, they must do the same. Every dollar of your and your parents' income and assets must be reported to a computer, which then crunches the numbers and decides how much you should pay for college. That's the starting point to figure your financial aid.

Nobody will ask about Grandma's money. She could be holding your college nest egg, and it wouldn't be counted in determining how much aid you need. Now I'm not suggesting that your parents transfer all their mutual funds into Grandma's name so that you can get more financial aid. Although that would be a perfectly legal step to take, I'm not suggesting that they do this because some people might consider it unethical.

But say that Grandma, or Uncle John, or Aunt Cathy decides that your birthday present every year will be a $100 contribution toward your college education. Grandma can serve you better if she just tells you she's putting $100 aside for you and actually keeps it in her name. Then she can write a check when the time to pay tuition arrives.

Tell your parents they need an IRA

If your parents don't have an IRA, encourage them to start one fast. An IRA not only is a work-free income source (see the preceding section), but you also save taxes on the money put into it. And IRAs, as an added bonus, make you eligible for more financial aid. (I'm using IRA, the most common term, to include all tax-deferred retirement accounts that go by such names as 401[k], Keogh, and SEP.)

When you apply for financial aid and the government's computers calculate how much you should be expected to pay, they don't count your or your parents' assets in an IRA. Get as much into an IRA as the law and your family budget permit. You can read more on planning for college costs in Chapter 15 and *College Financial Aid For Dummies* (IDG Books Worldwide, Inc.) by Dr. Herm Davis and Joyce Lain Kennedy. To find out more on tax-deferred retirement accounts, check out *Personal Finance For Dummies,* 2nd Edition, by Eric Tyson (IDG Books Worldwide, Inc.), at a bookstore near you.

You've got lots of company

Take it from the experts. If you're not applying to Harvard or Yale, you have plenty of company. The students who shoot for the high-prestige colleges are a tiny, elite group.

A study by the U.S. Education Department found that only 6 percent of all college-bound seniors meet the five basic criteria required by highly selective colleges. That's about 150,000 of the 2.5 million students out there looking.

The five minimum criteria generally required by very selective schools:

✔ A grade point average of 3.5 on a scale in which 4.0 means all *A*s

✔ A score of 1180 on the SAT (1100 before the scoring changes of 1995)

✔ Four high school English credits; three credits each in math, science, and social studies; two credits in a foreign language

✔ Positive responses from teachers to a series of questions about the students

✔ Two school-related activities

When the cutoffs were lowered to a 3.0 grade point average and a 1000 SAT score, the government experts found just 19.5 percent of the college applicants made this cutoff. Don't shy away from college because the geniuses in your class are applying. Four of every five applications are filled out by regular people who took the time to have a life.

In Chapter 1, you can see a list of the 22 colleges that accept fewer than 35 percent of their applicants. That's 22 of the 1,500 four-year colleges in the country. If that list were expanded to colleges accepting fewer than half their applicants, it still would have only 78 names. More than 1,400 colleges take more than half the students who apply.

Part II
Finding the Right Colleges

The 5th Wave By Rich Tennant

@RICHTENNANT

"There are some questions you have to ask yourself before picking a college, son. What's their curriculum? Where are they located? How big are their doors?"

In this part . . .

Now the search begins. In this part, stroll, year by year, through the process of finding the colleges that fit you best. Chapters 3, 4, and 5 help you narrow the field to select the campuses that you want to visit. Chapter 6 offers advice on the visits, and Chapter 7 helps you deal with the interviews. Then, in Chapter 8, you can put together all your new knowledge to decide where you will apply.

Chapter 3

What You're Doing (And Not Doing)

*U*nder ideal conditions, your sophomore year is the time to start your serious search for a college. Conditions are ideal if you're reading this book as a sophomore or earlier. But nobody said that everybody's conditions are ideal. If you're starting your search as a senior you can still conduct a serious search for a college, and do it right, but this means you must crunch more work into a shorter time.

By all means, you want to find the colleges that best fit you, your educational needs, and your distinct, individual personality. This book offers sound advice for making those choices. But the choices must be yours. You and your best friend may follow the same advice and reach totally different conclusions, because you are two different people.

Nobody else can make the decision for you because nobody else is you. Others will have advice, some good, some not-so-hot. Accept all advice graciously, digest it, sort it out, and then decide where you want to spend several years of your life.

If you search for your college the right way, you can be a happy student. You won't be transferring somewhere else after your freshman year, like all your friends who didn't do their searches right.

You're Looking for Places Where You Can Thrive

If you haven't yet asked yourself the all-important question, ask now. Why do you want to go to college? If you answer truthfully, you'll probably give yourself a long list of reasons. Some will be education related (to learn more than you already know), some will be linked to your future (to get a job in your chosen field), some perhaps will be connected to your personal life (to learn to live away from home). To help yourself answer the important questions, here are some preliminary questions you can ask yourself. Nobody else needs to know your answers. So make sure that you tell yourself the truth.

Do I want to go to college because

- ✔ My friends are going?
- ✔ My parents expect me to go?
- ✔ I can make more money with a degree?
- ✔ I'm ready to live on my own?
- ✔ I want to learn how to be a doctor, teacher, engineer, and so on?
- ✔ I haven't learned as much as I think I should know?
- ✔ I'm not sure what I want to do, and I think college can help me find out?
- ✔ I can't think of anything better to do?

Mull your answers around for a while in your head. If you're a typical student, you have more than one reason for going to college. When you search for the right colleges, you want to look for places where all those needs — educational, career-oriented, personal — can be fully satisfied. You want to look for places where you can thrive, academically and socially, as a student and as a person.

If your goal is, say, to be a chemist, you want to look at more than just good chemistry programs. You may find an outstanding chemistry curriculum at a school whose personality severely clashes with yours. (Yes, colleges have personalities just like you. I get into that later in this chapter, in the section "You're Checking Personalities.") Then that particular college is not right for you. You may learn a lot of chemistry, but you won't be happy learning it. You won't thrive.

You're looking for colleges where everything comes together for you. Trust me, these colleges are out there. Finding these schools takes a little work, but when you find them, you'll be happy you invested the time.

You're Making Lists

Lists are a big part of your search process, so get ready for them. You can write them on a tablet. (Don't worry, only you have to read them.) You can make them look pretty on a word processor. If you're lucky enough to have the right software at your school or your library, you can have a computer compile some of them for you.

The first list already is made for you. This first list is a list of the 3,500-plus colleges across the country that award degrees and want your tuition money. This monster list can be found in any of those huge directories listed in Chapter 1 — *College Handbook, Barron's, Peterson's, Arco,* and many more — that sit on your guidance office shelves. You also can find this list in software programs sold by some of those directory publishers. I have not yet found such lists on the Internet, but it probably won't be long (when the publishers discover a way to charge us for accessing them) until they appear.

Start, ideally as a sophomore, by taking names from that long list. Keep your list in a safe place. Your list will get smaller and smaller until, early in your senior year, it will contain only the names of the colleges to which you'll apply.

You're Checking Personalities

A key part of your search, probably the most important part, is the personality check. After you find colleges that on paper (or on a computer screen) look like they may be right for you, you need to check them out in person to make sure.

You have your personality. Each college has its own personality. You must decide whether your personalities mesh or clash.

The personality check takes time, so allow at least two days for each school you're checking. But don't think of your visits in terms of just driving through a campus, looking at the pretty elm trees, and saying, "This is a nice place." That would be a wasted effort.

You have to get out of the car and talk to people. Even live with them for a while. These are the people with whom you'll spend four years. Are they good guys or jerks?

If you don't take the time for a personality check and then wind up in a community of jerks, the only person more disappointed than you will be me. It will mean I'm wrong. You'll be writing for applications to transfer to another college by October of your freshman year.

The personality check is so important that I devote chapters 6 and 7 to the work that goes into it.

You're Looking for Colleges

The title of this part of the book is "Finding the Right Colleges." Yes, that means more than one college. No single college is right for you, so don't panic if you can't find it.

What you will find, as your lists grow smaller and smaller, are several schools that seem like they can give you everything you need. As you check them out in person, you'll be convinced that three or four — maybe six or seven — of these schools are places where you can thrive. These schools are your right colleges.

You'll have one or two favorites. But you'll apply to more, just in case your top choices decide they don't want you or they don't give you enough money to make them affordable.

I know that when you send in your applications, you'll be comfortable with your decisions. You won't be biting your nails, like your friends, fearing the rejection letter that will ruin your life. You'll know that wherever you wind up, you'll be at a right college, a campus on which you can thrive.

Why You're Not Choosing a College

If you're tempted to add a college to your list for any of the reasons described in the following sections, resist it. Or you can yield to the temptation, add the school to your list, and then check the school out carefully to see whether it belongs on your list. But none of these reasons, by itself, has any validity in identifying a school at which you can thrive.

Someone else likes the college

Someone else isn't you. Just because thousands of other students decide that they want to go to College X doesn't mean College X is the place for you. College X could very well be right for you, but that has no relation whatever to how many other students like it.

If all your friends are flocking to Flagship State, and you think you'd like to be with your friends, fine. Put Flagship State on your list. But don't apply to the school just because your friends do. You're dealing with your life, not plans for a party. See whether Flagship State has what you need. See whether your personalities mesh. If this college is not a good fit for you, tell your friends you're going somewhere else. Maybe they'll follow you.

If an older sibling or friend you respect highly recommends the college she's attending, that's a perfectly good reason to put it on your list for a hard look. But such a recommendation is not a good reason to rush to the admission office, application in hand.

The college has prestige

If you want to go to Yale just so that you can say you're at Yale, fine. Apply to Yale and see whether you're accepted. But you don't need this book. The prestige of a college in the eyes of the world at large has absolutely no bearing on your ability to thrive on its campus.

True, graduates of some high-profile colleges do have a better chance of finding jobs in their chosen field. And if you have a field in mind, part of your search process will be to identify colleges that seem to be favored by those employers. Likelihood of employment is a valid ingredient to toss into the pot you're stirring to find a college. And occasionally, likelihood of employment is linked to a school's prestige. But the likelihood of employment is just one of many ingredients in the recipe. If you choose a college only because it gives you a good chance of finding work, you may be gainfully employed in four years, but you may be miserable until then.

The college is tough to get into

For some reason, the prestige of a college often is measured by how tough it is to get into. The number used in comparing that toughness is the school's *admission rate,* which is the percentage of applicants who are accepted. The lower the number, presumably, the better the school. When you think about low admission rates as an indicator of the better schools, that kind of comparison doesn't make much sense. Such a comparison is, well, dumb.

Look at Yale, which accepted 20 percent of the people who applied for its 1996 freshman class. That's one of the lowest admission rates in the country — but not the lowest. Princeton was lower, at 14 percent. Cooper Union in New York City was lower still, taking just 12 percent of its applicants. All three are good colleges, but do those numbers mean Princeton and Cooper Union are a little better than Yale? Of course not.

Those admission rates mean more students applied to Princeton and Cooper Union, in relation to the number of places in their freshman classes, than applied to Yale. The numbers may also mean that Princeton was more popular than Yale among the high school seniors of 1996. Or the numbers may mean Princeton did a better job of recruiting applicants. (One reason Princeton-type schools recruit applicants is so that they can publish lower admission rates in the college directories, thus appearing even more prestigious.)

And Cooper Union? This school always has an enormous number of applicants — and a low admission rate — because it charges no tuition. A tuition-free college certainly is attractive, but not necessarily better.

Your parents want you to go to the college

Some of my best friends are parents. I've even been known to practice parenthood myself. Parents as a group are generally well-meaning folks, but I'm fully aware that occasionally they can cause trouble.

And trouble does erupt in a search for a college. Parents frequently think they know best where their beloved offspring should go. They've known what's best for the kid all these years, and they can find no reason as to why their wisdom is diminished just because the kid is growing up.

Sometimes parental wisdom works. Parents and kids agree on what's best. Often, it doesn't. The parents' choice and the student's choice are on opposite ends of the spectrum. Much family stress ensues.

Well-meaning parents often overlook one little item. When their kid goes to college, they get to stay home. They don't have to commit four years of their lives to a strange place where they've never lived. The student's life is what is on the line, and picking a college has to be the student's decision.

At college time, your parents become advisers. They're very important advisers, to be sure. Accept their advice willingly and consider it thoughtfully. But in the end, the only person who will know what's right for you is you.

Your parents are also very likely your financial backers. Without their check, you may well be going nowhere. And their advice on how much they can afford will be a key element in your decision.

If Dad is a Princeton man and is urging you to go to Princeton to keep the family tradition alive, fine. Put Princeton on your list. Give it a hard look. Consider that your chances of being accepted are higher because you're the child of an alumnus. But if, after checking it out thoroughly, you decide that Princeton is not the right college for you, advise Dad politely that you're going somewhere else. If you'd rather not tell him yourself, hand him this book and I'll do it for you:

"Hey, Dad! Your daughter's no fool. You did such a good job raising an intelligent young woman that she's now ready to make some choices on her own about how she'd like to pursue her life. Back off from that Princeton stuff and have the confidence in her to let her choose the right college for herself."

The college ranks high in magazines

You've seen them. They're a lot of fun to read. They're the lists in national magazines that appear every year ranking colleges by whatever criteria the magazine's editors select. These lists tout the best colleges, the cheapest colleges, the best engineering colleges, the best college values, the best tiny colleges, and so on.

The magazine rankings serve some useful purposes. They give college presidents something to complain about. And the presidents take advantage of every opportunity to complain about how meaningless it is to try to compare colleges, whatever yardsticks are used.

The rankings also keep college public relations offices busy. While their presidents are out complaining, the PR folks at schools ranking high on the lists churn out press releases and recruiting literature trumpeting the news that their institution is in the Top Ten of Best Colleges with Red Brick Dormitories in the Great Plains States.

One list I've never seen in a magazine is Best Colleges for You. I'll bet you haven't seen one either. Only you can compile this list.

Some information in some of the magazine rankings will be useful to you. In the fine print, a few show you the data that they've gathered to come up with their lists. And total books in a college library, or the percentage of full professors per student, certainly is good to know, but such a number is hardly the information on which you would base a final decision.

The criteria used by magazines to rank colleges will most likely not be the same criteria that you, after careful thought, will use to decide which colleges fit you best. And those rankings that purport to tell you the value you get for your education dollar don't know how many dollars you will be required to spend. All they know is each school's published sticker price, which two of every three freshmen don't pay in full. I'll repeat that because it's so important. The rankings that tell you which colleges offer best value in relation to their costs do not know how much you'll be required to pay.

So read the rankings. Enjoy them. Chuckle over them with your friends when you see that Flagship State doesn't make the Best State Colleges Beginning with the Letter F. But don't use them to decide where you'll go to college.

How many applications?

How many applications should you send? Does a college know whether you apply somewhere else? Does it hurt your chances to apply to maybe a dozen schools? Those questions often are asked by students as they start thinking about college. And students who don't ask aloud probably are wondering to themselves.

The short answer: Don't worry about sending out too many applications. Every college in the country hopes it will be the only one receiving an application from you, but every college also knows it won't be so lucky. Most students these days apply to at least three or four schools. But the number is limited only by the time you have to complete the applications and the money you can afford in application fees. Most colleges these days want $40, $50 or $60 in a nonrefundable fee just for considering your application. Only you and your parents know how much you can afford. My best advice is that if you're pretty sure that you don't have a chance of making a school's cutoff, don't waste the $40.

Unless you're applying for an early decision (see Chapter 9), don't limit yourself to one college. You're just hurting yourself. If that one college says no, you'll have to scramble to find other colleges that have space left.

When you reach the end of the process of finding your right colleges in Chapter 8, you'll have four schools left on your list. I suggest that you apply to all four and then find two more that also should get your application.

Six is not a magic number. You'll know, after you complete the process, how many schools feel right for you. Apply to all of them, even if they number a dozen.

No, a college does not know where else you apply unless you tell the college. Some schools once shared that information, but the U.S. Justice Department told them it was a highly illegal, bad thing to do. The antitrust laws seem to prevent the sharing of this information. So the schools stopped sharing. You can safely apply to a dozen schools and none will know it. And if they do, they won't care.

Chapter 4
Tenth Grade — Starting Early

*T*enth grade (your sophomore year) may not be the only time to seriously start looking at colleges, but it's probably the best time. If you're ready to start as a freshman and make your college search a longer, more leisurely process, go ahead. Start early. If you're reading this as a junior or senior, you're not too late. You'll just have to hustle a little harder.

The advice in this chapter assumes that you're working under ideal conditions — that you have more than two years left before you walk across a stage to get your high school diploma. If that's not you, make adjustments to fit your time frame.

So now, early in your sophomore year, the time has come to do more than think about college. Get out a pen and a tablet. Or sit down at your computer and activate your word processor. You're about to make your first of many lists.

The First List — What's Important

The first list is easy. All the information you need for this list is in your head. To make this list, however, requires some thought. But that's easy, too, because you're a good student and you have those thinking gears well lubricated. Right?

If you've already read Chapter 2, remember that I suggest several questions to mull over for a while because you'll have to decide whether they're important to you. (If you haven't read Chapter 2, don't leave. I repeat the questions in the following sections.) To begin your serious search, you must now decide the importance of each item you've been mulling over. You'll use the most important ones to help compile your first list of colleges and to eliminate a whole bunch of other schools.

Review the items on your Mull List — the first questions you'll ask yourself about a college. (In case you've misplaced your list, I'm about to remind you what those questions are.) As you think about each item, assign it a score. Use any scoring scale you like: 1 to 5, A to E, whatever. Leave space to make notes for the items to which you assign high scores. That way you can remind yourself why you think they are important.

Distance

Do you want to leave home? If so, how far would you like to go? Does how often you get home during your college years matter to you? If you feel strongly about distance, score it high — and make a note about how far away you'd like to be.

Size

Is the number of students at your college important to you? Big schools and small schools each have pros and cons. Would you feel comfortable on a large campus that offers a wide array of activities, social life, and cultural opportunities, but where you could also get lost in the masses and be just a number in some giant classes? Would you like the small classes and individual attention more prevalent at smaller schools? Or would you be happy with a little of both worlds at a medium-sized institution? If the size of a college is important, score it high and make a note that you like large, small, or in between. If you don't really care, give size a low score.

Location

Do you care about the area around your college? You can find schools of all sizes in big cities, suburbs, small towns, and pastures. Assign a score to location. If you consider the location of your college to be important, remind yourself why.

Major

Do you know yet what field you'd like to pursue as a major? If you're like most sophomores, you have not firmly decided. So, majors offered by a college may not be important right now. But if you're leaning toward certain areas, you'll want to look at colleges that offer programs in those fields. And if you're certain which way you want to go, then major should get a high score on your list.

Housing

Do you want to live on campus? In a dorm? Is a large number of students living on a campus where life revolves around the dorms important? Or do you care whether most of your fellow students commute? Write housing on your list and score it high or low.

Students

Would you like a college where your sex (or the opposite sex) dominates the student population? Or would you be happier with an even balance between the genders? Is racial diversity important? If you're African-American, do you think that you would thrive at a predominantly black school? Or do you care? Assign a score to students.

The test score factor

Test score factor can be a sticky category. You probably weren't ready to think about it until your sophomore year, and maybe you're not ready even now. But give it a brief thought: Do you want to go to a college where you think that everyone else is smarter than you, or one where you think that everyone else is not quite so bright as you? Or how about a place where everyone seems to be about on your level? I digress for a paragraph or two to tell you why this category is sticky.

Colleges like to compare themselves with each other on the basis of how smart their students are. The problem is that no one has come up with a good way to do this. So the colleges use the only measuring rod available: their students' scores on college entrance tests, such as the SAT and ACT. If College X students have a 1250 SAT average and College Y students have 1200, College X can say something such as "nana-nana, boo-boo." And College X does.

Many schools publish their SAT or ACT scores in the college directories. Some schools report average scores. Others list ranges, usually the range into which the middle half of their students fall. (That means 25 percent score above the range, 25 percent score below.)

A Mull List

Here's an example of a Mull List made by the hypothetical student described in this chapter.

Item	Rating (A-E)	Comment
Distance	B+	Max 200 miles from home
Size	A	Not giant, not tiny
Location	A	Small town or suburbs
Major	E	Undecided
Housing	B	Would like dorm
Students	D	Coed campus
Test scores	C	Not fussy

But even those numbers don't always compare apples to apples. When the schools figure averages or ranges, some schools count all students' scores. Some schools count all but the jocks. Some schools count all but jocks and minorities. Other schools count all but jocks, minorities, and kids of alumni. Believe it or not, some schools count all who were accepted, whether or not they show up at the college. A bright student who applied to and was accepted at four colleges could have her SAT score calculated into four schools' averages, although she's attending only one of those schools.

You may hear a college admission officer — in a conversation with a colleague but never with you — describe a student as a NIP. That's an acronym for *Not In Profile,* which is jargon meaning students whose SAT scores aren't included in the published averages. NIPs most commonly are free-ride athletes, underrepresented minorities, and children of alumni — groups who tend to bring the college's test score averages down.

Comparing students' abilities by using just their SAT and ACT scores is sticky enough to start. Given the variety of methods used to calculate the published scores, such comparisons get even stickier.

The good news is that colleges know they have a problem and are trying to solve it. College presidents, admission officers, and representatives of publications that use those test scores in their national rankings have been meeting to seek a standard way of reporting scores with which all can live. By early 1997, they had many discussions but made few decisions. Even the most optimistic say that a standard reporting process won't be in place until 1999 or later.

Still, knowing all this, you can find out something from the test scores in the college directories. These scores can give you some clue to the academic talent among the student body — how well most students do on the SAT or ACT compared to you. Most schools break down their published SAT scores into their math and verbal scores, so you also can get an idea of how the students do in those areas. If you are thinking about an engineering major, for example, you'll want to pay closer attention to the math scores.

Do you want a school where the scores average in the same range as yours? Or where they're considerably higher or lower? Write SAT or test score on your list. If this factor is important, score it high. And make a note to remind yourself why.

You have just taken the first step toward finding your right colleges. This was not a test. The only correct answers are the ones you wrote. You made a list, and now you'll put it to good use.

The First Cut — Eliminating 3,100

Now you hit the books or the computer. Go to one of those college directories, two inches thick with 2,000 pages of fine print, resting on the shelves of your school guidance office. If you're lucky, your school will have spent $400 on a software program produced by the publisher of one of those directories (several are available) that will put the information you need at your fingertips with the click of a mouse and a few keystrokes. If your school has neither the software nor a directory — that is, if your guidance office isn't adequately equipped — try your local public library. The library should have at least one college directory in stock. (Another source is the library at a nearby college.)

When you see the book, don't go into shock. You don't have to the read the whole thing. That's why you made the list of important stuff. The directory has descriptions of more than 3,200 colleges, almost the entire universe of the country's degree-awarding institutions. You will eliminate more than 3,100 of them, and you'll do it in an hour or two. Okay, maybe eliminating all these schools will take you half a day. But consider the half day to be well spent. Besides, what else do you have to do on a Saturday morning in tenth grade? Detention?

If you can find a computer with a college search program on it — and more schools are buying them every year — this first cut can be made in less than an hour. Would you believe 20 minutes?

To illustrate the process, I make up some things about you. Say you live in the Midwest, in a suburb of Chicago. When you made your list of important stuff, you decided that you would like to stay in the Midwest, within a three-hour drive of home. You decided that neither a very large nor very small college appeals to you. You would like a campus with a substantial number of students and a variety of activities, but small enough that a professor might know who you are. And you have no desire to be in an urban area. Suburbs and small towns are okay, but cities aren't.

The factors you rated highest on your list are size, location, and distance. Housing was close to the top because you're looking forward to dorm life as part of your college experience. You have no strong feelings yet about a major, so it was at the bottom.

You open a college directory. Despite the intimidating appearance, the directory is designed to be user friendly. It contains indexes of schools, by state, in all kinds of categories. You go to the indexes and find this directory groups colleges into four sizes: small, medium, large, and very large. You see that the medium and large groups lumped together would give you colleges with enrollments between 1,000 and 7,500. That's an appealing size range.

The following are the possible ranges:

✔ Small, under 1,000

✔ Medium, 1,000–3,000

✔ Large, 3,000–7,500

✔ Very large, over 7,500

Your desire to stay close to home means you'll limit your search to Illinois, Indiana, and Wisconsin. You check the indexes for medium and large colleges in those three states that aren't in urban areas. That amounts to 58 schools. You notice that the list includes three institutes of technology and an art college. You have no desire to be an engineer or an artist, so you forget those. That leaves 54 schools.

Make Another List

Next, you make another list. This task takes a few hours with a directory, a few minutes on a computer. First, write down (or ask the computer to print) those 54 names. Then go through the directory briefly reading the descriptions of these schools. Make notes of things you find attractive or disenchanting beside each school's name on your list. Also note the address of each college's Web site, which most directories now include. You'll want the address later, when you're gathering more information. Don't bother with the price tag. At this point, you're not ruling out any college because of its cost.

If you're lucky and find a computer with a college search program on it, this job will be much faster. The computer compiles the lists, based on your important criteria, and finds the college descriptions for you to read. But you still have to read them, on the screen or from a printout.

To continue my example, at this point you're reading the descriptions and you find out that four colleges on your list are single-sex: two for men, two for women. You scratch the two that won't accept you. The list now contains 52 schools. You see that seven are predominantly commuter schools, with fewer than 20 percent of their students living on campus. That's not the kind of college you had in mind, so they go. You're down to 45 schools.

Congratulations! You have just eliminated more than 3,100 colleges, and identified 45 colleges that you'll consider. That number can change, up or down, as you gain more information, but 45 is a fine number to start with in tenth grade.

Put your list in a safe place. You'll need to refer to this list over the next year or so.

Remember, the reason 45 colleges are on your list is because I made up stuff about you and what's important to you. I did that simply to illustrate the process. The number of schools on your first list may be lower or higher. The number 45 is not sacred, nor is any other number that I use for illustration in the examples throughout this book.

Take the PSAT

 Yes, I know you take too many tests already. But you'll have a chance to take even more, unrelated to any of your classes, as you move through high school. The best thing you can do for yourself is take them all and take them often.

The first test you'll face as a sophomore is the PSAT. The test name was probably once an abbreviation for Preliminary SAT, because that's its principal role, but now the letters don't stand for anything. The test is just called the PSAT.

You'll also see the test described as the PSAT/NMSQT. Some students call this test "pee-sat num-squat," but the folks who own the test don't particularly like that pronunciation. Don't be confused: The PSAT and PSAT/NMSQT are exactly the same test. The letters that come after the slash, NMSQT, are an excellent reason to take the test at least twice.

NMSQT stands for National Merit Scholarship Qualifying Test. The people who distribute merit scholarships choose their national semifinalists solely on scores from the PSAT taken as a junior. If your PSAT score is high enough, you'll qualify as a semifinalist. And, of course, you can't be a national merit finalist unless you're a semifinalist.

But you're a sophomore. Why take the PSAT now? Because this is the first time that this test is available to you, plus you get two advantages. One, you become familiar with the test (it even identifies your strengths and weaknesses); so when your score counts for something a year later, you're not going in cold. Two, the test identifies your strong points and areas where you need work for its parent test, the SAT, which will be a key element in your college application.

The PSAT is a mini-SAT. The PSAT has the same types of questions, just fewer of them. The test lasts two hours (the SAT takes three). When the SAT was revised in 1993, the PSAT underwent similar revisions. After taking the PSAT, you receive a report showing how you did — whether right or wrong — on each question. You see what you must do to improve. Take the PSAT as a sophomore, when its score means nothing to your future, and you'll be better prepared to score high on the later tests that are meaningful.

Surf the Net

With your preliminary list of colleges tucked in a safe place, you'll spend the rest of your sophomore year trying to find out more about them. And you'll be looking for other colleges that might interest you enough to earn a place on your list. An increasingly valuable tool in this effort is the Internet, and you should take advantage of this technological advancement.

Hundreds of Web sites are out in cyberspace offering information about colleges, and many of these sites can be valuable in your search. To start, visit the colleges on your list that have their own home pages. (You recorded their addresses when you compiled your list.) See what these schools tell you about their admission requirements, course offerings, and campus life. Look for links to other data, such as student newspapers or course catalogs. But remember that a college uses its Web site to tell you only what it wants you to know. Read a Web site as you would an ad in a newspaper or magazine. A Web site is a college's cyberspace ad.

Dozens of college-search advice sites abound, some offering better advice than others. The problem, as with all Web surfing, is you don't know which sites are time-wasters until you get to those that are. A good place to begin searching for general college information is the College Board site at www.collegeboard.org. The information that this site provides and the sites to which it links you are accurate and up-to-date.

Even more valuable can be conversations on the Internet and computer bulletin boards with people who know about colleges — students, professors, or recent graduates. They can tell you the stuff you don't find in the college advertising.

How to Fair Well

One very efficient way to gain information on many colleges in a short time is at a college fair or college night. These events enable college representatives to set up booths — or just sit at tables — to distribute literature and talk to students about their schools.

College fairs are similar to dating services. The fairs put you and the college together, but finding romance is still up to the two of you.

Take advantage of the opportunity to chat with folks from as many colleges as you can. Ask any questions that occur to you. Don't feel that any question is too dumb because, whatever your question, college admission officers have heard even dumber ones. The officers' only job that night is to answer high school students' questions.

The bare-bones version of a fair is a high school's college night, to which colleges in the area are invited. More often these days, groups of high schools collaborate on a regional college night that attracts more colleges because the crowd is larger. Some colleges have networks of alumni across the country who volunteer to represent them at college nights. A rule of thumb is that alums know less about what's happening at their alma maters than employees of college admission offices. The other side of that coin is that alumni often are more candid about life on their campuses than the people who work at them.

The most elaborate fairs are the series arranged by the National Association for College Admission Counseling, held in convention centers and large hotels from coast to coast. These fairs attract hundreds of colleges and, often, thousands of students, many convoyed in from nearby areas in yellow buses. Notices are usually sent to high school guidance offices that are within a three-hour drive of the fair site. To get a schedule of the national fairs, write to College Fair Desk, NACAC (pronounced nack-ack), 1631 Prince St., Alexandria, VA 22314-2818.

When you go to a fair, look first for schools that are on your preliminary list. (Remember the hypothetical number 45?) Talk to their representatives and see what kind of vibes you get. If you'd like information that is not available in a school's directory listing — perhaps its freshman SAT range or something about its music program — ask at the fair. You may find out things that cause you to drop a school from your list or to consider a school more seriously.

Then visit other colleges at the fair. The term *fishing trip* may sound crude, but that's what you go on. You cast a line to see whether schools that didn't make your first cut have something to offer that will persuade you to reconsider them. Pay attention to your vibes. If you enjoy talking to someone from a college, if you discover good chemistry with an admission officer, chances are that chemistry might extend throughout the campus. If the college is close to your requirements in size, location, major, or whatever, it will deserve a spot on your list so that you can find out whether that energy is campus-wide.

Open All That Mail

Another reason to take the PSAT your sophomore year is that the volume of mail with your name on it will increase. If your PSAT score is pretty high, the mail could become fairly heavy.

Mail in itself isn't that much fun. But this mail will help you learn more about colleges in the comfort of your own bedroom, while exerting no more energy than you use to slice open envelopes.

Material will come from colleges close to home and hundreds of miles away, from some colleges on your preliminary list and from some you are certain you don't want, and even from some schools that you don't even know exist.

The mail will contain flowery form letters asking for some of your time so that you can find out about the colleges, brochures, perhaps catalogs, and other literature with pretty pictures of smiling students on scenic campuses. Some of the mail could even contain information that's valuable to you.

Why are all these schools sending you stuff? How do they know you exist? Why is Lenoir-Rhyne interested in you when you've never heard of Lenoir or Rhyne?

You, just as your friends on the football team, are being recruited. These colleges got your name the old-fashioned way: They bought it, for about 15 cents. When you took the PSAT, you filled in a form providing personal data about yourself. You also checked a box saying your name could be given to colleges and then promptly forgot about doing so. (If you didn't check the box, you should have. Despite the jokes that college mail produces among students, this mail has enough pertinent information to make the little effort you spend opening the envelopes worthwhile.)

The College Board, the outfit that owns the PSAT, keeps a database of the personal information all test takers provide. Colleges buy names of students who meet their requirements from the database. Suppose that Lenoir-Rhyne wants to target students over a certain PSAT score in Maryland, Delaware, and Pennsylvania. The school buys a list of those students. Should you fit that description, you'll hear from Lenoir-Rhyne.

If nothing else, the volume of your mail is an early indication of how desirable a college applicant you will be. Colleges only recruit students they want. The more mail you get, the more colleges want you.

Open all the mail. If mail is from a college in your Top 45, read it thoroughly and file it in the same safe place you tucked your list. Glance at the stuff from the other schools and see whether anything makes you stop and say "Hmmm." If it does, peruse the literature with care. You may want to add that college to your list.

After the first mailing, most respectable colleges won't bother you again unless you express an interest. Most colleges include a card that you can return if you want to find out more. If you're interested, return the card.

Talk to People

Another source of information is plain, simple conversation. Talking to people can be a valuable source, especially if you're talking with someone whose opinions you trust. As a sophomore, gather information from wherever you can find it. You seek information specifically about the colleges on your preliminary list as your likely choices, but at this early stage, you're accepting advice about any school. The following sections describe potential sources of information.

Friends

You know people who go to college, who have older siblings that go to college, who have visited colleges. Your own older siblings probably qualify. Talk to them all. Solicit their opinions. Don't treat everything they say as gospel; just file their words to consider with all your other information.

Parents' friends

Many of your parents' friends no doubt went to college and know others who did. Ask them for opinions. And act grateful when opinions are delivered.

Internet friends

If you're active on the Net, you probably have a group of regular correspondents with whom you're trading opinions on trigonometry, baseball players, music groups, and software programs. Some of them likely are searching for colleges. Some may have already found their right schools. Ask them for advice. And share some of the stuff you have found out. You can even tell them about this book.

Teachers

Teachers are in the grapevine. They have had their own college experiences and they talk regularly with former students who are or have been in college. Teachers with whom you feel comfortable can be excellent sources of advice. Keep them apprised of what you're doing, the lists you're making, and the reasons you're making them. If you chat with a certain teacher throughout your college-search process, he or she will likely be ready and willing to help when the time comes to write a letter of recommendation.

Counselors

For a college-bound student, a good counselor is a gold mine. Good counselors maintain regular contact with college admission offices and understand the way they make their decisions. If you have a good counselor, talk to her often and listen to her advice. If your counselor knows you well, she can guide you to colleges that fit you best.

Unfortunately, not all high school students have good counselors. Many students have the kind who can learn a good deal by reading this book. Unfortunately, I know of no quick way to tell whether a counselor is competent. You can get an indication, though, by asking about the admission standards at a nearby college that attracts many students from your school. If the counselor gives you a clear, straight answer, he probably knows what's he's talking about. If he refers you to a directory to look it up for yourself, assume he's the other kind.

Regardless of how competent your counselor is, though, make a point to regularly check the shelves in the counseling center. Colleges near and far will send your school literature they want you to read. If something interests you, read it.

Take a Stroll on a Campus

Tenth grade is not too early to make a campus visit. This first visit isn't a formal visit, when you interview people, but a get-acquainted, information-gathering tour.

Go to a college in your area and spend an hour or two walking around. Drop into the student center and see how students spend their leisure time. Walk around a dorm or two. Read the bulletin boards to see what's happening. Pick up a copy of the student newspaper to see what the current campus issues are.

Keep your eyes open and observe as much as you can. Talk to people if you have the opportunity. Even make notes, if you're comfortable doing so. You'll find out some things about that college that can give you clues as to what you might like or not like in the college you choose. Stroll into the admissions office and see what information it's giving away. But don't bother with any formal interviews yet. Tenth grade is too early, for you and the college, to talk seriously about your plans. That talk comes later.

If an older friend or relative lives in a college dorm, try to elicit an invitation for an overnight visit. The best way to find out how college students live is to live with them.

Take Time to Think

While you are collecting and storing information about colleges, stop for a minute every so often and think about what you're finding out and about yourself. Has anything changed since you made the list of important stuff? Do you find yourself leaning toward a particular type of college? Do you have a feeling, strong or otherwise, for what you'd like to study in college?

When you're a junior, more decisions must be made. You'll have to think about them then. If you think about the questions before it's time to come up with answers, those decisions are much easier to make.

Chapter 5

Eleventh Grade — Starting Later

● ●

In This Chapter

▶ Thinking major thoughts

▶ Making the cut a little deeper

▶ What not to worry about . . . yet

▶ Seeking specific information

▶ All about those dreaded tests

▶ Should you pay for help?

▶ Trimming the list way down

● ●

*I*t's halftime. You've finished your first two years of high school. Your record is on the books. You can do nothing to change it.

The second half is about to start. Grades 11 and 12 are still blank slates. The accomplishments you record on those slates are the most significant portion of your high school record that you eventually send to colleges. And one thing that impresses a college admission officer is a record that improves each year. Such a record shows that you are peaking at the right time. To find out more about how colleges look at you, see Chapter 9.

If your academic record is not as sparkling as you'd like it to be, you still have time to do something about it. A strong finish after a slow start looks better than an excellent record in ninth and tenth grades that deteriorates in the later years. So work on your academics now. Make your last two high school years stand out.

As you begin your junior year, you need to narrow and refine the list of colleges you're considering. You're about to take the initiative and let some colleges know you are seriously interested in them. You must trim your list to a number that's workable so that you can start to communicate with colleges without giving up time for important things, like an *A* in chemistry.

First you need to see where you are. To illustrate the process, I assume stuff about you as I do in Chapter 4. As you read, substitute your own experiences for my assumptions.

Keep Thinking about a Major

You've been thinking about a major since you made the first list of colleges and realized that you had no idea what you want to study. (If you haven't made a list yet, you can find out how to do so in Chapter 4.) Your junior year is the time for you to collect all your random thoughts, put them together in a package, and see what it looks like.

Say that you glanced at lists of majors offered by colleges and found some of them very long. They range from aeronautical engineering to zoology, often with more than 100 fields in between. Some majors you immediately ruled out — majors like Arabic, fashion design, medieval studies and wetlands engineering. (If you really are interested in Arabic or medieval studies, forget I said that. But you get the point. Some things just don't turn you on.)

As a sophomore, you became aware that you like to write. You enjoy the challenge of creating sentences out of words. You find that writing a paper is not the onerous chore that frustrates some of your classmates. You signed up for the school newspaper and found you like communicating information in writing. Or perhaps you've found the same enjoyment tinkering in a biology lab or making a computer do what you tell it.

In your summer job at a day camp, you had a chance to help coach a little kids' softball team. You found satisfaction in showing a young boy how to do something, maybe something as simple as catching a ball in a glove. You liked the spark in his eyes when he learned how to do it. And you liked the role you played in causing that spark. You wonder if you can do other things to create more sparks. Becoming a full-time coach or teacher comes to mind, but you're not sure you'd like either one. For the moment, though, you don't rule them out. At least you have some evidence you can do it. Maybe you had a summer job in an office and discovered that you have a talent for making columns of numbers balance. Whatever your experience, you're discovering abilities you never knew you had.

These thoughts are the kinds that help you focus on selecting a college major. Now you'll put all these thoughts together. You'll consider English, a field in which you can go many ways with a writing talent. The broad field of communications appeals to you because that's what you've been doing well — communicating with students through the school paper and with little kids on the playground. Journalism is a possibility. You'll keep education in the back of your mind, but the idea of dealing with students every day isn't that attractive. As a student, you know how tough they can be. Something in the future may change your thinking entirely, but for now that's the package your thoughts produce.

Refine Your List Further

Go back to the preliminary list you made as a sophomore with 45 (or whatever your number) colleges on it. (If you need to read more about making a preliminary list, see Chapter 4.) The list is a little different than when you first tucked it away in a drawer or a computer file. Since then, you've found out some things. Friends told you about two colleges that have reputations as party schools, where fraternity and sorority life dominates. You like to party occasionally, but it's not your top priority in life. You already deleted those two schools. In a report on crime statistics at colleges, you read about a crime-ridden campus that was on your list and scratched it. That cut the list to 42 colleges.

During your visits to college fairs, you found four schools not on your list that grabbed your attention. One school impressed you with its journalism program, and a chat with its representative got you thinking about a journalism major. The four missed your first cut because they're larger than the 7,500-student limit you used for your search. You added their names. Back up to 46.

Then you heard some good things from a teacher about a small college in Michigan where the faculty excels in teaching creative writing. You decided to find out more. Up to 47.

Now, you're ready to make a deeper cut of your list. You look at the list again and ponder it. You notice those two single-sex colleges are still there. You now know you want a campus with a good gender balance. You draw lines through those schools' names. Down to 45.

You wonder about your size requirements. You walked around a campus with 1,100 students. It felt too small for you. You think you'd like something larger with a wider variety of things to do. You decide to eliminate colleges with enrollments under 2,000. You check the notes on your list where you recorded each school's size. You count 16 that have sub-2,000 populations. They go. Your list has shrunk to 29.

Now about your major, the key element you didn't include in the important stuff for your original cut. You go back to the large college directory (or the guidance office computer) and check the majors offered by each of the remaining 29. They all have English. No surprise. You find 22 have some kind of communications major, but only 5 offer a specific major in journalism. And all but 3 of the 29 will train you to be a teacher with an education major.

You decide to narrow your focus again. You confine your search to the schools that offer majors in communications, journalism, and education, just in case you decide to go for some combination of the three. You recheck the list and see that 21 colleges qualify. Delete the others. You now have a list of your 21 semifinalists.

Remember: Just as 45 was not a hard-and-fast number for your first list, 21 is the same. It's simply a number to illustrate the process. I got to 21 because I assumed stuff about you. Your list of semifinalists could include 11 colleges, or 31, or any other number.

Only you know what the number should be because only you know what's important to you.

What You're Not Worrying About

You still didn't think about some things when you cut your list to 21 because your junior year is still too early to worry about them or because they're not important.

Money

Eventually you'll worry about money, but not yet. Early in your junior year is too soon to eliminate any college because of cost. Remember, two-thirds of all college freshmen pay less than the price published in directories. You have no idea yet how much you'll be expected to pay. So let's face it: Worrying about cost at this point is a waste of valuable energy. (You can read about finding money in Chapters 11 through 15. You can read more about not worrying about money in Chapter 2.)

Personality

Every college has a personality. Before you apply anywhere, check out your finalists to see whether your personalities mesh. But right now, you're determining which colleges deserve the honor of a personality check. First things first.

Selectivity

As you narrowed the field, you didn't bother to look at the percentage of applicants a college accepts. (Maybe you did, out of curiosity, but you didn't write the number down.) A college's selectivity, usually measured by its acceptance rate, has no bearing on whether it's a right college for you.

A low acceptance percentage means only that a whole lot more students apply than get in. This percentage is directly related to the popularity of a college among last year's high school seniors. And last year's seniors' opinions — unless you're getting one in person from someone you know — are not important in your search.

National rankings

At no time during your deliberations did you look at a magazine to see how a college fared in national rankings. Okay, you looked, but you didn't let it influence your decisions. You have no idea whether the criteria used by magazine editors are close to the criteria you desire in a college. Now that your list is down to 21, pick up a magazine and look — just for fun. See whether the magazine editors' choices agree with yours. Interesting, isn't it? And you can wonder a little about students who base their entire college-going decision on what they read in magazines. (More on magazine rankings in Chapter 3.)

Actively Seeking Information

With 21 colleges in your semifinals, you're starting to take the initiative. You're going after information rather than waiting for it to come to you.

The first step is sending a letter to each school on your list. Relax. You don't have to create 21 different letters. You can type one on a computer and print it 21 times, each with a different address and perhaps a few changed words. If you're lucky and have a college search program in the guidance office computer, it should contain a sample letter you can use as a model.

Your letter should go to the college admissions office. It should tell the dean of admission that his or her college is one of 21 you're seriously considering and contain a phrase or two explaining why. You don't need to get into an elaborate explanation. Something simple, like "because Old Siwash offers majors in communications and education," will suffice.

Frank J. Fussy
Dean of Admissions
9999 Nittpickie Hall
Flagship State University
Flagship, IL 55555

Dear Dean Fussy:

I am a junior at James Whitcomb Riley High School in Pumpkinville, Indiana. I am seeking information on colleges that may fit my needs after graduation. Because Flagship State offers majors in English, journalism, and education, your school is on the list of colleges to which I am writing.

Please send me all available information on your admission requirements, courses, campus housing, and financial aid. Please also include anything else you would like me to know about Flagship State that will help me make an informed decision.

Sincerely,

Stephanie Student

Figure 5-1:
A typical
first letter.

Ask the dean to send you all available information on admission requirements, financial aid, student housing, the majors to which you're leaning, and anything else that will help you learn about the school. Include a sentence or two about yourself, saying that you're a junior and play a mean trombone.

Address the letter personally to the dean of admission (or director or whatever the head person is called). The name and address are in most college directories.

The dean probably won't read your letter. A secretary will open your letter, gather the literature usually sent on such requests, and ship it to you with a form letter presigned by the dean. But your letter will be filed. And if you eventually apply to Old Siwash, the initial letter may become part of your application file. When an admission officer glances at it and sees you cared enough to find out the dean's name, you will make a favorable impression. Remember, little things count.

While you wait for the return mail, continue to talk to people — friends, teachers, and so on — about colleges they think might fit you. Mention the colleges to which you've written and see whether their names produce any opinions. Thank them graciously for their advice and file their words for future consideration.

Tests Don't Have to Be Painful

Yes, tests are tough. They're stressful. They make your palms moist. Those standardized tests where you must answer questions and race the clock at the same time are the worst. And the reason they cause stress is because they produce a result — a grade or a numerical score.

Calm down. Relax. I know relaxing is difficult at test time, but it can be done. The less you worry about your score, the less stress you will feel. And the less stress you feel, the better you'll do. Dozens of books have been written, and whole courses are offered, full of test-taking advice. Here's some in one simple sentence that comes with no extra fee: Take each test once just for fun.

Take a trial run

If you take a test when its score means nothing, you'll be familiar with it when it counts and you won't risk a thing. You'll discover what types of questions the test asks. You'll know what to expect when you take it again later. The test will be a friend, not a stranger. Experience shows you'll score higher on a later try than on that first, no-count try. You'll have less stress.

A practice round, of course, is not always possible. Your geometry teacher offers his final exam just once. But for the biggies — the PSAT, SAT, and ACT — a trial run is available.

PSAT

In Chapter 4, I suggest taking the PSAT as a sophomore. But that's just a trial run. Take it again in the fall of your junior year when its score means something.

The PSAT itself is practice for the SAT. The PSAT contains the same kinds of questions. But its other, more important role is as a qualifier for National Merit Scholarships. Each year, hundreds of students are named National Merit semifinalists solely because of their scores on the PSAT in eleventh grade.

If you become a National Merit finalist, college doors suddenly fling open. Presidents of schools you haven't contacted send you personal letters. Financial aid is plentiful. The Merit Scholarships themselves, which range from $500 up, are just part of the bounty. Colleges are more receptive to Merit Scholars because they like to have Merit Scholars on their campuses. Some even issue press releases announcing how many they have. But you can't become a Merit Scholar unless you're first a semifinalist. And you can't become a semifinalist unless you take the PSAT as a junior.

Surprisingly, many students don't know that this test leads to scholarship money. The evidence is plentiful. I've heard many sad tales from students who might have been Merit Scholars but aren't — because they didn't take the PSAT as a junior. They take the PSAT as sophomores and then forget it. And whenever I write about the PSAT, I think of John who has a full four-year free ride to Eckerd College in Florida because he's a Merit Scholar. Daily he thanks his eleventh-grade English teacher who insisted that he take the PSAT.

Take the PSAT as a sophomore for practice. Take the test again in the fall of your junior year when its score could open gates to your future. And in both instances, the PSAT will be practice for its older sibling, the SAT.

SAT

For 65 years, since it was first administered in the 1920s, the SAT was officially known as the Scholastic Aptitude Test. For most of those years, everyone concerned called it simply the *S A T*. Then the people who own the test, an outfit called the College Board, decided to go with the trend and change the name. The test became just the SAT.

A few years later, the College Board decided that name changing was so much fun, they'd change the test's name again. The SAT became the SAT I. Other tests the College Board administers (which I discuss later in this chapter) became SAT II. But because just about everyone still calls that important college admission exam the SAT, this book calls it the SAT. If you see the term SAT I, it means the same test that you, your parents, and grandparents know fondly as the SAT. (And the folks who publish this book embraced the new name in a volume of good advice called *SAT I For Dummies,* 2nd Edition, by Suzee Vlk [IDG Books Worldwide, Inc.] at a bookstore near you.)

Don't be confused by the two names. Some directories now publish colleges' SAT I scores. Some report SAT scores. Under either name, these scores are from the same test.

What's new about SAT I

When the good old SAT became the new-fangled SAT I in 1994, it got more than a new name. Some of its traditional sections were overhauled and questions were redesigned because its owners said they wanted to make it more relevant to the way students learn these days. As the College Board unveiled the SAT I with considerable fanfare, it was described as a "reasoning test." Those words are still used in some of its literature.

The SAT I still has a verbal section and a math section, and each is still scored on a range of 200 to 800. The test still consumes three hours of a Saturday morning. The big difference is fewer multiple choice questions, on which you can make educated guesses if you're not sure of an answer, and more questions to make you think.

The verbal section has four reading passages followed by a series of questions to see whether you understood what you read. The math section has questions that require you do to computation at your desk and fill in answers on a grid. And, yes, calculators now are allowed in the testing room for the SAT and PSAT.

In 1995, more changes arrived, but you see them only in your scores. The changes were called *recentering*, a process of shaking up the scoring system so that it's totally unrecognizable by anyone who knew how it worked in the past. Starting with the SAT I given in spring 1995, the new system took effect.

The problem, as the SAT folks see it, is that the national average score traditionally was around 900. That offended their sense of neatness. If the test is scored on a range of 400 to 1600, they figure the national average should be right in the middle: 1000. So they adjusted the scoring to make it happen. A student who scored 900 in 1995 now scores 1000 or more (depending on the mix of math and verbal scores) by answering the same questions the same way. Most other scores also increased but a few went down. Don't ask why. Just trust The College Board.

So if you take the test this year and think you scored higher than your older brother, think again.

The SAT also is available for practice but, unlike the PSAT, your practice score shows up on your record. This practice score just won't count if your second score is higher — and it probably will be.

The SAT is offered three or four times (sometimes more) each school year in every school district. Take it in the fall of eleventh grade, soon after you've taken the PSAT. Then take the SAT again in the spring. If you're a typical student, your spring score will be higher. The national average for students taking the SAT a second time is a 40-point increase. That's another very important fact worth repeating. For students taking the SAT a second time, the average score is 40 points higher. Most of that increase is attributed to students' familiarity with the test the second time around. And just about every college in the country will look only at your higher score for admission purposes.

SAT scores: New versus old

Here's how the new scores for the SAT I college admission test compare with the old.

For example, if you got a 600 verbal score in 1994, took the test again in 1996 and answered the same questions correctly, your score climbed to 670. But a 600 math score is still 600. It seems the verbal scores were more off center and needed greater adjustment than the math scores.

Verbal

Old	New	Old	New
730 – 800	800	250 – 520	80 points higher
710 – 720	70 points higher	220 – 240	70 points higher
610 – 700	60 points higher	210	270
530 – 600	70 points higher	200	230

Math

Old	New	Old	New
780 – 800	800	390 – 440	40 points higher
770	790	320 – 380	50 points higher
750 – 760	10 points higher	290 – 310	40 points higher
720 – 740	Unchanged	270 – 280	30 points higher
660 – 710	10 points lower	260	280
600 – 650	Unchanged	250	260
550 – 590	10 points higher	240	240
500 – 540	20 points higher	230	220
450 – 490	30 points higher	200 – 220	200

For those of you who scrutinize while you read, you may have noticed (from the table) that certain scores are missing from the *New* column. Nice catch. Some old scores can't be converted to these particular new scores, such as a new Math score of 210 or a new Verbal score of 770. But these new scores can be earned in the new system.

If you still don't like your score after taking the SAT twice, you can get a third shot in the fall of your senior year. And the College Board is making the sign-up process to take the test easier. You now can register for the SAT on the Internet, at the College Board Web site: www.collegeboard.org

Here's a tip to keep the perspiration from your palms. An SAT (or ACT) score will be an important part of your college application, but it won't be the only part. Not a single selective college in the country accepts or rejects applicants solely on the basis of test scores.

If a friend insists you can't get into Dartmouth unless you have a 1300 SAT, tell your friend he's wrong. Check a directory or computer program and you'll see that the middle half of Dartmouth's freshman SAT scores ranges from 1450 to 1260. That means 25 percent of Dartmouth's freshmen — one of every four — have scores below 1260. Of course, 25 percent also have scores above 1450.

ACT

ACT is an acronym for *American College Test.* This test is developed and administered by an organization in Iowa City known, appropriately, as the American College Testing Program.

The ACT often is considered a substitute for the SAT because that's how it's used. Some colleges, mostly in the Midwest and South, prefer an ACT score. SAT scores are in demand by colleges mainly on the East and West Coasts. But in these enlightened times, almost any college accepts either test. If a school says it prefers the ACT, that doesn't mean an SAT score makes you ineligible.

Although their roles are similar, the SAT and ACT are different kinds of tests. The SAT is designed to measure your ability to do college work. The ACT measures your knowledge of specific subjects: English, science, math, and so on.

Like the SAT (or SAT I, if you want to be official), the ACT is offered several times each year. Take the ACT first in the fall of your junior year. Then take it again (and again, and again, if you desire), and your score likely will go up. And just as with the SAT, colleges count only your highest ACT score. Don't punish yourself, however, by taking the SAT or ACT more than three or four times. By the fourth try, you've probably scored as high as you ever will. And some colleges frown on students who keep trying more than four times.

SAT II

Until the College Board's great name-changing orgy of 1994, these tests were known as Achievement Tests. They're still *achievement tests,* designed to measure your knowledge of specific subjects, but they now live under the SAT umbrella.

At last count, the College Board offers 16 different SAT IIs. (Or should the plural be SATs II?) You can take one in biology, chemistry, physics, writing, literature, two kinds of history, three levels of math, and six foreign languages.

Each is an hour-long exam that usually is offered on the same seven Saturday mornings as the SAT I. The ideal time to take an SAT II is when you have just completed a class in biology, chemistry, or whatever, and your knowledge of the subject is at a peak.

Some selective colleges ask for scores in certain SAT II tests. All colleges like to see these test scores. If you plan to major in engineering, for example, an admission officer hopes to see SAT II scores in math and a science or two. A good rule to follow is anytime in your junior or senior years that you're finishing a class for which an SAT II is available, take it. You do have to pay a fee to take the test — but it's cheaper to take the test and possibly not have to take the college course if you do well enough. You can get college credit for high scores on this test, and the credit counts toward your degree at some schools. Because you're not sure where you're going to go at this point, take the test — it may save you thousands of dollars.

And here's a vote for going back to the old name, Achievement Tests, which told you what they really are. SAT II sounds like an admission exam for second-level colleges. The name change adds to confusion instead of eliminating it.

Keep Opening the Mail

They're still coming. Those brochures with pretty pictures of happy students show up in your mail box with annoying regularity. Stop complaining and enjoy the attention you're getting. This volume of mail shows how popular you are. Some people out there want you, and your tuition money, or they wouldn't spend their own dollars to send you all that stuff.

The more mail you get, the more schools care enough to buy your name on a mailing list. As any dean of admission might say: "We only buy the kids we want." Isn't it nice to be wanted?

Open all the mail. If the mail is from a school on your list, read it carefully and file it with all the other stuff you've been collecting. Glance at the literature from other colleges to see whether anything they say whets your appetite.

Revisit a Fair

As a sophomore, you went to a college fair to help narrow your list of colleges. (To read more about the college fair, see Chapter 4.) Go back, a year later, for the same reason with a shorter list. You now are more focused on the type of college that interests you. Your list is down to 21 colleges or whatever number of schools you have selected. Prepare a list of questions to which you still want answers and ask them in person to college representatives at the fair. And do more than just listen to the answers. Be alert for the kind of vibes you're getting in conversation with the college officials. Trust your instincts. If you get the feeling that College X has a personality that won't mesh with yours, put that feeling into the equation when you make your decision. You're looking for a place to spend four years or more of your life. Your personal comfort level must be a key factor in deciding where that place will be.

In my own visits to college fairs, I have encountered students who arrived with their lists narrowed to two or three schools. As they visited the booths of those schools, the conversations with admission officers — and the vibes they received — convinced them on the spot which of the two or three schools were right for them. Things may not work out so neatly for you, but live conversations with college folks in a fair setting can be extremely helpful in steering you toward, or away from, certain campuses.

To Pay or Not to Pay for Help?

 Some of the unsolicited mail arriving during your eleventh-grade days won't be from colleges. People will write offering to help you find a college or find the money to pay for college. You may see ads in newspapers, perhaps even your school paper, promoting such services. Of course, these people and services want you to pay a fee in exchange for their help.

They trumpet the promise that for one low payment — it could be as low as $50 or as high as $500 — they can guarantee to find a college that will accept you or a scholarship for which you're eligible.

Are they worth the money? That's up to you. Most of them are legitimate businesses that do provide a service. Only you can decide whether the service is worth the price. To help you make that decision, I tell you how they work.

At a recent trade show for people who want to open their own businesses, I acted like I was interested in buying a scholarship search service and signed up for that company's 30-minute presentation. To make sure I didn't miss anything, I signed up a second time.

I discovered that the company maintains a computerized database of thousands of scholarships at its home office in a western state. For a one-time fee, I can buy the right to sell the company's scholarship data to students in my area. The company supplies forms for my student-customers to fill out, providing a wide array of information on their interests, club memberships, religions, ethnic backgrounds, parents' occupations, and their likely college majors.

I send the students' forms to the home office. The company plugs the information into its computer and sends back a list of scholarships for which each student might qualify. I pay the company a fee of, say, $50 for each form it processes. And I charge the student any price I desire over $50. I can charge $60 and make $10 a customer, or charge $500 and make $450 a customer.

Notice that the search services' ads don't promise to find you money. They guarantee finding scholarships for which you're eligible. They give you a list of potential money sources, and you have to take charge of obtaining the money from there.

The services that guarantee finding a college work the same way. They give you a list of schools where, based on your academic record, you're a sure shot to get in. Some schools on the list are open-admission schools that take anyone with a high school diploma. But you still must apply.

Here's the catch. The computer database that churns out scholarship lists for a fee is almost identical to computer programs I have used for free. Several times. I used one in a college library. I used one in a public library. I used one in a Florida high school's counseling center.

Software that matches students to private scholarships is developed by many of the same companies that publish college directories. The software is marketed to schools and libraries and, perhaps, to companies that sell lists.

The computer program that finds colleges for a fee is just like the program you can use, if you're lucky, to compile your first list in tenth grade. And if you don't have access to a computer program, you can use scholarship directories available in most public libraries and well-stocked high school counseling centers.

You can pay for a college or scholarship search service. Or you can do the search yourself at no cost. The result will be the same. The question you must answer is Do you want to pay someone else to do the work and save you the time?

Most search services are legitimate, but some aren't. A few scams take your money and run. Unless you personally know some satisfied customers, don't pay for a service before checking it out. Call your local Better Business Bureau and ask whether it has had any complaints. Or ask the service for some past customers' names and phone numbers as references. (Then call them.) If the service refuses to identify past customers, steer clear.

The National Association of Student Financial Aid Administrators, in a handbook for high school counselors, issues this warning: "These search services need to be used with care after a thorough investigation of the service they render. A guarantee that a certain number of sources will be found might simply mean that the service will tell the student he or she can apply for federal aid programs. There is no need to pay a search service to identify these programs. Furthermore, a little time and effort on the part of the student in the reference section of a library will probably unearth sources of assistance."

What about Test Help?

You'll also find some people trying to sell you prep courses for the SAT and ACT. Some may promise you something like a 30- to 50-point increase if you complete their course. Again, the decision to spend the money is yours. College admission officers have mixed feelings about the benefits of the prep courses.

There's no way a few classes will increase your math and verbal skills that are measured by the SAT. But they can give you test-taking skills and make you comfortable with the test. Of course, you can do that yourself by taking the test in the fall for practice and then taking it again in the spring. As I mention earlier in the chapter, the national average is a 40-point increase on the second try.

If you really want to practice, you can start taking the SAT for fun as early as seventh grade. Then just take it once a year thereafter to see how your scores improve. By your junior year, the SAT will be an old friend — and it will cost a lot less than a $300 prep course.

If you feel like spending money on a prep course, it certainly won't hurt. I don't think a prep course will give your test score the 100-point boost you need to make a difference in an admission office. You must decide whether your money, and your time, can be better invested on other things.

The Final Cut (Think of It as Spring-Cleaning)

It's spring of eleventh grade. You've put in a lot of work over the last two years collecting information. Each of the 21 colleges to which you wrote responded with a packet of literature about its campus, its courses, its housing, and its costs. Most colleges also sent catalogs describing course offerings and included applications for admission.

You tried to read everything. Occasionally you feel as if you have information overload. You don't have many spare bytes left on the hard disk in your head.

Now you need to trim the list again. You can decide what information you don't need, clear it out, and toss it away. The next cut, and the final cut for the first stage of the college-finding process, will produce a list of right schools that you like well enough to visit for a personality check.

Go back to your file. Take out your list and all the brochures, catalogs, and notes stored with it. As you glance at the names of the 21 colleges on your list, you get the feeling that this decision might be easy.

You already have a few emotional favorites, colleges that lit a spark when you read about them or talked to their people at a fair. One college comes highly recommended by your favorite English teacher. As you read the catalogs, three others impressed you with their journalism programs. You look at your list and start crossing out those that have given you no reason to think about them any longer. You find you've crossed out 11 of the 21 names.

You go back to your notes to refresh your memory. You notice that three of the remaining ten have enrollments between 2,000 and 2,500. Now you think that might be a little too small for you, and none of the three is among your top choices. Those three go. Your list is down to seven.

Think of it. You started with a book (or computer program) containing 3,200 colleges. With a little time and effort, you found seven colleges that could be right for you. But next come the most vital questions: What do they look like in person? Can you thrive on their campuses? The only way to find answers is to visit them.

I've said it before, I'm saying it now, and this won't be the last time. Every college has a personality. You can find out whether your personalities mesh or clash by spending some time with each other.

After you visit the seven colleges, you'll return home ready to decide which of them you will honor with an application.

Just as in the other examples that illustrate the process, seven is not a magic number. You have selected seven schools to visit because I assumed stuff about you as we cut names from your lists. Your number could be higher than seven or it could be lower. Some students have been known to visit 25 or 30 schools before making a decision.

Chapter 6

The Campus Visit

Going to college is a commitment. You're agreeing to spend two or four or more years of your life at a certain place with a certain group of people. If you live to be 80, that's still five percent of your life that will be spent at college. Would you commit to live even a month with a person you haven't met? Of course not. So don't decide where to spend your college years without first meeting the college. As a sage adviser once said, "Have a date before you rent a hall for the wedding".

You Won't Know Until You Go

You may think that you like a certain college in the mountains, on the edge of a small town, with about 1,500 students. From its literature, the school sounds like an idyllic spot to earn a degree. Then you get there and find that it's dominated by neat freaks who get haircuts every week and ridicule roommates who leave socks on the floor.

Neat freaks aren't reported in the catalogs. And they make you uncomfortable. But if you show up as a freshman without visiting the campus before you apply, you're stuck in Neat Freak Land for at least nine months. And you spend a miserable nine months hoping someone will take you as a transfer.

Many students transfer after their first or second year of college. If you talk to transfer students candidly about the reason why, the most common answer is that the first college "wasn't what I expected." And if you ask another question, you'll find that their expectations came without the benefit of a campus visit.

Tales abound of students heading to a prestigious college, or to the college where their crowd is going, with no idea of what lies ahead. They're unhappy from week one.

You're not looking for a college because it has prestige or because it's popular with your friends. You're looking for a college that's right for you, where you can grow academically and socially. If your friends decide to go there, too, so much the better. But if they don't, and it's a right college for you, you'll quickly make new friends.

Personality Check

The biggest test in locating a right college is the personality check. That bears repeating and remembering. Be sure to test the college with a first-hand personality check. To do so, visit the campus, meet officials, talk to students, eat in dining halls, and, if you can manage it, spend the night.

The concept of a college personality was not invented for this book. Students have been using the word for years. One of the nation's outstanding high school students rejected offers from Ivy League colleges because he found the state university near his home had a personality better suited to his taste.

If you read Chapters 4 and 5, I assumed some things about you, and what's important to you, that shrunk the number of colleges you're considering to seven. If you haven't read those chapters, take my word for it and assume that your final list of possible colleges contains seven schools that you've determined may be right for you. You can find out for you how right they are by paying them a visit. This way, you can know whether these schools are right, up close and personal.

Set Your Visit for Spring or Fall

The best time for you to visit colleges, in terms of convenience, is during the summer, when you're not burdened by the pressures of high school. But at most colleges, summer is the worst time for a personality check. Nobody's on campus in the summer. Well, hardly anybody is. A few students who are taking summer classes and the professors who are teaching them are sweating through June and July, but by August, they're gone, too. In the summer, you can get a nice view of the shade trees, stroll through empty dorms, visit the student union, if it's open, and not much else.

The best time to get a genuine feel for a college's personality is when all students are on campus, all classes are in session, and all systems are go. That's spring and fall. Ideally you've identified the colleges you want to visit in the spring of eleventh grade. So the ideal times for your visits are during April and May of your junior year or September and October of your senior year.

Check the college catalogs to see when classes end for the summer. You don't want to visit during final exam week because no one will talk to you. At some schools, finals are as early as the end of April. On other campuses, they don't come until June. A few colleges, public and private, do have classes in full swing through the summer. You can identify them from the catalogs, too.

Allow two days for each campus visit because staying overnight — even if it's in a motel — is important. If the college is within easy driving distance, plan to drive there in the morning, spend the afternoon, evening, and following morning gathering information, and then drive home the second afternoon.

Don't make your visit a spur-of-the-moment trip. Plan it at least two weeks in advance. After selecting dates that are good for you, call the college admission office for an appointment. The most essential of all the essential items in your visit is a two-way interview between you and an admission officer. You want to be sure that an admission officer is available to talk.

If you show up unannounced, you may find nobody home. Or an admission officer may adjust her schedule to fit you into an already busy day. Being human, she'd find that adjustment a bit irritating. Her first impression of you would be negative, and that's not the impression you want to create.

With two weeks notice, an admission office can usually schedule sufficient time for a leisurely chat. Call for the appointment and then build the rest of your visit around it.

Cover the Four Essentials

To accomplish its purpose, each campus visit requires four essential elements. Make sure that you:

- ✔ Plan an interview with an admission officer.
- ✔ Arrange an interview with a financial aid officer.
- ✔ Find opportunities to talk to students.
- ✔ Stay overnight, preferably in a dorm.

Other things you can do, such as talking to professors and sitting in on classes, can help you gauge the college's personality. But these four elements are essential.

The admission office

The admission office does much more than read applications and decide who gets into its college. It's the liaison operation between the college and all potential students at all stages of the college-seeking process. Admission officers tried to recruit you at college fairs. They sent you brochures with pretty pictures of smiling students. They answered your requests for catalogs and other information. And they will try to recruit you once again, after they decide that you are their kind of student.

The admission office interview is a two-way street. You're both — the student and the college — trying to impress each other while also trying to decide whether you really like each other. The interview is the most important part of your visit because, if you decide to apply to the college, the interview becomes a key in determining your acceptance. This book devotes a whole chapter (the next one) to the admission office interview because it's so important. After you have digested all the following advice about the rest of your visit, read Chapter 7 to find out more about the interview.

The financial aid office

You haven't thought about money all this time. (Right?) Now you need to give money a thought.

Eventually you must decide where you'll go to college, based on which schools have accepted you and how much they expect you to pay. The financial aid officers are the folks who decide how much their college expects you to pay — that is, how close to the sticker price your tab will be. When you visit the campus, you need to begin a conversation with these officers.

After you make an appointment with the admission office, you can call the financial aid office and ask for some time to chat. On most campuses, the two offices are in the same building.

Tell the aid officer that you have an appointment with the admission office and, while you're there, you'd like to get information about your prospects for financial aid. He will probably welcome you eagerly because he doesn't get much company. Very few student-visitors think about dropping in. Indeed, very few prospective students know that the financial aid office exists until they receive word on their grants and loans after they're accepted for admission.

During your visit, offer some information about your family's financial condition: your parents' income range, their ballpark net worth, any money you have stashed away. With that general information, the aid officer can at least estimate whether you'll receive any cash at the school. Some brave financial aid people may even venture an educated guess as to how much money you'll receive. But their guess will be only an educated guess. No one knows for sure how much aid you will get until your application data is pushed through a computer.

But, believe it or not, that's not the main reason you're there. If you read Chapter 12, you'll be able to make the same financial aid calculations yourself. No, you dropped in to meet a financial aid officer and to let him meet you. You hope he'll remember you favorably. When the time comes to assemble your aid package, an image of you as a nice, friendly person can't hurt. The financial aid officer will be dealing with thousands of students whom he knows only as names on a computer screen. If he can put a pleasant personality with a name, so much the better for you.

And when you need to call the financial aid office with questions, you'll be more comfortable knowing the person on the other end of the line and knowing that he knows you.

The students

Before you left home, you nailed down firm times for campus interviews. But during the rest of your visit you want to wing it — on a freelance search for information. One of your best sources for information will be the people most plentiful on campus, the students.

College students are among the most opinionated of human beings. They usually have strong feelings about what's right and what's wrong with their schools, and they have no qualms about sharing those views. Some students that are now in college say they found out more from other students on their campus visits than from any other source. No surprise.

Be sure to seek out students wherever the opportunity exists — the library, a cafeteria, a walk across campus. If students look like they have time to talk, talk to them. Ask about the classes, the professors, the social life, and the housing conditions. You probably won't have to ask many questions to produce a stream of opinions.

As you talk to students, you also can find out a lot about them. And that's important because the key ingredient in a college's personality is its students. Their collective approach to life determines whether a college is a party school or nerd haven, liberal or conservative, clean-cut or grungy. In conversations with students, you can quickly get a feel for which way the campus leans in these and other areas that may be important to you.

If you're leaning toward a particular field of study, look for students majoring in that area. A good way to find them is to hang around the building where that department is located and its classes held. In large universities, personalities can differ among specific colleges, schools, and academic departments.

The overnight stay

The best way to discover a person's true personality is to spend a night at his place, wake up in the morning, and see how that person acts at breakfast. The same is true of a college.

The overnight stay is the most important way to find out exactly what you want to know about the school. No other part of the visit will have as much impact on your opinions.

The reason you're visiting the college is to decide whether it's a place where you can thrive and be comfortable for four years. You can find out a little about a college by walking around for a few hours talking to people. You can find out much more by spending the night in a dorm, if you can manage it, or at a local motel. The overnight stay gives you a feel for the campus after hours, when classes end, professors go home, and students do whatever they do.

A night in a dorm gives you the best view of how students live. For a few hours you can experience life as a student at this college. And what better way to know whether you like something than to try it?

Many colleges will arrange an overnight dorm stay if a visiting student asks for it. Almost all colleges require advance notice. When you call the admission office for an appointment, ask whether a night in a dorm room is possible.

If the college can't arrange it, you're on your own. Try to find a student who can give you a spare bunk or a floor to spread out a sleeping bag. If you become friendly with a student you meet during your strolls around campus, ask about a place to stay. Remember, that student was in your shoes a year or two ago and knows why you're there and what you're trying to find out. Many students are happy to show off their dorm to a visitor for a night. If your parents are with you, let them go to the motel. You stay in the dorm.

Meet others on the floor. Find out the personality of the dorm you're staying in. Ask about the other dorms. What are the students' interests? What do they talk about? Complain about? You're going to want to know about the dorm that goes without heat until February when the temperatures dip below freezing soon after November.

If you can't find a dorm room, a motel on or near campus is second best. From the motel, you still have a chance to check out the campus after dark. You may want to ask where students gather for evening social life and then drop in to join them. In the morning, you'll have a fresh outlook on everything you discovered the previous day. You'll likely think of some new questions that you want answered before you leave.

You Can Do Even More

The four essentials of a campus visit (described in this chapter in the "Cover the Four Essentials" section) won't take all your time. You'll have a few hours to look elsewhere for information. The following sections are some places you can look.

Visit a professor

If you're leaning toward a college major, you'll want to find out more about the school's courses in that area than what you can read in the catalog. You also may like to get a sense of the types of people — professors and students — involved in the field.

Students aren't the only ones who like to talk. Professors do, too. Talking to students is a large part of their daily lives. If you're leaning toward chemistry, call the chemistry department before you leave campus and ask whether you can visit a professor. Mention that you're thinking about a chemistry major. The person answering the phone, probably a secretary or administrative assistant of some kind, either has the authority to schedule an appointment or can suggest a good time to drop by when professors are available.

When you chat with a professor, try to do two things:

✔ Get information about the chemistry curriculum and the requirements for a chemistry major.

✔ Tell the professor why you're interested in chemistry. Talk about what you've accomplished in chemistry as a high school student.

A fact of college life is that faculty departments covet students who major in their areas. And the better the student, the more fervent the coveting. The more majors a department has, the easier it can justify its existence to administrators who prepare budgets. If you impress a professor as the kind of student she would like to have, she could drop a note to the admission office saying so. Perhaps you might even suggest this idea to her. That note will go into your file. When your application arrives, this professor's note will become part of the package reviewed by admission officers who decide whether you get in.

The note can go a long way. Recommendations from faculty are not treated lightly.

Sit in on classes

Classes, after all, are the reason you'll be going to college. Sit in on one or two while you're there to see what vibes you get. You're going to be spending a lot of time either in classes or on your way to classes for a couple of years — you'd better find out what they're like.

When you talk to a professor, ask whether you can visit one of his classes. If he doesn't have one soon, he might refer you to a colleague who does. Interest in attending a chemistry class is clear evidence of a sincere interest in chemistry.

If you can't get into a class with a professor's help, try some students. If you spend a night in a dorm, ask one of your new friends whether you can tag along to her first class the next day.

Unless you're at a small college, where all the classes have fewer than 30 students, you should check large and small classes. Your reactions will be different in each. Find a large class of several hundred students in an auditorium with a professor lecturing from a stage. Ask yourself, are you comfortable in that kind of setting? Do you like the idea that the professor has no way to find time for individual attention to several hundred students? Sit through the class. Think about the situation. The experience may change some items you think are important about a college. You also can ask the admission office for a list of classes required for all freshmen and show up at one of those.

Display your talent

Well, maybe you shouldn't display your talent, but at least let people know it exists. If you have a certain talent (and you think that you're pretty good at it) — perhaps playing a musical instrument or acting in school plays — mention it in your admission office interview. Then drop into the music (or theater, or whatever) department and mention it again.

Tell someone in the music department that you play a decent trombone (they won't ask to hear it — yet), that you're thinking about applying to this college, and that you'd like to know about the opportunities for trombonists to develop their skills.

Departments that rely on special talents, such as music and theater, are eager to find talented students, whether or not they are music or drama majors.

Read the paper

A fine source of campus information, available without talking to anyone, is the student newspaper. It's usually available in the student center, dorm lobbies, and other popular campus spots. The student newspaper can give you a quick briefing on the current hot campus issues and a feel for what students at their college think is important. Many student newspapers are now reproduced on the college's Web site. If you have access to the Internet, try to read the school's paper in advance. Reading the paper can give you a feel for the campus and suggest some questions that you may want to ask before you go to visit the campus.

On many campuses, the student paper is a self-supported activity, free of control by the college administration. In those papers, student journalists are inclined to discuss issues as candidly as they would in their dorm rooms.

Journalists, as a group, tend to be more outspoken than the rest of the population, and student journalists are no exception. That makes the student newspaper office a fine source of information. Drop into the newspaper office, explain who you are and why you're there, and ask for a copy of the paper to read. Then, unless everyone seems to be scurrying to meet a deadline, strike up a conversation with a staff member or two. You'll be surprised how much you can find out so quickly.

Do Mom and Dad Really Have to Come Along?

Your parents, I'm sure, are fine people. And they have key roles to play in helping you find right colleges.

Go back and read that last sentence again. They have key roles to play in helping you find right colleges. Notice that word *helping*. Your parents certainly can be a big help, but that's all they can be. Finding a college must be your effort and your decision. After all, it's your life on the line. It's you who will be attending classes, writing term papers and living in dorms. When decision time comes, only you can know what's right for you.

As they read this section, some parents are scoffing. They're thinking, "My kid can't decide where she's going to college because she's not paying the bill." When they think about it a little longer, they'll realize that's only half true. Their kid's choices may be limited by the amount they can afford to spend, but within that limit the kid — the student — must decide what's right for her. And that monetary limit will become flexible if the student decides to borrow money for college. (You can read much, much more about all this money stuff in Chapters 11 through 15.)

Should your parents go along on your campus visits? If it's at all possible, yes, absolutely. Parents will see things and hear things that you don't. Simple arithmetic tells you that six eyes and six ears see and hear more than two of each. And parents will think of questions to ask that may not occur to you. Back in the motel room, or on the drive home, you can compare notes and come up with better opinions about the college than if you were gathering information with no help.

Should your parents accompany you on your interviews? Yes, for all the preceding reasons. At the financial aid office, they'll surely think of questions. And they'll probably be able to offer a more accurate description of their financial condition than you would. (To find out more about your parents' roles in the interview, take a look at Chapter 7.)

A group tour? It's harmless

When you visit a campus, don't be surprised if other students are there looking, just like you — 2.5 million of you are seeking a college. Some may show up at Flagship State the same day as you. Indeed, the college admissions office may have arranged it that way.

When you call ahead for an appointment, an admission officer may suggest that you arrive in time for a tour with other visiting students. If it fits your schedule, do so. A group tour is harmless and can be another information source.

In the busy visitor seasons of spring and fall, group tours are held several times a week. Prospective students are assembled in a meeting room, hear a brief talk about how wonderful the college is, and then are introduced to a student who leads a campus tour.

The tour offers live views of scenes you already have seen in the brochures. The student escort is working for the admission office and probably will describe the scenes in words written by the admission office. When you ask a question, it's likely to be one for which the admission office has supplied an answer.

The student tour guide, though, can help you start the rest of your personality check. Ask where students hang out in their spare time. Ask about the most popular student cafeteria. Ask about the newspaper office. If you haven't lined up a dorm room for the night, ask him about the chances of finding one. He may be working for the college, but he's still a student. And one reason he was hired for the job is because he likes to talk.

Campus visits produce the best results when you and your parents work enthusiastically within your separate roles. You are the customer. You are inspecting a product to see whether you want to buy it. You also are trying to decide where to spend four years of your life. Apply the information you collect toward those two goals.

Your parents are advisers. Welcome their advice. Consider it seriously because they undoubtedly are wise people. And it might be nice to thank them for it. But it's still your decision.

If You're Older

A campus visit is just as important for students whose high school years are in the past. You, as much as your younger colleagues, need to see whether a college's personality fits your lifestyle. You need to know whether it's a college that enthusiastically welcomes older students or one that focuses only on the young. The best way to find out is to visit the school.

When you visit a campus, an admission officer can fill the same role as the high school counselor. She can offer good advice on whether her college is the right place to pursue your goal. (If it isn't, she can steer you to potential right places.) She can talk about the courses you need and, if necessary, set you up with a faculty member to talk in more detail. She can tell you how the admission criteria differ for you as an adult and offer a realistic estimate on your chances of being admitted. She can tell you what activities and organizations exist to serve older students.

After talking to an admission officer, don't forget those people who have the most intimate knowledge of any college, its students. Stroll the campus and drop into the student center to see how many older students are in view. Chat with a few of them about the opportunities and problems that confront students of mature years. You'll likely find out just as much from other adult students about how you will fit in at a college as you will from the admission office.

Follow Up When You Get Home

The colleges you visited have not forgotten you. Don't forget them.

Within two days after your return, drop notes in the mail to everyone you talked to at length on the campus. Remember even the students. Thank them for giving you their time and advice. Mention something specific from each conversation so that it doesn't read like a form letter. Your note will convey the impression that you're a considerate person, a doer, and someone they would like to have on their campus. The letters will help your cause if you eventually apply.

A file with your name on it exists in the admission office. It was created when you first wrote for a catalog. By now, it contains any notes made during your interview, perhaps some notes sent over from the financial aid office, and possibly a note from a professor. When your thank-you note arrives, it will go into the file. So, in time, will your application for admission.

When an admission officer opens your file to decide whether you should be accepted to his college, he'll see the thank-you note from your visit. Little things count.

Chapter 7
The Interview

. . . .

In This Chapter

▶ Why bother with an interview?

▶ You'll accomplish two goals

▶ What to bring, wear, ask, and tell

▶ What are the college's goals?

▶ After the interview is over

. . . .

*N*obody makes prep courses for an interview. But an interview with an admission officer can be more stressful — and play a more important role in determining where you go to college — than any test you take on a Saturday morning. Although a lot of people would like to take your money to help you get a higher SAT score, no one is in business to help you impress a college admission officer in a one-on-one setting. But don't fret: You have this book.

A Two-Way Street

The interview, first and foremost, is a conversation. Two people, you and an admission officer, sit down together in the same room for the same reason. You want information that the other person can provide.

You are a buyer shopping for right colleges. You are visiting Flagship State to determine whether it is to stay on your shopping list. The admission officer has answers to many of the questions that can help you make that decision.

If you decide that Flagship State is right for you, and eventually submit an application, you hope Flagship's admission officers think highly enough about you to accept you. So the interview also is your chance to provide information about yourself that can help them make their decision.

The admission officer enters the interview with the same goals. She knows you're interested in Flagship, or you wouldn't have called for an appointment. She hopes to get information about you that will help her decide whether Flagship wants you.

And if Flagship eventually decides that it does want you, the admission officer hopes that you think highly enough about it to accept an offer of admission. So the interview is the admission officer's chance to convince you that Flagship needs to be at the top of your list.

The two of you have identical goals: getting and giving information. The goals are equal. Neither takes priority. You need to put as much effort into finding out about Flagship as you do informing Flagship about you. The interview is a two-way street.

Relax and Enjoy Your Interview

The prospect of an interview can work up a little stress in anyone. A job applicant preparing to meet a potential employer, or a public official about to be grilled by *60 Minutes,* feels the same kind of apprehension as a student walking into an admission office. Face it, an interview puts you on stage, alone, with no supporting cast. The outcome depends totally on you. But a little tension isn't all bad; it will probably keep you alert. As long as it's just a little, and doesn't get in the way of your thinking about what to say, some tension can help.

This interview is important. It's the one and only opportunity an admission officer has to connect a face and personality with the information he has on paper or a computer screen. It's the one chance you have to tell a college about yourself in your own voice, to convey stuff that just won't fit anywhere in the application package.

I've been watching admission officers work for 15 years. I've sat in on committee meetings where decisions have been made from New England to Chicago to Southern California. And I've found that far more decisions to admit — or reject — applicants turn on an interview rather than on a 30-point difference on an SAT score. (I've yet to see a decision made based on a 30-point difference in an SAT score.)

Now that you're beginning to feel some tension, here's something to relieve it. Remember what I said in the preceding paragraphs. You and the interviewer are in the same boat. You're talking to each other to get information for your own goals. And just as you want to impress him, he wants very much to impress you.

If the college decides that you are right for its campus, it knows that other colleges will make the same decision. Then they'll all be competing for you. After you're accepted, the admission officer who interviewed you will be on the phone inviting you to a reception where high college officials will try to persuade you to enroll at their beautiful campus. An admission officer is well aware that the interview is his first — and maybe last — chance to make a good impression on you.

So you and the admission officer go into the interview with the same two goals — to decide whether you like the other person and to make that person like you. You are both the interviewer and the interviewee. Each of you wants to gather information while informing. The admission officer has a definite advantage because he does this every day. This chapter helps you level the field.

Do You Really Need an Interview?

Yes, you really need an interview. Don't even think about applying to a college until you have had a chance to sit down face-to-face with an admission officer, for two reasons.

✔ **You are trying to find colleges that are right for you, and you have many questions that you'd like answered.** Admission officers are the only people on campus who get paid to answer questions from potential students. They have a vast amount of information about their schools in their heads. Remember, recruiting is part of their job. Asking your questions in person is much more productive than writing a letter. If the answer leaves something out, you can come right back with another question.

✔ **Everyone on this planet has done something that doesn't look so good in writing, but would certainly look better with a personal explanation.** For you it may be a *C* in geometry on a report card that otherwise has all *A*s and *B*s. Or it may be your decision to quit high school band as a sophomore and rejoin as a junior. On paper, a *C* is not impressive. And flipping on and off the band indicates a lack of commitment. But if you could tell someone that the teacher in that particular geometry class gave no grade higher than *C*, or that you dropped out of the band because your mother got sick and you had to take some responsibility for your little brother, both events look a lot better. The interview is your chance to explain.

Although all colleges would love to talk to every applicant, very few require an interview these days. And the number that do continues to dwindle. As tuitions keep climbing, colleges feel they can't insist that interested students spend the money to travel to their campuses. Schools that require or strongly encourage interviews — mainly the highly selective types, such as Ivy League colleges — usually have a network of alumni across the country who interview students in their areas and report to the admission office. Some alums get paid for the effort, some volunteer. Alumni as a rule know less about what's going on at their alma maters than the people who work on campus.

Many students feel that if an interview isn't required, why bother? They haven't read this book.

Would you marry someone you never met? The college interview is the ultimate in blind dating. Why pass up your chance to see whether the admission officer is a wimpy jerk or whether she's got a wonderful personality?

You're not going to apply to a college until you've walked its campus, talked to its people, and checked its personality. And while you're there, you will interview an admission officer. If a Princeton or a Dartmouth offers you an interview with Albert Alumnus, a lawyer in your hometown, you take it. But you visit the campus and talk to an admission officer, too.

Your Two Goals

During the interview, you have two goals: to find out about the college and to tell the college about yourself. You need to go into the interview ready to talk about both subjects — the college and you. Be prepared to ask questions that add to your knowledge of this school and help you decide whether it's one you want to favor with an application. And be prepared to make sure that the college — represented by the admission officer — knows enough about you to think that you're a student it wants.

If you apply to the college, you want the admission officer to have a favorable impression of you, even before reading your application. The interview is your shot at creating that impression. People who don't go for an interview start with no impression at all.

First a few things to avoid. The following can hurt your chances instead of help them:

✔ **Don't ask questions to which you should already know the answers.**
If you got a brochure that tells you 75 percent of the freshmen live in dorms, don't ask how many freshmen live in dorms. That tells the admission officer that you aren't really serious about this college, at least not serious enough to read the information it has sent. Ask instead about your chances of becoming part of the 75 percent who live in dorms.

On your way to the campus, or just before you leave home, review everything you know about the college. Make some notes, if it'll help your memory. Your goal is to find new information, not cover ground you've already trampled.

✔ **Don't be shy, especially in talking about yourself.** Resist the natural tendency to downplay your achievements. Colleges like to see students with enough self-confidence to express pride in what they've done. If you won a Rotary Club award for organizing a cleanup of a local park, mention it. Sure, the admission officer will see that you won the award when she reads your application. But if you tell her about it in person before the application gets there — give her a sort of preview — she'll have it in her notes when she picks up your application. And as she starts to read your application, she'll already have a favorable impression. That's one of your goals.

✔ **Don't be pushy or overbearing.** Shyness is one extreme, pushiness is the other. Try to stay comfortably between the two. Although you should mention your achievements, don't reel them off in a manner that says, "Hey, lady, you should be impressed." Don't try to convince the admissions officer that as a physicist you're the second Einstein. To colleges, self-confidence is a virtue. Braggarts are usually not welcome.

With those warnings heeded, your goals will be accomplished by asking and telling: Asking about the college and telling about yourself. Try to be relaxed. If you can't really relax, try to fake it. Remember, the admission officer's goals are the same as yours.

What to bring

Bring to the interview anything that you think will help you. A note pad and pen or pencil are probably essential. Feel free to take notes as you talk. The admission officer will surely be doing it. Your notes will be invaluable later when you try to remember everything you heard and found out. And they'll come in handy when you send your follow-up letter. (More on that later in this chapter.)

Your questions

Bring a list of questions as a memory jogger, to remind yourself what you want to know. It can be on the same pad that you use to take notes. If you have questions about something that you read in the college literature, you may want to bring the brochure or catalog so that you can refer to it specifically. When you ask about housing, you can point to a brochure you brought and say, "It says in here that 75 percent of the freshmen live in dorms. What do I have to do to get into that 75 percent?" That will be a clear sign that you care enough to read through the material.

High school transcript

Bring a copy of your high school transcript. Some admission officers like to see it. Others aren't interested. But your transcript is a good thing to have in a folder on your lap. The interview will be the only time you have to discuss your transcript with an admission officer face-to-face. It's your chance to explain that C in geometry in your own words.

A smile

Also bring a smile. And use it often. Everyone likes to see smiling people. If you smile frequently, an admission officer can't help thinking nice thoughts about you, even if you do have a C in geometry.

What to wear

Dress casually. No jeans, shorts, or denim jackets. But no suits, ties, or good dresses are necessary either. Colleges are casual places. Professors go to work in flannel shirts. Students usually wear as little as they can without freezing or breaking a law. The admission officer may be a little dressed up because she has to deal with the public. (That's you.) But neither she nor anyone else expects you to show up dressed for a fancy restaurant. A clean shirt or blouse and a decent pair of slacks will work fine.

What to ask

Ask about anything that concerns you, interests you, intrigues you, or helps you decide whether this is a right college. You probably had a list of questions prepared before you left home. If you had a chance to stroll around the campus before your interview, additional questions may have come to mind. Your parents probably have some, too, that they'll ask if they come with you. The following are some possible questions for your list:

✔ **How tough will it be to earn a degree in four years?** Is there a chance that you could get shut out of some necessary courses due to lack of space, and get pushed into a fifth or sixth year?

✔ **How secure are the residence halls?** Federal law requires the college to make security information available, including campus crime statistics, to every applicant. Many don't wait for students to apply, but send it out earlier to those who request literature. If you don't yet have the college's security report, ask for a copy. If you got the report in the mail, it likely raised some questions. The interview is the time to ask.

✔ **How much college credit can you get for Advanced Placement courses in high school?** Do you need a minimum score, say a 4 or 5, on an AP test to get credit? Is AP credit automatic, or must you ask for it to get it?

✔ **How many freshman courses are taught by graduate students instead of full-fledged professors?** The larger the college, the more likely the faculty is concentrating on research and letting the teaching assistants take over the lower-level classes.

✔ **What's the typical class size?** In classes of 30 or fewer students, you likely will have a chance to build some individual rapport with the professor. If most classes are larger, it's something to consider in your decision.

✔ **What's important in deciding whether an applicant is accepted?** How much weight does an SAT or ACT score have? You probably won't be told the real scoring system used to grade applications. The admission officer probably will say something like your high school record is most important, and all the other information, such as test scores, merely supplements it. That will be true as far as it goes, which isn't very far. (More about how colleges look at you in Chapter 9.)

✔ **How easy is it to get into campus residence halls?** What's available off-campus for students who don't live in dorms? Is off-campus housing certified or inspected by the college? How do you find off-campus housing? Does the college produce lists? Or must you check bulletin boards and read classified ads?

✔ **Do certain dorms have certain lifestyles?** Are some dorms coed, some single-sex? Are some quiet dorms with rules on music and radios? Do some have alcohol-free floors with the rules enforced? Check the admission officer's answers later with students. See whether they agree.

✔ **How does the faculty advising system work?** Is a professor expected to give you advice on which courses to take? Or do you arrange your own schedule and take it to a prof for a rubber-stamp signature? The admissions officer will tell you how the system is supposed to work. You'll find out how it really works by talking to students.

  ✔ **How big are fraternities and sororities in campus life?** It will be interesting to compare the perspective of the admission office and students on this one. On some campuses, the Greek life is very important; on others, it's not. The answer to this question will let you know which kind of campus it is.

  ✔ **What are your chances of being accepted?** With a quick glance at your high school record, an admission officer can tell whether you're in the ballpark of students her school wants.

If you're an older student, ask about the services offered to adults. Does the school have organizations and social events exclusively for beyond-25 students? Is some housing reserved for adults? The answers you get will help you decide how adult-friendly a campus may be.

Ask the questions confidently and politely but, please, not belligerently. The interview is not a cross-examination. It's a fact-finding mission. If you don't receive satisfactory answers, ask again politely. If you still aren't satisfied, that's something to consider when you decide whether this college is right for you.

What to tell

An interview has no set format. The admission officer may begin by asking about you, asking why you are interested in the college, or asking whether you have any questions. At some point, however, the conversation will turn to you and what you've done.

Offer some information about what you're doing in high school, the courses you have taken, and the activities in which you're involved. Mention the areas that interest you enough that you're leaning toward them as a college major. If, as in the examples of earlier chapters, you've discovered a talent for writing and an interest in helping kids, tell her you're thinking about some combination of English, journalism, and education. A good admission officer will respond with good advice on how to best serve those interests at her college.

If you have a special talent, such as the saxophone or the stage, mention it, too. The admission officer could call someone in the music or theater department to set up an interview for you.

If you read Chapter 9 before your interview, you'll know that some things on your school records will raise questions when your application arrives. Anticipate those questions by offering answers during the interview. The answers will be in your folder, in the interviewer's notes, before the questions arise.

Above all, be honest. Honesty is an essential virtue on college campuses. Voluntary honesty is fervently desired. Explain briefly to the admissions officer the process you're using to find colleges and how it brought you to her office. Mention some of the schools you've visited or are about to visit. Tell her what factors you'll be using to make a decision. She'll appreciate your honesty. If you apply, you'll have a few points on her scorecard already.

And be honest about who you are. Don't try to act like someone else because you think it might make a better impression. An admission officer can quickly tell whether the you she sees is the real you. She's had a lot of experience recognizing students who are putting on acts.

Even more important than being honest is avoiding dishonesty. Remember the girl whose acceptance by Harvard was withdrawn after the news came out that she killed her mother five years earlier? Harvard did not reject her for killing her mother. It told her to go elsewhere because she lied about it on her application.

The entire college community is built on a foundation of truth. If the admission office suspects you're not truthful, you have no chance of getting in.

Kisses of death

Here are some interview *kisses of death* — things you can do to convince a college quickly that it doesn't want you:

- Use the word like in every sentence.

- Chew gum.

- Answer a question in monosyllables rather than whole sentences.

- Look at the floor when you talk.

- Ask questions to which you should know answers. (Do you have a math major?)

- Use the phrase you know in every sentence.

- Use a smart-mouth wisecrack to avoid answering a question.

- Let your parents take control.

- Perform — put on an act instead of having a natural conversation.

And for best supporting role . . . your parents

Your parents have a role in almost every aspect of your college planning process, and it's always the same role. I say it in chapters before and after this one, and I'm saying it again now. Your parents are advisers. They have much expert advice to bring to your decision. You should welcome it and seriously consider it. But the final decision on how and where to spend four years of your life is yours.

If your parents want to accompany you on the interview, welcome them enthusiastically. The admission office also will welcome them. Even if your parents don't want to go along, encourage them to join you. Three minds remembering what was said will produce more information than one. And they'll undoubtedly have a question or two that doesn't occur to you.

But remember, it's your interview. You are the captain of your team. Your parents are going along with you, not vice versa. Admission officers say a quick way to create a negative first impression is to let your parents take control of the interview.

A serious blunder, which unfortunately does occur, is for Mom or Dad to arrive at the admission office and announce, "I've brought my son for his interview." The admission office wants to talk to you, not your parents. The admission officer will be nice to them because they are your parents. But allowing your parents to control the interview will be a big step toward a rejection letter.

Colleges Have Goals, Too

The college, like you, has two goals in the interview. It wants to find out things about you that it won't find on your application, and it wants to convince you that its campus is a fine place to be a student. As I said before, a college admission officer wears two hats. He is at the same time keeper of the gates and recruiter. And not all interviews are equal. He could be more recruiter than gatekeeper, depending on how much he likes you.

College is still a buyer's market. Each year's freshman classes have more spots than there are high school graduates to fill them. If the admission officer feels you're an attractive student likely to be accepted, he'll spend more of his energy trying to recruit you. The only schools where recruiting isn't a part of the interview are the few dozen high-prestige campuses — Harvard, Stanford, Duke, and so on — that get four times more applications than they need.

But supposing that you're not the second Einstein, the admission officer will be assessing you as a prospect for his college — looking for things that won't show up on the paper you submit. Do you speak well, or do you answer questions in monosyllables? Do have you a decent vocabulary, or do you insist on using the words like and you know in every sentence? Do you seem to be self-confident? Do have you a sense of humor? Can you laugh at a joke? Are you really serious about this college or just on a fishing trip? Your actions will answer these questions. And the right answers, in this case, are pretty obvious.

A rehearsal could hurt

Some people, perhaps even your parents, may offer what they think is good advice. They'll suggest that you practice for an interview. Someone may even volunteer to videotape a practice interview so that you can see for yourself how you do.

Be polite, but decline the offer. A rehearsal can backfire on you in a couple of different ways.

It can make a two-way street one-way.

The interview is a two-way conversation. Ideally, you're finding out as much about the college as it's finding out about you. Practicing before you go puts undue importance on your need to impress the admission officer.

Yes, you want to make a good impression. But it may not matter at all what kind of impression you make. Your first goal in the interview is to decide whether the college is right for you. That's why you're on the campus. If your mind

is preoccupied with impressing an admission officer — because you have practiced how to do it — your mind won't have much room to store the information you need to collect. You want to think about what you're going to say only in a general sense — do not write it down, don't practice it, and do not act it out on videotape.

Practice can turn a conversation into a performance.

To make the best possible impression, you must be yourself. If you rehearse an interview, and maybe see some things on a tape you don't like, you'll be tempted to change your natural conversational style just for the interview. Don't do it! You will be performing — putting on an act — instead of having a mutually beneficial chat. Astute admission officers (even those who aren't so astute) can spot a performance quickly. It will backfire into a negative impression.

Whew, the Interview Is Over, What Now?

As the interview progresses, the admission officer will be taking notes. These notes will go into your file, the one first created when you wrote for information. When your application arrives, it enters the same file. At some point soon after that, an admission officer — probably the same one who interviewed you — will pick up your folder and read everything the college knows about you, including the notes from the interview. He will read for about 15 minutes and then give you a score that will go a long way in determining whether you are accepted or rejected.

That's all the time you get — 15 minutes — to make a first impression on the college gatekeepers. As a gatekeeper reads his interview notes, you will want him to remember you as someone he would like to have around for four years.

When you get home from your campus visits and interviews, your information search has ended. You now need to put together everything to decide where you'd like to go to college.

Chapter 8

Decision Time

· ·

In This Chapter

▶ Apply, apply, apply

▶ Can you make the reach?

▶ Why you need a safety valve

▶ Is an early decision a good idea?

· ·

*Y*ou knew this day would finally come. You've had some fun since your sophomore year looking for colleges, and you've done some work. You have visited some pleasant campuses and met interesting people and some who weren't so interesting. Now you're home after your final college visit. And you're about to enter a new phase of the process. Sometime in the fall of your high school senior year, you need to stop shopping and make the decision to buy.

This chapter is brief. Most of the stuff you need to know came earlier in the book as you were searching for your right colleges. It will also come later, as you try to convince the colleges that they want you. And a large chunk of your new knowledge arrives as you look for money. But decision time deserves a chapter of its own because it's the turning point in the college planning process. Decision time is when you stop gathering information about colleges and start providing it to them — on applications and essays and statements and even tax returns. It's when your relationship with the college admission office changes from recruit to applicant.

More important for you, decision time is when you identify three, four, or more colleges that you feel will be the best fit for you. Places where you believe that you'll thrive academically and socially. Places where you're comfortable investing four years of your life. Then you'll get on with the task of applying to them and deciding which ones you can afford.

The three kinds of admission

All colleges fall into one of three categories in deciding who can pass through their gates as students.

✔ **Selective:** These colleges have firm applications deadlines, usually in January or February, but many are moving their deadlines into mid-December. They let all applicants know their fate in late March or early April. All give successful applicants until May 1 to decide whether they'll enroll. After May 1, they fill unclaimed places by taking names off their wait list. (You can read more wait lists in Chapter 17.)

✔ **Rolling admission:** These colleges accept and reject applicants until their freshman classes are full. They usually publish a date at which they begin considering applications. If they publish a deadline, it's the date that they *expect* to be full. But it could happen earlier. You'll know how you fare earlier at a rolling admission school, but that's no reason to choose it over a selective college.

✔ **Open admission:** These colleges take anyone with a high school diploma or its equivalent until classes begin or space is gone. Almost all two-year colleges are open admission.

You can tell which type of admission policy a college uses from its directory lists. Selective schools have a firm application deadline. Rolling admission and open admission usually use those terms to describe their process.

How Many Applications?

How many colleges you apply to is a decision that only you can make, but here's some good advice. Don't rule out any school at which you truly feel you can be comfortable as a student. Do rule out all the others.

By now you probably have one or two favorites. You have made your top choices, where you'll sign up immediately if they accept you and give you enough financial aid. These are your favorites because you found yourself comfortable with all aspects of the campuses — including the curriculum, the professors, the students. You especially enjoyed your night in the dorm. But a couple of other colleges are out there that you feel could serve your needs nicely as well. You could be happy and thrive at either of them if your top-choice colleges don't accept you.

Okay, you have identified four right colleges. Not bad considering you started with 3,500. Now apply to all four and see what happens.

Whoa! I know what some of you are thinking. Why make yourself extra work? Why not just apply to your top two choices and, if they turn you down, go on to the next two? Bad idea for one big reason: If you wait, you may be shut out. In Chapter 1, I describe the three basic types of admission policies used by most colleges. For readers who didn't start at Chapter 1, see the sidebar "The three kinds of admission."

If your third and fourth choices are selective colleges, their application deadlines will have passed by the time your top choices make a decision. If they have rolling admission, these schools are accepting applicants as they apply. By the time you check in, their freshman classes may be full.

The most efficient approach for you is to submit all your applications at the same time. Ideally, that time is December or early January of your senior year.

And four applications is not four times the work. Much of the information you provide can be used on the form for all four colleges. (You can read more on applying in Chapter 10.) But four applications is four times the money. Every college wants an application fee, usually in the $40 to $75 range, just to start reading your application. If you have a budget of a couple of hundred dollars for application fees, four is no problem. If your budget is tight, the fee is a factor to consider.

Should you go for the reach?

Then there's the college you like, but you feel is probably too tough. With your high school record, your chances of getting in look like a long shot. Its SAT average is 1300; your score is 1210. It looks for students in the top 10 percent of their high school class; you just made the top 15 percent. It wants three years of a foreign language; you have two years of Spanish.

In admissions office language, that college is a *reach* for you. That means you probably won't make it, but your credentials are close enough that it can't hurt to try. If you have an experienced high school counselor, ask her about the chances of getting in with your credentials. She may have seen others in your situation try. And don't forget, another application means another application fee.

If you feel like it's worth a gamble, send Reach U. an application, too. It will mean, maybe, another hour's worth of work. What's the worst that can happen? Reach U. may say no. But you could get lucky. It's a gamble where you have little to lose and much to gain.

Everyone needs a safety valve

You still have one more college to identify. A college that needs to be on every student's list. The place you're sure that you can go if all else fails. It's your safety valve.

Imagine the worst case scenario. All the schools that you applied to (hypothetically) in the preceding sections of this chapter say, "Sorry, we've filled our class with other people." What a horrible thought! But in case it happens, you need to be prepared.

The more likely scenario is a money problem. Your top two choices accept you, but don't give you enough financial aid to meet your full need. In reality, that's the same as rejecting you. Admissions officers call that type of situation *admit-deny*. They say they want you, to make you feel good, but they really don't because they won't come up with the cash. (To find out more about getting money, read Chapters 11–15).

Or suppose that these colleges offer you what they think is enough money, but you disagree. Even with a substantial aid package, you don't think you can afford any of your top choices. Then what? You're prepared with a school that you know will accept you and whose price tag you know you can meet. It's your safety valve.

Almost all high school seniors, at some point in the process, worry that they aren't good enough for any of their top-choice colleges. They can end all those worries the same way, with the safety valve option.

How do you determine your own safety valve school? Look for one that will accept you and that you're sure you can afford, even without financial aid. It can be the local community college or a nearby four-year college that takes any high school graduate. It could be Safety State in the next town, where your academic record makes acceptance a sure thing.

Chances are good you won't even need a safety valve. But because you're a wise college-bound student, you should identify one and apply to it. You want to be certain that when your friends head to college, you won't be staying home.

Is an Early Decision a Good Idea?

Another option to consider is applying early. Most selective colleges offer the chance to apply in November or December of your senior year, and they'll give you a decision before January 1. The early options come with many names. The most common are Early Decision and Early Action. Each plan has its own rules. Regardless of what they're called, each offers a big advantage to you and the college:

- ✔ The plus for you is that you discover quickly whether your top-choice college will accept you. If it does, the process ends successfully in the middle of your senior year. If it doesn't, you have time to apply to other schools.

- ✔ The advantage to the college is that it signs up a committed freshman — one who is sure to be there in the fall. If you apply to four colleges and are accepted by all, three will be disappointed when you decide not to enroll. For them, an Early Decision eliminates the disappointment.

You may have heard some horror stories about colleges filling their classes with early decisions and having no space for students who apply later. Some of your older friends who applied to college in recent years may be suggesting that you apply early so that you don't get shut out. Your parents may be getting the same advice from parents of older students. Don't let that kind of well-meaning advice panic you into a decision that you may regret.

Yes, some of those rumors are based in fact. A dozen or so very selective colleges, back around 1995, began accepting more students on early decision for the preceeding reason. They wanted more students committed to their school in December and fewer who they would have to beg to enroll in April. (To find out more on how colleges beg, read Chapter 16.) The expanded early decision produced some unfortunate results. Some highly qualified students — students the Harvards, Dartmouths, and Princetons would like to have — applied during the regular process and found, indeed, the freshman classes with fewer available places. These highly qualified students wound up at places such as Lafayette, Williams, and Rice, pushing out students who normally would attend colleges like Lafayette, Williams, and Rice. The ripple effect frustrated thousands.

The selective colleges that started the ripples had second thoughts. They have pulled back on the number of students that they're accepting on early decision. The pressure to get in early or be shut out is being relieved.

Consider an early application only if you've found one college that stands out in your mind above all others, a definite first choice. The price you must pay for being accepted early is a commitment to enroll. You must agree in writing not to apply anywhere else — or to withdraw all other applications if you're accepted.

And Now ... You Begin a Whole New Ball Game

Get ready. This is the start of a whole new game. You have identified six colleges, including a reach and a safety valve, to which you'll apply. Now you must tell them about yourself in a way that will make them eager to have you as a student.

As I say in Chapter 7, an admission officer spends about 15 minutes reading each application and then gives it a score that often determines the applicant's fate. You're about to request your 15 minutes in the sun at six admission offices.

Part III
Getting In

The 5th Wave   By Rich Tennant

"I'm glad we visited the campus. It's a hard school to get into. The entrance exam to get into the parking lot was three pages long."

In this part . . .

This part is where you'll get to work on making yourself look pretty. This book can't make you look pretty on its own. It needs your help. You can make yourself attractive enough that the colleges you have selected will want you.

Chapter 9 explains what colleges find attractive about students. Chapter 10 offers advice on what you can do to meet the colleges' expectations, including a step-by-step stroll through a typical application.

Chapter 9

How Colleges Look at You

....

In This Chapter

▶ Examining your academic record

▶ Understanding what test scores tell

▶ Choosing activities you can stick to

▶ Knowing the power of letters of recommendation

▶ Avoiding essay phobia

▶ Looking at how high your high school stands

▶ Putting all the pieces together

▶ Determining whether you can get a break because you're special

....

Dispel the mystery. The qualities that make some students more attractive than others to the nation's colleges are not hard to understand. Some colleges may try to make you think that admission selection is a mysterious process that you, the poor uninitiated applicant, are just too green to comprehend. When you ask about how colleges make their admission decisions, they'll answer in generalities such as, "The most important thing we look at is your high school record." That's true, but only a small part of the truth. This chapter gives you the rest of the story.

If you ask an admission officer to show you the scoring system that her school uses to grade applications, she may deny that one exists. Or she may say something like, "It's proprietary information that we don't share with the public." Hey, that means you. You're the public. You're also the buyer of the services the college is selling. If a college won't tell you how it will score your request to become a student, that's something to consider when you decide where you'll apply.

At a few enlightened colleges, an admission officer will answer your question by pulling out his scoring grid, or numerical table, or whatever he uses, and explain exactly how each part of your application will be weighed against all other parts. Unfortunately, too few colleges are enlightened yet. But you can be, simply by reading this chapter. And, if you would like to enlighten a few admission officers, take this book on your campus visits. The book will enjoy the trip.

The Stuff Colleges Look For

All colleges are essentially looking for the same thing. First, they want good students. Good students make professors happy. And the last thing an admission officer needs is a bunch of professors complaining about the quality of the students in their classes. Good students also warm the hearts of college presidents who can brag about them on fund-raising trips to alumni groups. And good students make it easier for colleges to fill their primary roles — places of learning through an interchange of ideas. So a good student is every college's first priority.

Second, colleges want students who do more than study. They want people who will get out of their dorm rooms and mingle. A typical college takes pride in being a community, and wants students who will be productive citizens of its community. It looks for students who are likely to

- ✔ Volunteer
- ✔ Join organizations
- ✔ Assume leadership roles
- ✔ Work for the newspaper
- ✔ Shoot photos for the PR office
- ✔ Help when help is needed
- ✔ Get involved in things other than classrooms

That's why special talents, such as, yes playing the trombone, are desirable.

Given those two basic qualities of an attractive applicant — being a good student who does more than study — beauty will be in the eye of the beholder. Every college builds on those two qualities to meet its own particular needs. Colleges even define those qualities differently. A good student at Harvard, for example, is different from a good student at South Dakota State because the Harvard student likely arrived with much higher academic credentials. An active student at Frostburg State, nestled in the western Maryland mountains, is different from an active student at New York University in the heart of a huge city.

Some colleges, because of their roles in life, have distinct preferences for certain types of students. Ohio State, because it's subsidized by the state of Ohio, has a preference for Ohioans. Brigham Young University, a creation of the Mormon church, has a student body that is predominantly Mormon. Georgia Tech likes students who want to be engineers. College of the Ozarks in Missouri, which charges no tuition, gives priority to low-income students.

Notre Dame (which no longer gives a break to Catholics) publishes literature saying that a certain percentage of each freshman class is reserved for children of alumni. However, this literature doesn't mention the spots reserved for recommendations by the football coach.

The varieties each school builds into its preferences are endless. In an experiment a few years ago, I gave the University of Chicago and the University of Pennsylvania — two very selective colleges — applications from three hypothetical students and asked them to pick just one. They made different choices. Chicago chose a student who expressed herself well in writing and seemed to be a real intellectual. Penn took one who looked like the most active contributor to its campus community.

You can get a feel for the preferences of a particular college by reading its literature and talking to people — especially students. They know, probably better than anyone else, what their college is all about.

Given the variety of preferences, however, almost every school uses certain fundamental approaches in looking at applicants and gauging their beauty. The application you send to colleges will have basic components that are viewed in very similar ways at every admission office. Together, those parts paint a portrait of you and everything you've done since you entered high school. An admission officer will spend about 15 minutes looking at that picture and then decide whether he likes you well enough to allow you to enter. The following sections look at each part of the portrait, one-by-one.

First Things First — Your Academic Record

When an admission officer says your high school record is the most important item in your application, believe her. The first piece of paper to be scanned during your 15 minutes in the sun is your high school transcript. Remember, the first priority everywhere is to enroll good students. The transcript tells what kind of student you are.

She'll look at your grades, of course. The more *A*s she sees, the better. She'll frown if she sees a lot of *C*s and *D*s. But if she's at a college that's the least bit choosy about who it accepts, your grades won't be the first thing to get her attention. First she wants to see what courses you took. How many Advanced Placement and honors courses are on your record. (All transcripts identify AP and honors courses.) She's looking to see whether you challenged yourself with the toughest offerings on your high school's menu.

The International Baccalaureate (also known as IB), an advanced curriculum for top students that is being used in more high schools each year, is considered equal to — sometimes even tougher than — AP courses when the rigor of a student's classes is weighed, Every time I say something about AP courses, it also applies to IB.

Then she'll check out your *solids*. That's admission office shorthand for how many years you have spent in the five solid academic areas — English, math, science, social studies, and foreign language. Some colleges want a minimum of two or three years in each, or they won't consider you. All colleges want to see four years of solids.

It's an accepted fact at colleges everywhere that, all things being equal, a student with four years of high school English, math, and science gets in before an applicant with three years. For the same reason, a student who takes four AP or IB courses has a big edge over his friend at the same school who takes none. Colleges call it *academic rigor*. Admission officers want to see you take the toughest stuff. If you shy away from the tough stuff in high school, they figure you'll bring the same attitude to college.

If the admission officer sees no AP courses — or just one or two — on your record, she'll flip to your school's profile. (It's normally stapled to the transcript.) Almost every high school these days publishes a profile. Usually the profile is a single printed sheet filled with vital statistics about the school, including its curriculum. If she sees that your school offers only one or two AP courses, no problem. You didn't have the opportunity. But if 12 AP courses were available and you took only 1 or 2, she wonders about your willingness to take on challenges. The score she gives you won't be as high as it could have been.

A tough B or a snap A?

It's a question students ask every year. Is it better to take an Advanced Placement course and get a *B*, or a regular course in the same subject for an *A*? The answer from admission officers across the land is always the same: Get the tough *B*. The tough *B* shows you care enough about your mind to stretch it. Colleges like mind-stretching students. Sure, your GPA may drop a notch or two with that *B*, and it may blow your shot at being valedictorian. But, believe it or not, thousands of valedictorians each year don't get into their first-choice colleges. (There are 20,664 high schools in the country. That means 20,664 valedictorians. Freshman classes at the eight Ivy League colleges total 13,249. You need more than a transcript with all *A*s to make it.)

At one time, some picky colleges penalized students whose schools didn't offer AP courses. They simply counted the AP and honors classes on your transcript. If your school didn't have any, it was your problem for going to that school. Colleges with that attitude are moving away from it now. Not only was it unfair, but the law of supply and demand came into play. With the demand for students greater than the supply, those colleges found themselves arbitrarily eliminating some fine students. The key question now asked is, What did you do with what you had?

Andrew Weller, admission director at Marymount University in Virginia, says he would "rather see someone trying, and getting a B, than chickening their way through a high school curriculum." Taking tougher courses, says Weller, "even if you don't get an *A*, shows a lot of character and academic rigor." Or as many deans of admission put it: "First we look at what you've done. Then we look at how well you've done it."

Even your GPA should weigh less

Your 5.23 GPA may impress your parents and your neighbors. Even your high school principal may be a little awed. But it means nothing to a college admission officer because he doesn't know what your 5.23 means. You do because you know how your high school weights various grades to give more points for tougher courses. Weighted GPAs are good for high schools to identify students who really are doing the best. But these GPAs are meaningless to colleges because every high school uses its own weighting system. Is your 5.23 better than a 4.76 at a school in the next county? Nobody knows for sure.

At many admission offices, the grades on your transcript are quickly recalculated into an unweighted GPA, with all *A*s worth four points. Thus, 4.0 is the absolute maximum. The admission officer then weights your score with his own points for your AP and honors courses. This way every application he reads is weighted the same. Your school could save him some time if it reports an unweighted GPA on your transcript. He'd like that.

After reading and analyzing your academic record (in less time, by the way, than it took you to read this section), the admission officer will give you a score for academics. This score may be on a numerical scale, say 1 to 6. It may be a letter grade. Or it may be a combination of the two. Whichever, it's the score that will carry the most weight in determining whether you get an acceptance letter.

Does your class rank matter?

Every college likes to see where you rank in your senior class. Your rank tells how well you've done compared to everyone else at your school. Some say they prefer students in the top 10 or 20 percent. But class rank is not as important as it used to be because colleges are starting to realize that they don't know how good everyone else in your school is. Colleges, with a few exceptions, will note your class rank on their scorecards, but it won't be as crucial as other factors in their final decisions.

For those few exceptions, however, your class rank is crucial. In some states, admission to state universities is determined by a formula that includes class rank in its calculation.

How to help yourself

Now that you know all this, you can help yourself. Your high school record starting as a freshman is the first and most important thing a college looks at. If you're not yet a freshman, you have time to plan your high school schedule accordingly. Work out a curriculum path that will take you to AP courses by your senior year. Talk to a counselor about your strengths and weaknesses, and which of the big five solids you should stick with for four years.

If your freshman year is in your past, some of your high school record is already written in stone. Sorry (or perhaps happily), there's nothing you can do about it. But you can still work on the unfinished part. A record that improves as you move through high school is looked upon favorably. The opposite, a strong freshman or sophomore record followed by a slump, won't impress many admission officers.

The most important year on your high school transcript is your senior year. Colleges like to see your record getting stronger every year. That means you're performing at your best as you come to them. Many colleges, including most selective schools, want to see your grades for the second half of your senior year even after they've accepted you. They'll ask your high school to send your final transcript.

Seniors who kiss off their spring semester because they think it doesn't matter have been shocked to find their college acceptance revoked due to their poor performance. Borderline students often are admitted on the condition that their full senior-year grades are satisfactory.

Lois Mazzuca, a counselor at Glenbrook North High in the Chicago suburbs, tells of a student accepted by a highly selective college who got a letter from that college asking why his senior grades suddenly plunged. "He shared that letter with the world," says Mazzuca. "It had such a ripple effect on the kids coming behind him that I could run to that admission office and kiss those people."

Your Test Scores — How Much Do They Matter?

Before she puts down your transcript, the admission officer will note your scores on the SAT or ACT. They'll tell her a lot — but not what some of you might think. She's not looking to see whether you score below a cutoff point so that she can toss your application in the trash. If that's the way it worked, she could save time by checking your SAT score first.

(If you haven't read Chapter 5, this book uses SAT to mean the test now officially designated as SAT I. It's the test called the SAT for 60 years.)

At most colleges, test scores are guidelines. The SAT, despite its other uses, was designed to measure a student's ability to handle college work, and that's still its main job. The ACT measures ability in specific subject areas. Each college, for its own purposes, prefers one or the other, but almost all accept either one. Unless you're looking at one of the few colleges that don't require tests scores with their applications (Bowdoin, Bates, and Middlebury are among the most notable), you must take the SAT or ACT before you apply. But as I said, the scores are only guidelines. They're used most often to group students in ranges of ability. (For more about college entrance exams and when to take them, see Chapter 5.)

An SAT score in the 1400s does make you more attractive than a score in the 1200s. But an admission officer won't give a second thought to the difference between a 1450 and 1420 or a 1200 and 1230. It's likely he won't even think of you as, say, a 1200 applicant but rather as a 700 and a 500. Your math and verbal scores will be considered as separate entities.

Depending on your major, a low score on one portion of the test can have little influence on your fate. If you want to be an engineer, for example, you should demonstrate a strong aptitude for math, but your ability with words is less important. If you intend to major in English, the reverse is true. The highest SAT scores in the country are at California Institute of Technology (which likes to be known as Caltech), where 91 percent of the degrees are awarded in engineering, math, and science. At Caltech, 75 percent of the freshmen have SAT math scores over 720 and verbal scores over 600.

At some colleges, usually the very picky that get four times as many applicants as they need, candidates are considered in order of their test scores. All the 1400s or higher are scrutinized, and accepted or rejected. Then they move on to the 1300s, 1200s, and so on, until they have accepted enough to fill the class.

But still the scores are just guidelines. College admission officers are more interested in what you've done for four years than for four hours on a Saturday morning. They know that some students just don't test well. And they're beginning to realize that test scores aren't totally accurate in predicting college performance. Most colleges still want them because they're nice numbers to have. But their importance in the admission decision dwindles every year.

The exceptions to all of the preceding (aren't there always exceptions?) are the few state universities that accept students solely on a combination of grades and SAT scores. Your GPA determines the minimum test score needed to get in. The lower your grades, the higher the test score necessary.

If you've taken the SAT II (otherwise known as achievement tests) in specific subjects, those scores also are on your transcript. The admission officer will note them on his scorecard, and they likely will be figured in your final score. SAT II scores in subjects of your intended major may count more than others.

Sign on — and Stick to — Activities

Colleges deeply desire active students. The student who shows a willingness to get involved is much more attractive than one who spends her whole high school career working on her GPA. But students who know this fact often make a serious mistake. They confuse involvement with volume. They think the number of activities they join is more important than what they do in those activities. They're wrong.

Don't be a *list padder.* That's an admission officer's term, usually derogatory, for a student who joins every club and organization in sight so that he can list it on his application. List padders don't score very high on the activities section of the admission office scorecard.

List padders are easy to spot. They have long lists of activities, often more than one page, neatly typed on the latest word processor and churned out by a laser printer. On the surface, the lists appear impressive. Below the surface, nothing. They report nothing to show that they ever attended a meeting or contributed in any way to the groups they joined.

"We're trying to shape a class of students with strengths in different areas," says Steve Syverson, dean of enrollment management at Wisconsin's Lawrence University. "Students who are okay in a bunch of things are not nearly as attractive as a student with depth in one."

Colleges want contributors, not joiners. They want people who persevere in an activity, not those who bounce from fad to fad. Ideally they want leaders. But they'll take committed followers too. Commitment is the key. A student who works for four years on the school newspaper, moving to a more responsible position each year, scores higher — much higher — than one who joins 12 organizations and contributes nothing. And she'll score higher than one who moves from the newspaper to the yearbook to the photo club.

When the admission officer looks at your activities, in school and in your community, he'll think about how they translate to his campus. In what ways, he wonders, will you contribute? If you served on student government, did you take the initiative on a project that improved your school? If you were in the Russian club, did you organize any kind of cross-cultural event? If you're leaning toward science, did you do independent work after school in the biology lab? Did you teach a kids' class at your church or just go to church every Sunday? Are you a Boy Scout or an Eagle Scout? Have you shown you can make a commitment? Concentrate on what interests you. That's where you'll make the most commitment.

How to help yourself

Now that you know all this, make the smart choice. Resist the temptation to pad your list. Find one or two activities that truly interest you — within or outside school — and get involved. Stick with them. Accept responsibility. Become a leader, even the leader. You'll be much more impressive at a college admission office than your friends who just keep joining things.

Getting Recommendations That Count

The most overlooked and often underrated items in a college application are recommendations from your teachers and counselor. But they can be important. I've seen admission decisions made on borderline applications by what admission officers were reading between the lines of recommendation letters. They spent minutes analyzing every phrase.

Most colleges want recommendations from at least one teacher and a counselor. Some request more. Colleges look to recommendations to tell them things about you that they won't find out anywhere else. They hope to learn what kind of person you are. They already know from your transcript what kind of student you are.

The recommendation letters gain importance if you are a marginal candidate, teetering on the fence between acceptance and denial. Your score from an admission officer's initial 15-minute review wasn't high enough to get you in or low enough to keep you out. (More on how decisions are made later in this chapter.) By this time, your application is likely out of the hands of the first admission officer and before a committee. Your grades, your test scores, and your activities got you this far. Now the committee is looking for something to separate you from the other students with whom you're competing for the final spots. That's when the committee carefully scans the recommendations, hoping to find something on which it can hang a decision, for better or worse.

Unfortunately, too many teachers and lackadaisical counselors kiss off recommendations as chores to get out of the way. They don't think much about what they're saying. They use nonspecific trite sentences that give the impression they've written the same letter 75 times. And they probably have. It's easier for a busy teacher to compose a one-size-fits-all letter than try to individualize recommendations for 75 students.

Those letters don't help you. In fact, they hurt. The admission officer will conclude that you must not be much if a teacher can't say anything more than a few platitudes. I remember well an admission officer at the University of Chicago reading a counselor's letter and commenting, "We're asked to take a lot on faith. This counselor says, 'Admit her, she's one of the best I've ever counseled.' I want to know why."

Keep in mind that you have some control over who writes the letters and what they say. If you're unlucky and have a poor counselor, you're probably stuck with that person, unless you feel like complaining to the head counselor or your principal. But you can choose a teacher to recommend you. And by the time you're applying to colleges, you have probably developed a rapport with a few teachers whom you respect and who know you well as a student and a person. Pick one and ask him to write a letter for you. Give him a few weeks' notice so that he doesn't have to do it overnight after grading papers. Chat with him about what he might tell the college that will enhance its knowledge of you. Tell him why you're interested in that particular college. Remind him things you've done. You can even give him a list of stuff you've accomplished. Teachers are busy people who sometimes forget things.

And remind the teacher and counselor who are writing recommendations that the college doesn't want to read stuff about you that it already knows. If they ask how you know that, show them this book.

Ten signs your teacher doesn't care

With apologies to David Letterman, here's a list (from the Home Office in Sarasota, Florida) of the Top Ten Phrases Teachers Can Use in Recommendation Letters to Show That They Don't Care Whether Their Students Get into College.

10. **I recommend Suzy for your consideration.** (There's a difference between consideration and admission. College admission officers recognize it.)

9. **Jason is definitely college material.** (If he isn't, he shouldn't be applying.)

8. **Michelle is involved in a wide range of school activities.** (Michelle already told them that.)

7. **Steve's test scores are above average.** (They know Steve's scores, and they know what the average is.)

6. **Rebecca appears to be enthusiastic in all my classes.** (If the teacher doesn't know Rebecca well enough to know if she really is enthusiastic, the officers won't give much weight to anything else you say.)

5. **Christopher may well be equipped to handle the most rigorous college work.** (Then again, he may well not be.)

4. **Jennifer is one of the best I've ever taught.** (They don't know who else you taught.)

3. **The quality in Richard that teachers appreciate most is his personality.** (That doesn't say much for his schoolwork.)

2. **When Kathryn speaks, others listen.** (A tired cliché is a clear sign of a letter written without much thought.)

And the Number One Phrase Teachers Can Use in Recommendation Letters to Show That They Don't Care Whether Their Students Get into College . . .

1. **In case you didn't notice, Brian took six AP courses and got all As.** (Hey! They noticed. That's their job.)

The Essay Made Easy

The most work involved in applying to a college, and the most stressful part of the process, is writing an essay. Most colleges want at least one. Some want two. Others, like those state schools that work on GPA/SAT admission formulas, don't require you to write anything.

If you're applying to five colleges, chances are that at least three will want to read something you've written just for them. And the stress builds because you have no idea what they really want you to say, what kind of writing style they prefer, or what kind of reaction your essay will produce. At least you didn't know any of that stuff until now. Sit tight, you're about to find out.

Colleges want an essay for three reasons. One is the same reason they want letters of recommendation: They hope to learn something about you that the rest of your application doesn't tell them. This time they want to hear it in your own words. They also are seeking insight into how you think and how you write.

Some colleges assign a topic for the essay. Some offer a list of topics and let you choose. Most colleges just give you a general suggestion, such as "an experience that has special meaning to you," and let you take it from there. Well, take it and run.

 Think about something in your life that was truly meaningful. It could be something as far back as fourth grade, when you discovered the joys of solving math problems, or as recently as this year, when you were tinkering in the physics lab. It could be bird watching, working at a hospital, or tutoring little kids. Think about why you remember it so well. Then try to organize those thoughts into sentences and paragraphs. If the suggested topic is "an issue that concerns you," think about what stirs your emotions. Student apathy? Phony politicians? Polluting the environment? Then think about why you feel so strongly about the issue.

The whys have it

As you write, remember the *why*. As the admission officer reads, she'll invariably ask "Why?" Why do you feel strongly about this subject? Why is this topic important to you? Knowing you're against pollution is nice, but why does it make you react with such passion? Without the why, your essay is incomplete. Tell the admission officer why you care. That's what she wants to read: Why you care.

Most important, be yourself. Don't force your writing into a style that doesn't reflect your personality because that's what you think a college wants. It's not! A college wants to know about you. It reads your essay to find out about you. Tell it about you. Be yourself.

 Remember also that a sense of humor is a desirable trait. Let some of your show in your essay. Don't overdo it, however. Don't let your attempt to be funny subordinate your message. But if you let a little wit appear to lighten up your writing, you'll earn an extra point or two. Again, be yourself. Don't force it.

And remember to give yourself enough time. After you write your first draft of your essay, you'll want to put it aside for a few days and then come back and look at it with fresh eyes. Odds are you'll find ways to improve it when you read it again. And you'll want to ask a teacher you respect to react to it, plus check it for style and grammar.

So start thinking seriously about the essay a few weeks before it must be done. The worst approach you can take is to start writing the night before you put your application in the mail.

The big don'ts

The following lists a number of things you should not do regarding your essay:

- ✔ **Don't use your essay to summarize your high school accomplishments.** The admission officer already has read them on your application. Telling him something he already knows is a sure way to get a big zero on his scorecard — and for your essay to fall accidentally into his trash basket.

- ✔ **Don't write about your summer trip to Europe (or your week at the beach) unless you can convince an admission officer that it was a meaningful experience.** He'll be hard to convince. Too many of your friends will be writing on those topics. And these essays usually say more about their parents' vacation preferences than about themselves.

- ✔ **Don't give the admissions officer a choice.** Don't say "Here are a whole bunch of meaningful experiences. I can't decide which is most important, so you pick one." Hey, that's not his job. If you can't decide, don't expect him to decide for you. The admission officer's job, when he reads that, is to give you a zero and let your essay slide into the trash.

Okay, so I've been exaggerating a little. Admission officers don't routinely toss essays in the trash. But perhaps once a year they can't resist the temptation to pick one up gingerly between forefinger and thumb and let it fall in an appropriate place. More than likely that one is a written analysis of a student's high school activities list.

How to help yourself

If you read Chapter 2, you may already be helping yourself prepare for the essay. In Chapter 2, I suggest that you keep a diary because it forces you to use writing skills and to think about what's important to you. If you've been doing that, you have had daily practice writing coherently about yourself, the main skill you'll need for the essay.

Your diary is now a record of the important stuff in your life. It can jog your memory. A diary entry could be the first sentence of your essay.

Essays: The good and the bad

An essay won't help or hurt your application just because of the subject you choose to write about. It's what you say about the subject, and how you say it, that counts.

Say two high school students spent their summers in Florida working on projects to save the swampland. A noble cause, indeed. Both decided to write about their experiences in their application essays. One drew rave reviews at the admission office. The other got a "Yecch!"

Here's how the two essays began:

Poor: When I was in Florida last summer, I really liked working in the Everglades. It's a neat place with alligators and other endangered wildlife.

Good: Most people visiting Florida see the Everglades as a large swamp to be avoided. I had the opportunity to see the Everglades as a place where I could make a contribution to preserving life.

How Does Your High School Measure Up?

It's time to shoot down a myth. You know, the one that says there's a master list ranking every high school in the United States, 1 through 20,664, that selective colleges use to pick their students. Well, there is no such thing.

Every year some students, and more often parents, ask about this list. They heard about it from a friend, who got it firsthand from a good source. They want to know where their kid's school ranks, and is that why he can't get into Harvard. I repeat, there is no such list. Even if I wanted to compile one (and I thought about it), where would I start? How do you compare high schools? What criteria do you use to rank them? Number of teachers with master's degrees?

Having destroyed that myth, I'll offer a fact. Some high schools do a better job than others preparing their graduates. Colleges know the difference. Students at a high school that consistently graduates people ready to handle the most rigorous college work have an edge getting into selective colleges.

How do colleges know?

For one thing, colleges have records. When a typical admission committee meets to consider a group of students, each member has a computer printout showing how other students from the same high schools have performed at that college. It's a record they don't ignore. They're looking for good students who can handle their professors' work. If a high school has sent them such students in the past, they have reason to believe it will send them more.

They also know about high schools from personal experience. Admission officers usually are assigned responsibility for specific geographic areas from which their college gets most of its students. One of their jobs is to visit high schools, know what they do, how they grade, and the rigor of their curriculum. An admission officer's opinion of a high school, when offered to colleagues at a committee meeting, is accepted as fact. The admission officer who knows your school probably will be the one who reads your application first.

What does this mean to you?

If you're a very good student, in the eyes of the college to which you apply, the strength of your high school means nothing. If you're a borderline applicant, the strength of your school may get you in. But then so can your trombone.

If you're reading this before high school and have a choice about which high school to attend, you may want to consider one that sends a high percentage of its students to college. You can find out the percentage by asking for a copy of the school's profile, the fact sheet that it sends out with its transcripts.

Scoring System Stuff

Every college uses a scoring system to rank its applicants. Most colleges won't talk about it. Some even deny it.

The admission officer who first reads your application, and probably the one with whom you talked on your campus visit, assigns the score. The items most commonly considered are

- Unweighted GPA
- Honors, AP, and IB courses
- Test scores
- Activities
- Teacher and counselor recommendations
- Content and writing style of your essay

Some colleges also give points for class rank and impressions formed during an interview. Each item gets a score, say on a scale of 1 to 6, and then the subscores are added for a total.

At some colleges, if your first score is high enough, you're an automatic *admit*. If it's too low, you're a *deny*. That means you're gone. But most admission offices require an application to be read twice and use the combined scores for automatic acceptance or rejection.

In most cases, the automatic admits are less than half the number of students needed to fill the freshman class. So then the staff must turn to the great mass in the middle. Decisions on those candidates usually go to the admission committee, which typically is the entire admission office staff, chaired by the dean or director. This step is when recommendation letters are scrutinized with careful eyes. Even at this stage, those first scores are meaningful. It's not unusual for a committee to consider candidates in descending order of their scores and stop when they have enough.

Yes, You're Special, But Will Colleges Think So?

At every college, hundreds of applicants fall into categories considered outside the normal scoring process. The applicants may be called lucky. Colleges like to call them *special*. In the admissions office, being special means being attractive.

You can be special in two ways. You can get special consideration because of who you are. Or you can get extra points because you have a special talent. In either case, that's good for you.

When you checked out admission requirements for colleges in those thick directories, you may have noticed that many include a sentence beginning with, "Special consideration is given to . . . ." The sentence most often ends with "minorities." Sometimes it says "minorities and children of alumni." Those sentences are true, but they're not the whole truth. Many more students than minorities and alumni kids enjoy the luck of special consideration. In some cases, it's luck they were born with. In others, it's luck they've made on their own.

Either way, special consideration means students are removed from the large pool of applicants and considered only in competition with other students in their own smaller pool. In the case of minorities, special consideration often is called affirmative action. To be consistent, colleges should say that groups of other students are being affirmatively acted upon, too.

The Diversity Goal

Much of the special consideration offered to college students has its roots in a special word: diversity. A diverse student body is a goal on many — probably most — campuses. And diversity means many things, often depending on how a college defines the word to meet its goals.

A college is more than classrooms and elm trees. It's a community in which students learn from each other. Each college builds its community to meet its own particular goals and to enhance the students' interactive learning. The school may want a student body that is widely varied by family background, by special talent, by geographic origin, by extracurricular interests, by socioeconomic status, by ethnicity, and, yes, by race. The goals that are derived from the desire for diversity play a large role in much of the special consideration I describe in the following sections.

Minorities

It's a fact that some minorities aren't represented on some campuses in proportion to their numbers in the population. It's also a fact that some colleges have policies, set by their presidents or boards of trustees, to fix that imbalance. To meet that goal, they must accept a higher percentage of applicants from some minority groups.

The admission office calls them underrepresented minorities. On predominantly white campuses, the term *underrepresented minorities* usually includes African-Americans, Hispanics, and Native Americans.

How does special consideration work? Say a dean of admission, to meet her president's goal, must have 60 African-Americans in her next freshman class. She has 350 African-American applicants. History shows that for every four African-Americans accepted by this college, one eventually enrolls. (Enrollment percentages differ by college.) To get 60 African-American freshmen then, the dean must accept 240 applicants. So her 350 African-American candidates go into their own pool, where they compete with each other for 240 letters of acceptance. Those are much better odds than the odds for students not being specially considered.

Special consideration for minorities often is called *affirmative action,* the term used when minorities get the same type of break in the workplace and elsewhere. Affirmative action for minorities is less prevalent in college admission offices now than it was a few years ago. One federal court has ruled it unconstitutional to use race as a factor in admission decisions. The California legislature has prohibited affirmative action in that state's public universities.

Kids of alumni

Minorities get special consideration to correct an imbalance. The other large group of people becomes special for a different reason: money. Deans and college presidents will speak at length about graduates of Old Siwash being part of the Old Siwash Family, and how they like to give family members a break at admission time. When you hear that kind of talk, wave the smoke from your eyes. Children of alumni get a break at a parent's college, but the size of the break is directly related to the parent's generosity.

Children of alumni are called *legacies.* Get familiar with that word. You'll hear students on campus called legacies. You'll hear students calling themselves legacies. Legacies are students who get special consideration because of their parents.

From the college's perspective, giving children of alumni special consideration is good business. All colleges, even those that get state subsidies, need outside sources of cash. They regularly solicit contributions from alumni, many of whom regularly respond. In exchange for his help, Albert Alum knows that when his daughter applies to Old Siwash, she won't be in the regular pool with the masses. Princeton's veteran dean of admission, Fred Hargadon, was quoted in a campus publication as saying, "The question is not whether there should be alumni preference but how extensive it should be."

When Albert Alum's daughter, Alice, applies to Old Siwash, she immediately will be recognized as a legacy because the application form asks for the colleges of the student's parents. Her application is pulled from the pile and shipped to the college alumni office, or development office, or both.

Most colleges have a development office. *Development,* on college campuses, is a euphemism for fundraising. Almost all colleges have alumni offices whose main job is also fundraising. In some cases, the two offices are combined.

At the alumni office, Alice's application gets a grade — colleges call it a legacy rating — say on a scale of A to E. It has nothing to do with her academic record or her trombone talent. It is based solely on her father's generosity to Old Siwash. If old Albert gives $100,000 every time the college asks, Alice will get an A. If he responds occasionally with a $25 check, she'll get an E.

Her application then returns to the admission office. Typically, if she has a legacy rating of A or B, she'll be accepted, regardless of what the rest of her application shows. A grade of C or lower puts her back in the pool where her legacy status gives her an edge as she competes with everyone else.

Here's one example of the size of the legacy break. At Haverford College outside Philadelphia, 43 percent of all applicants are accepted. Among legacies, 86 percent get in. At most private colleges, those differences are about the same.

Tuba players

Playing a musical instrument also can earn you a break at the admission office. The size of the break depends on how well you play and the need for your instrument on that campus.

Face it, trombone players are pretty common. If you play a mean trombone and impress the band director with your tapes, he may send a note to the admission office saying your trombone is the kind of talent Old Siwash needs.

If you play a tuba, or bassoon, or something else that few of your generation master, you may have a bigger break. If the band's only tuba players are graduating this year, the director becomes desperate. He already has informed the admission office of the urgent need for tubas. When your application arrives with "playing the tuba" among your activities, you zoom to the head of the applicant class.

Deans of admission at selective colleges say recommendations from band directors and all faculty get the same weight as recommendations from coaches. Well, maybe. At least they say that.

The tuba factor also works when, say, the physics department is bugging the admission office to find more physics majors. If you show up expressing a desire to major in physics, you get special consideration. If the physics faculty's influence is strong, all potential physics majors may be put in a separate applicant pool to compete against each other.

Athletes

The special consideration given to athletes is special, indeed. But knowing how it works will not help you. If you want to know how athletes get into college, ask one of your high school coaches. He's probably lining up spots for three or four kids right now.

Athletes who get special consideration — male and female — fall into two general categories depending on where their schools rank in the national college sports hierarchy. The categories are those that give full free rides to jocks and those that don't.

All college sports programs belong to one of three divisions — known appropriately as Divisions 1, 2, and 3 — established by the National Collegiate Athletic Association. (Each division is made up of subcategories.) Each college selects a division for each of its sports, thereby agreeing to play by that division's rules. Georgetown University, for example, plays basketball in Division 1 and football in Division 3. The divisions indicate, among other things, the level of competition. Division 1 is the toughest.

The recruitment and enrollment of college athletes are governed firmly by the NCAA's rules for each division. A college stepping even slightly over the line faces stiff penalties. The rules — including such things as number of times athletes can visit campuses and when coaches can visit athletes' homes — are spelled out in books even thicker than the directories you've been reading. Colleges employ people full-time to make sure that they abide by the rules.

Most colleges in Divisions 1 and 2 — where full athletic scholarships are offered — use the NCAA's minimum academic standards as their own standards for admitting jocks. That standard is a combination of grade-point average and SAT or ACT score, with the required test score lower as GPA increases. The standard also is lower than most colleges use for other students. But anyone a coach recommends who meets the NCAA standard is in.

There are, of course, exceptions. Colleges such as Stanford, Duke, Rice, and Vanderbilt — among others — impose higher academic standards on athletes than the NCAA requires.

In Division 3, where athletic scholarships aren't allowed, admission officers generally consider a coach's recommendation favorably but insist jocks meet the minimum academic criteria. Coaches at those colleges don't recommend athletes who won't qualify academically.

The bottom line for athletes capable of performing at the college level is that they don't need this book. They don't have to seek colleges. The college coaches will contact them. The coaching/scouting network is so pervasive that very few good high school jocks go unnoticed.

Kids from North Dakota

Colleges pride themselves on diversity among their students, and they mean more than just ethnic diversity. Geographic diversity is also a goal. Some colleges love to send out brochures saying they have students from all 50 states, but they're foiled because the admission office can't find anyone from North Dakota.

If you don't mind traveling, you may have a better chance of getting into a college where few students from your area apply. A Montana applicant will get into Harvard over a New York student with identical credentials. That's a fact of life. Live with it.

Geographic diversity normally is a goal of private colleges. State universities exist first to serve residents of their own states. Out-of-staters are accepted to fill the classes, but get few breaks at the admission office. For example, the University of North Carolina-Chapel Hill accepts only 13 percent of the non-North Carolinians who apply. That's a tougher ticket than Harvard.

Kids of plumbers

Admission officers call it socioeconomic diversity. They want their student body to include kids of bankers and kids of plumbers. But more bankers' kids apply than plumbers' kids. So when they see a plumber's kid — that is, anyone from a family with a blue-collar background — he gets extra points on the scorecard for the diversity he'll bring. An applicant who will be the first generation of her family attending college gets even more bonus points.

Kids with cash

The hottest debate raging at admission officers' conventions these days is whether a student's wealth should be considered in admission decisions. The purists loudly argue no. They insist colleges should stick with the tradition of need-blind admissions, which means students are accepted on their merit, without considering their ability to pay. Ten years ago, almost every college in the country did it that way.

On the other side are the pragmatists who say: "Hey. Times are tough. We need the cash. Students who can pay the full bill, and won't need some of our money in financial aid, should get an advantage." On those campuses, when the admission process gets down to its final borderline decisions, a student who can afford the full price may have an edge.

But at last count, those colleges that consider money in their admission decisions were in a minority in the debate. (More about paying college bills in Part IV.)

If You're Over 25

The application process for older students is the same as for the kids. You send in the forms, probably write an essay, and wait for the news. But the way they look at you in the admission office will be different.

Each college will have its own procedure for judging your qualifications, and you should ask about it when you talk to an admission officer. Most probably will want a high school transcript, even if high school was 30 years ago. The longer you've been out of school, the less influence your high school record will have.

Your activities and your work experience will get much more attention than your high school grades. The college likely will ask you to write about a meaningful life experience, either as a formal essay or as a supplement to your application. For people who have been out in the world, meaningful life experiences are legitimate substitutes for high school academic records. It's that different perspective — the mature view — that you will bring to the student body to increase its diversity that adds to your attractiveness.

On some campuses, college credit is offered to adults for life experiences. That credit reduces the number of courses necessary to earn a degree. Ask about it at the admission office.

And don't sweat the prospect of joining a bunch of kids on a Saturday morning in an SAT testing room. You probably won't be asked to take the test again. If you took the SAT or ACT in high school, a college will look at that score. A few exceptions — there always are exceptions — require a recent SAT score for adults to use as a measure of your ability to handle college work. Each college admission office will tell you its requirement over the phone.

Chapter 10

How to Look Your Best

*1*t's time to discover another fact of life. A college will decide whether it likes you in one way, and one way only: by reading about you. You can have an exuberant, charming personality that makes people like you the instant they meet you. You can wear a smile every waking hour. But unless that personality and smile come through when a college admission officer reads about you, it won't help your chances of being accepted to the college.

Most of what the admission officer reads will be words on paper — or on a computer screen — that have been submitted by you. They are words, and a few numbers, on the bundle of pages you lovingly prepared and submitted as your college application. True, the admission officer also will have notes from your interview last spring when you displayed that charming personality. But when decision time comes, he'll be reading those notes, too. Reading is an admission officer's number one job.

Your number one job now, as you prepare your application, is to convince him that his college wants you. As I say in other chapters, the admission officer spends about 15 minutes reading your application and related documents, including his own notes. The score he gives you after those 15 minutes may get you into the college or keep you out. But that score certainly will go a long way toward determining your fate. (The scoring system is described in Chapter 9.)

In Chapter 8, I assume that you'll apply to six colleges (a made-up number to illustrate the decision process). I assume that you wrote to those colleges requesting application materials. Now those materials are all assembled in a neat pile on your desk. Each separate packet is about eight pages long, not counting instructions. You have a stack of about 60 pages in front of you, and you're thinking, "Hey, this is work."

Relax. It's not as bad as it looks. Three of the six colleges use what's called the Common Application. You fill it out once, run it through a copier, and you have three applications ready to go. Plus, not all of those pages are for you. Some must be delivered to a teacher and a counselor for their input.

So you approach the pile not with fear but with caution. You know this is your big chance to sell yourself to the colleges you've selected. You have been building a good record through four years of high school, and you don't want to blow it now by being careless.

When and How to Apply

You don't have much of a choice on when to apply. The colleges set their time frames for considering applications and you either meet their schedules or get left out. But depending on the college, you may have a choice on how to apply. More colleges each year allow you to perform the task on a computer screen instead of on paper.

The early bird gets the edge

The best time to apply depends on the colleges to which you're applying, and the admission systems they use. If a school has a firm, published application deadline, be sure that your application gets there by the deadline. Tardiness is not a desirable trait. Most deadlines are in January or February for the class arriving the following September. Some deadlines are as early as mid-December.

Here's something to remember. At least 99 percent of college applicants in the United States wait for the deadlines to send their stuff. But you're no dummy. You're going to help your own cause by submitting your application a few weeks early, before the mailbags start piling up on an admission officer's desk. This way, she can have more than 15 minutes to focus on your application. (If you're among the 99 percent who procrastinate, you may want to consider one of those overnight delivery services to guarantee its on-time arrival.)

If you're applying to a college that uses rolling admission, get your application in as soon as the school will take it. Rolling admission means applicants are considered, and accepted or rejected, as they show up. It's essentially first come, first served. If you wait too long, the freshman class could be full. (You can find out more on rolling and open admissions in Chapter 9.)

Open admission colleges, including almost all two-year colleges, usually take anyone who qualifies until classes begin. But now some are shutting their doors when they get too full. As with other colleges, the earlier you apply, the better.

Should you shoot for an Early Decision?

A few hundred of the more selective colleges offer the chance to apply, and be accepted, before the full-scale application process begins. Decisions on early applicants usually are made by December of the senior year. (More about early decisions in Chapter 8.) They're called Early Decision or Early Action or Early Admission, but they all work pretty much the same.

Don't even think about applying early anywhere unless you're 100 percent sure that it's the college you want. The price a college charges for giving you an Early Decision is your commitment to attend if accepted. Some colleges make you promise to apply nowhere else until they decide on you. Others require you to withdraw all other applications if they say yes.

If you have settled on one college and are sure you won't be enticed by any others, it's your chance to get a decision out of the way and enjoy the spring, while your friends are biting their nails waiting for the mail.

The advantages of applying by computer

If you have access to a computer, technology can make your task easier. Almost half the nation's colleges now accept applications on computer diskette. They give you the application on disk, and you fill it out on your computer screen and ship it back. Some colleges want just the disk returned; others want the disk with a paper printout.

The Common Application (which I talk about in the next section) is also available on diskette. You can get one in your school counseling center or from the National Association of Secondary School Principals' main office, 1904 Association Drive, Reston, VA, 22091.

A newer trend, which has appeared at a small number of colleges, is application by modem. You can send your forms via modem and phone lines directly into the admission office computer. If your college offers such a service, it'll let you know.

What a Break! A Common Application

If you're lucky, all the colleges you're considering will accept the Common Application. That means you have to fill out only one form and run it through a decent copier for every school on your list.

The Common App, as it's known, is an eight-page form devised by the National Association of Secondary School Principals (NASSP) to help students save time. (Principals want you to have time for important things like high school term papers and band concerts.) NASSP figured that you need to fill out only one application to serve the needs of any college. The Common App's popularity among admission offices started to grow in 1994, when Harvard decided to accept it as a substitute for its own application. When Harvard does something, others rush to follow.

At last count, 165 colleges use the Common App as their official application college and the number is growing by about 10 a year. Other's will take it if you send it to them. So before you fill out unnecessary forms, ask the admission offices at your colleges whether the Common Application is acceptable.

Electronic versions of an application form similar to the Common Application are available at several private companies' Web sites. But before you send a college an application produced by a private company, make sure the college will accept it.

Copies of this form are sent each year to every high school's counseling center. If your school is out, check with your principal about ordering more Common Apps. (Your principal probably belongs to the NASSP.) Or ask for the form from the college. Any school that accepts the Common App should have copies at its admission office.

Enough of the preliminaries. It's time to make yourself look beautiful, on paper or on a computer screen. Because the Common Application is so common, and because it's so similar to other applications, I walk through filling it out line by line.

Vital statistics

Take a look at the first page. It'll be easy. There's a long list of colleges at the top that accept the Common Application. It's not a complete list because other schools signed up after the form was printed. And some that don't formally sign up to use the Common App will accept it if you send it.

The Personal Data shown in Figure 10-1 is pretty simple stuff. If you don't know your name, address, and birthdate, even this book can't help you. Notice the line that asks about possible areas of academic concentration or a major. If you're leaning at all toward certain majors, mention them here. That's something the admission office likes to know, and it could be that the faculty in one of those areas is clamoring for students. The hypothetical student I assumed you to be in earlier chapters would write "English, journalism, education." If you're leaning toward a science major but aren't sure which science you prefer, just write science. If you truly are undecided, check the undecided box.

PERSONAL DATA

Legal name: _____
Last   *First*   *Middle (complete)*   *Jr., etc.*   *Sex*

Prefer to be called: _____ (nickname) Former last name(s) if any: _____

Are you applying as a ☐ freshman or ☐ transfer student? For the term beginning: _____

Permanent home address: _____
Number and Street

_____
City or Town   *County*   *State*   *Zip*

If different from the above, please give your mailing address for all admission correspondence:

Mailing address: _____
Number and Street

_____ Use until: _____
City or Town   *State*   *Zip*   *Date*

Telephone at mailing address: _____/_____ Permanent home telephone: _____/_____
    Area Code *Number*   *Area Code* *Number*

Birthdate: _____ Citizenship: ☐ U.S. ☐ Permanent Resident U.S. ☐ Other _____ Visa type _____
  Month Day Year   *Country*

Possible area(s) of academic concentration/major: _____ or undecided ☐

Special college or division if applicable: _____

Possible career or professional plans: _____ or undecided ☐

Will you be a candidate for financial aid? ☐ Yes ☐ No If yes, the appropriate form(s) was/will be filed on: _____

The following items are optional: Social Security number, if any: ☐☐☐ - ☐☐ - ☐☐☐☐

Place of birth: _____ Marital status: _____
  City   *State*   *Country*

First language, if other than English: _____ Language spoken at home: _____

How would you describe yourself? Check any that apply.

☐ American Indian, Alaskan Native (tribal affiliation _____) ☐ Mexican American, Mexican

☐ Native Hawaiian, Pacific Islander ☐ African American, Black

☐ Asian American, Asian (including Indian subcontinent) (country _____) ☐ White, Anglo, Caucasian

☐ Hispanic, Latino (including Puerto Rican) (country _____) ☐ Other (Specify _____)

Figure 10-1:
Personal
Data for the
Common
Application.

A key question in this section of the application is the last one, asking if you are seeking financial aid. If you read Chapter 9, you know that some colleges give a break to students who can afford the full sticker price. You know that there's no way you can meet the cost of this college without some help. But you're tempted to check No, just in case this is a college where no-aid students have an edge. Resist the temptation. As soon as your financial aid application arrives on campus, the financial aid office computer will tell the admission office computer. The admission office will know you lied. Dishonesty is fatal. Your application will be dead in the water. Remember that the girl who applied to Harvard was rejected not for killing her mother, but for lying about it on her application.

The Educational Data section, shown in Figure 10-2, is also no sweat. You may have to ask your counselor for her fax number and your school's ACT/CEEB code number. If she doesn't know those numbers, don't rely too strongly on her advice in other areas.

The top of page two asks for more vital statistics, as shown in Figure 10-3. You should have no problem remembering the schools that you've attended and your scores on all those — who can forget them? — SATs, I and II. International students who have taken the TOEFL, Test of English as a Foreign Language, should fill in the date and scoring information in this section. (Turn to Chapter 19 for more information on TOEFL and international students.)

Figure 10-2:
Educational
Data for the
Common
Application.

EDUCATIONAL DATA

School you attend now _____ Date of entry _____

Address _____ ACT/CEEB code number _____
             City   *State*   *Zip Code*

Date of secondary graduation _____ Is your school public? _____ private? _____ parochial? _____

College counselor: Name: _____ Position: _____

School telelephone: _____ / _____   School FAX: _____ / _____
                Area Code   *Number*   *Area Code*   *Number*   **APP**

List all other secondary schools, including summer schools and programs you have attended beginning with ninth grade.

Name of School   Location (City, State, Zip)   Dates Attended

List all colleges at which you have taken courses for credit and list names of courses on a separate sheet. Please have a transcript sent from each institution as soon as possible.

Name of College   Location (City, State, Zip)   Degree Candidate?   Dates Attended

If not currently attending school, please check here: ☐   Describe in detail, on a separate sheet, your activities since last enrolled.

Figure 10-3:
Educational
Data
(Continued)
for the
Common
Application.

TEST INFORMATION. Be sure to note the tests required for each institution to which you are applying. The official scores from the appropriate testing agency must be submitted to each institution as soon as possible. Please list your test plans below.

	SAT I (or SAT)	SAT II: Subject Tests (or Achievement Tests)	American College Test (ACT)	Test of English as a Foreign Language (TOEFL)
Dates taken/				
to be taken				
Scores				
	Verbal *Math*		*(Composite)*	

Family stuff

The section labeled Family in Figure 10-4 at the bottom of page two of the application looks pretty routine, but some of the information it wants may be important. It could make you a special person deserving special consideration. Your parents' colleges will determine whether you're the most special person of all, a legacy. Your parents' background also could make you special. If they have blue-collar jobs or didn't go to college, you could be a student who will bring socioeconomic diversity to a campus. Special, indeed. (A full description of special students is in Chapter 9.)

If you're first, you get a break

If you're the first person in your family to go to college, let the college know. You can provide a widely sought commodity — diversity.

Most colleges want a diverse student body — and diversity of family life is a key ingredient in the mix. Many colleges give breaks in the admission process to the campus. First-in-the-family students are rare. (More on diversity in Chapter 9.)

It's probably no surprise that students whose parents went to college are more likely to have college in their plans. A 1995 survey by a group called Postsecondary Education

Opportunities found that kids whose parents earned degrees are twice as likely to go to college as kids from noncollege parents.

If you're the first in your family to take the step, make it clear somewhere on your application, An essay built around the factors in you're decision, explaining why you decided college is for you, would be a fine way to do it. You could ask a teacher to mention the fact in a recommendation letter. And where the application asks for parents' colleges, don't leave the lines blank. Write none.

FAMILY

Mother's full name: _____ Is she living? _____

Home address if different from yours: _____

Occupation: _____
       (Describe briefly)   *(Name of business or organization)*

Name of college (if any): _____ Degree: _____ Year: _____

Name of professional or graduate school (if any): _____ Degree: _____ Year: _____

Father's full name: _____ Is he living? _____

Home address if different from yours: _____

Occupation: _____
       (Describe briefly)   *(Name of business or organization)*

Name of college (if any): _____ Degree: _____ Year: _____

Name of professional or graduate school (if any): _____ Degree: _____ Year: _____

If not with both parents, with whom do you make your permanent home: _____

Please check if parents are ☐ separated ☐ divorced ☐ other _____

Please give names and ages of your brothers or sisters. If they have attended college, give the names of the institutions attended, degrees, and approximate dates:

_____

_____

Figure 10-4:
Family Data for the Common Application.

ACADEMIC HONORS

Briefly describe any scholastic distinctions or honors you have won beginning with ninth grade:

_____

_____

_____

_____

Figure 10-5:
Awards Data for the Common Application.

School stuff

Now look at the next page of the application, headed School Report. Remove it and the three following pages and set them aside. They go to school — to a teacher and counselor — for those all-important recommendations.

Wow, you've finished six of eight pages, and it feels like you've just begun! This is a snap, right? Well, not really. Settle down because you still have some work to do.

Awards

At the top of page seven, the form wants to know about "scholastic distinctions or honors," as shown in Figure 10-5. That means awards. Mention every award you received in high school, small or large. Don't forget that certificate you earned in Latin class, the Rotary Club student of the month award, and your prize in the science fair. And mention the award your school newspaper won while you were the number two editor. That's a school-related honor. If you have more awards than will fit neatly on those three lines, don't try to cram them all in. Attach a list on a separate sheet.

This section may seem like a simple recitation of facts, but it's more. It's one test of your ability to understand and follow instructions. Notice the form asks you to list awards beginning in ninth grade. Do it that way. List them in the order that you earned them, chronologically, not in the order that you think about them. Some admission officers won't pay attention to the order, but some will. Don't take a chance.

EXTRACURRICULAR, PERSONAL, AND VOLUNTEER ACTIVITIES

Please list your principal extracurricular, community, and family activities and hobbies in the order of their interest to you. Include specific events and/or major accomplishments such as musical instrument played, varsity letters earned, etc. Please (✓) in the right column those activities you hope to pursue in college.

Activity	Grade level or post-secondary (p.s.) 9 10 11 12 PS	Approximate time spent — Hours per week / Weeks per year	Positions held, honors won, or letters earned	Do you plan to participate in college?

Figure 10-6: Activities Data for the Common Application.

In case you're wondering, don't include the blue ribbon you won for showing your prize hog at the county fair. And don't list the trophy for winning the all-county, under-17 female singles tennis tournament. Those are fine accomplishments, but they're not scholastic honors. You can list hog shows and tennis tournaments later as activities. And you can talk more about hogs in your essay, if they're an important part of your life.

And don't mention any of those pseudo-awards from companies that put your name in a national directory so that you and your relatives will buy the book. Admission officers recognize those so-called awards for what they are — clever marketing tactics by book publishers.

Activities

The next section of the form, shown in Figure 10-6, gets careful scrutiny in the admission office. This section is often the second item read, after your transcript. It asks for a list of your activities during high school, and it wants all activities: school-related, personal, community, church, and family. If you have more than the seven activities for which space is allotted, attach a separate sheet. It won't be the only attached sheet the admission officer reads that day, or even that hour.

Take time and think about your activities. Be sure that you remember all of them since ninth grade. (That magic diary I suggest in Chapter 2 would certainly help here.) Don't forget your volunteer work at a hospital, your Boy Scout positions, and the time you worked the stopwatch for the Special Olympics. They're activities. The college wants to know about them because they tell something about you.

This part is another place where the admission officer finds out whether you can follow instructions. Unlike the awards list you just finished, your activities should not be in chronological order. Check that first sentence of the introduction. It says "in the order of their interest to you." You must decide how important all your activities are and tell the college by the order in which you list them. Be careful. The order of your list often gets as much attention in an admission office as the list itself. The college wants to know all the things you did, sure, but it also wants to know what you care about. This is one of the places that the school gets that information.

I advise you to be careful with your list because applications can be seriously damaged by the order in which activities appear. If you quit the school paper after ninth grade, but it's first on your list above activities you've pursued for four years, all sorts of questions pop into an admissions officer's mind. One of them is, "Does he really understand what he reads?"

A quick piece of advice before you put your list to paper (or disk). Two sections later, the application asks you to write about your most meaningful activity. What you write shows some consistency in your thought processes (and colleges love consistent thought processes) if the activity you write about as most meaningful is at the top of this list of activities. Of course, if you want to make a distinction between important and meaningful, charge ahead.

In the column headed "Positions held . . ." mention any leadership role you assumed or honor you earned in an activity. If you were an Eagle Scout, president of your Junior Achievement company, scheduler for hospital volunteers, or Sunday school teacher, say so. Any position of that type indicates an ability to lead and, in college, leadership is a very desirable trait. Try to come up with some contribution to each of your activities that can be described in this column. Too many blanks peg you as a dreaded list padder, one who joins for the sake of joining and contributes nothing. Colleges don't like list padders.

If you lean at all toward the pursuit of an activity in college, check the box that says you plan to participate. You can always change your mind later. Colleges fervently covet active students. And if the school has a special need for one of your talents on campus, it may make you a special person worthy of special consideration. Wouldn't you like to be a recipient of affirmative action for trombonists?

If you must use a separate sheet to continue your list, be sure to include all the information requested on the form. Report the years you were involved in each activity and the time you spent by the hour and by the week. If you overlook any of the requested items, you may get points off for carelessness.

Jobs

The list of jobs you held, near the bottom of page seven, shown in Figure 10-7, also tells the admission officer something about you. The list could show an interest not reflected anywhere else on your application. If you worked at a hospital instead of volunteering, for example, this is the place to report it. Consistent employment also can be a mitigating factor for an unimpressive activities list.

If you had more than three jobs during the last three years, use a separate sheet. Don't cram two on a line. That makes an admission officer squint, and squinting produces negative reactions.

WORK EXPERIENCE

List any job (including summer employment) you have held during the past three years.

Specific nature of work	Employer	Approximate dates of employment	Approximate no. of hours spent per week

In the space provided below, briefly discuss which of these activities (extracurricular and personal activities or work experience) has had the most meaning for you, and why.

_____

_____

_____

_____

_____

Figure 10-7:
Work
Experience
for the
Common
Application.

You get to talk

At last, you can stop answering questions and say something on your own. At the bottom of the page, you're asked to pick an activity or a job that has "had the most meaning" for you and explain why. To show you're consistent, writing about the activity that heads your list as most important is smart. But if consistency is not your thing, pick another meaningful activity.

Two things about your statement matter most: what you say and how you say it. Admission officers read the statement the same way they read your longer essay to find out how you write, how you think, and what you care about. Many addmission officers compare this statement with your essay looking for, yes, consistency.

If you put some real effort into your formal essay, displaying your outstanding writing talent, and then kiss off the meaningful activity statement with a few mundane sentences, questions will surely arise in an admission officer's head. One may well be, "Who wrote the essay for you?"

Watch out: Another follow-the-instructions trap is in the meaningful activity statement. Until now, you've been attaching separate sheets when the form doesn't provide enough space for your answers. Don't do it here. Look at those first five words: "In the space provided below." Confine your statement to the five lines on the form. A word processor can get a lot of characters into those five long lines.

The essay needs to answer why

The application form calls it a Personal Statement, shown in Figure 10-8, but students everywhere know it as the essay. You've been working on it for weeks before you even picked up an application. Your favorite English teacher checked it for grammar and writing style. Now you must fine-tune it to meet the instructions on the application.

The instructions are general enough that any well-conceived essay will work, perhaps with a few adjustments.

You get a choice of

- ✔ Evaluating an experience in your life
- ✔ Discussing a national, local, or personal issue
- ✔ Describing how one person has influenced your life

There's not much that won't fit into one of these categories. The essays that won't fit are those that should not be written.

In Chapter 9, I discuss how a college looks at an essay and tell you what brings smiles to an admission officer's face and what gets tossed in the trash. Some of that advice deserves to be repeated here. If you write about your summer trip to Europe and can make it fit Category 1 by evaluating it as a meaningful experience, it will work well. If you can't, it will be one of hundreds of trite essays submitted every year about a summer trip to somewhere.

PERSONAL STATEMENT

This personal statement helps us become acquainted with you in ways different from courses, grades, test scores, and other objective data. *It enables you to demonstrate your ability to organize thoughts and express yourself. Please write an essay about one of the topics listed below.* You may attach extra pages (same size, please) if your essay exceeds the limits of this page.

1) Evaluate a significant experience or achievement that has special meaning to you.
2) Discuss some issue of personal, local, or national concern and its importance to you.
3) Indicate a person who has had a significant influence on you, and describe that influence.

I understand that: (1) it is my responsibility to report any changes in my schedule to the colleges to which I am applying, and (2) *if I am an Early Action or Early Decision Candidate, that I must attach a letter with this application notifying that college of my intent.*

My signature below indicates that all information in my application is complete, factually correct, and honestly presented.

Signature _____ Date _____

These colleges are committed to administer all educational policies and activities without discrimination on the basis of race, color, religion, national or ethnic origin, age, handicap, or sex. The admissions process at private undergraduate institutions is exempt from the federal regulation implementing Title IX of the Education Amendments of 1972.

Figure 10-8:
The essay for the Common Application.

If you write about the need to save the Everglades, and make it fit Category 2 by explaining why saving the Everglades is important to you, it will put many points on your scorecard. If you ignore that essential point — why you care — your essay is trash-basket material.

Admission officers want you to know why they're reading your essay. They tell you at the top of the page in italics so that you won't miss it. Your essay will show how you can "organize thoughts and express yourself." But that's not the whole story. They want to learn from your essay something about you that they can't find elsewhere in your application. A regurgitation of your activities list is the quickest way to get a large zero under Essay on an admission officer's scorecard.

Admission officers also want to know what you care about and why. I've told you that their favorite questions begin with "why." That's what they're asking as they read what you have written. Why? Give them an answer.

Notice that the instructions don't specify a length for the essay. You can write as much or as little as you desire. But some colleges that use their own form will ask for a certain length. Abide by the request. If the form asks for 500 words, don't write 1,000. That's one of the most blatant signs that you can't follow instructions.

About Those Recommendation Letters

When you finish the essay and sign your name at the bottom of the last page, your application still isn't ready for the mail. You must deal with the four middle pages that you set aside. They're the ones where others get the chance to offer information about you. The two pages labeled School Report go to your counselor. The two Teacher Evaluation pages, shown in Figures 10-9, 10-10, and 10-11, go to a teacher of your choice.

At some high schools, the teacher and counselor will return their recommendations to you to be mailed with your applications. Other schools will send the recommendations separately because these schools think that you shouldn't see them. Neither approach is dominant. The split is about 50-50. And how the recommendations are mailed doesn't matter, as long as all pieces of the package get to the admission office.

Please return a photocopy of this sheet to the appropriate admissions office(s) in the envelope(s) provided you by this student.

Teacher's Name (please print or type) _____ Position _____

Secondary School _____

School Address _____
_____Street_____City_____State_____Zip

BACKGROUND INFORMATION

How long have you known this student and in what context? _____

What are the first words that come to your mind to describe this student? _____
_____

List the courses you have taught this student, noting for each the student's year in school (10th, 11th, 12th) and the level of course difficulty (AP, accelerated, honors, elective, etc.). _____

(See reverse side) **TE**

Figure 10-9:
Teacher
Recommen-
dation.

Figure 10-10:
Teacher
evaluation.

EVALUATION

Please feel free to write whatever you think is important about this student, including a description of academic and personal characteristics. We are particularly interested in the candidate's intellectual promise, motivation, relative maturity, integrity, independence, originality, initiative, leadership potential, capacity for growth, special talents, and enthusiasm. We welcome information that will help us to differentiate this student from others.

RATINGS

Compared to other college-bound students whom you have taught, check how you would rate this student in terms of academic skills and potential:

No basis		Below Average	Average	Good (above average)	Very Good (well above average)	Excellent (top 10%)	One of the top few encountered in my career
	Creative, original thought						
	Motivation						
	Independence, initiative						
	Intellectual ability						
	Academic achievement						
	Written expression of ideas						
	Effective class discussion						
	Disciplined work habits						
	Potential for growth						
	SUMMARY EVALUATION						

Signature _____ Date _____

Figure 10-11:
Teacher
ratings.

The teacher's role

The most important part of the application's two pages that you take to a teacher is the blank space at the top of page two, shown in Figure 10-10. That's where he uses his own words to tell the college why it wants you as a student.

Most teachers can write fine recommendations — if they have the time and the inclination. To make sure that your teacher has enough time, see that you give him the form at least two weeks before you need it back.

Teachers are busy people. Preparing lesson plans, grading papers, and supervising activities take a lot of their after-school time. Writing letters for students is another chore heaped on top of all the rest. That's why, even with enough time, a teacher may not be inclined to put enough thought into a recommendation. She wants to get it done and get on with something else. And then the recommendation may be one of those trite boilerplate efforts that do you more harm than good. (I discuss letters of recommendation in Chapter 9.)

It's your job to find a teacher who will put thought and effort into what he writes. By the time you're a senior, you know some teachers fairly well. Some teachers know you as a person as well as a student. They even genuinely like you. They want you to succeed. They will take the time to find the words that will convince an admission officer to accept you. (If a teacher doesn't know what those words are, have him read Chapter 9.)

Don't worry about the section in the Teacher's Evaluation labeled Ratings — where you'll get a rating in skills such as creative thinking, class discussion, and work habits. Teachers are taught early in their training that all their students are excellent. A teacher rarely will check any box but excellent in any category for any student. (Maybe they're afraid of being sued.) Admission officers know this. When they see a good or very good rating, it can be fatal to an applicant's chances.

The counselor's role

The college looks to the counselor as the representative of your high school. That's why she gets the School Report shown in Figure 10-12. One of her key roles is attaching the first piece of paper an admission officer looks at, your transcript. The other is her written recommendation, an example of which is shown in Figure 10-13.

In a typical high school, you don't get to choose a counselor, but must take the one assigned. So you can't search for a counselor who is your friend, as you can with a teacher. If a counselor knows you well and understands your strengths and weaknesses, you're in luck. If she can tell the college things about you that it won't find out elsewhere and tell them in a way that convinces the college that it wants you she has done her job well. But if you're in a large school where each counselor is responsible for 150 to 200 students, chances are he knows you only as a record in his computer. That will come through on the first page of his report, and the admission office won't be looking for much more.

TO THE SECONDARY SCHOOL COLLEGE COUNSELOR:

After filling in the blanks below, use both sides of this form to describe the applicant.

This candidate ranks _____ in a class of _____ students and has a cumulative grade point average of _____ on a _____ scale.

The rank covers a period from _____ to _____. If a precise rank is not available, please indicate rank to the
                              (mo./yr.)   *(mo./yr.)*

nearest tenth from the top. The rank is weighted _____ unweighted _____. How many students share this rank _____

Of this candidate's graduating class, _____% plan to attend a four-year college.

In comparison to other college preparatory students *at our school*, the applicant's course selection is:
☐ most demanding   ☐ demanding   ☐ average   ☐ less than demanding.

How long have you known the applicant, and in what context? _____

What are the first words that come to your mind to describe the applicant? _____

_____

Counselor's name (please print or type): _____   _____
                                                                              Signature

Position: _____   School: _____

School address: _____   Date: _____

Office telelephone: _____ / _____   Office FAX: _____ / _____
                    Area Code   *Number*   *Area Code*   *Number*

School CEEB/ACT Code ☐ ☐ ☐ ☐ ☐ ☐

Please Note: Attach applicant's official transcript, including courses in progress. Include, if available, a school profile and transcript legend. (Please check transcript copies for readability.)

(See reverse side) **SR**

Figure 10-12: School Report.

Unfortunately for students, in counselors you have to take potluck. Regardless of what you get from the pot, though, you can help yourself by making sure that your counselor knows you. In schools where the student-counselor ratio is 200 to 1, that's not automatic. Find opportunities to talk to him during the school year. Sit down, if possible, for a minute or two to chat about what you've been doing. Ask him for advice. When letter-writing time comes, you may stand out in his memory from the rest of the pack.

Be Sure You Don't . . .

In the sections preceding this one, this chapter talks about making you look good. To end the discussion, I must offer warnings about how you can make yourself look bad. Little things can produce big negative reactions in the minds of harried admission officers. And negative reactions you don't need.

Please feel free to write whatever you think is important about this student, including a description of academic and personal characteristics. We are particularly interested in the candidate's intellectual promise, motivation, relative maturity, integrity, independence, originality, initiative, leadership potential, capacity for growth, special talents, and enthusiasm. We welcome information that will help us to differentiate this student from others.

Figure 10-13: Counselor's Evaluation.

(Optional) I recommend this student: ☐ With reservation   ☐ Fairly strongly   ☐ Strongly   ☐ Enthusiastically

✔ **Don't use that white goopy stuff to correct errors.** Patches of white across an application are ugly. Remember that 453 of every 500 college applicants are neat freaks, and you don't want to look a mess. If you don't have access to a computer and must use a typewriter, those cute little ribbons that backspace and erase at the same time can correct your errors without being noticed.

✔ **Don't make extra work for an admission officer.** Give him the information he expects when and where he expects it. For example, don't say "See transcript" where the form asks for your SAT score. Sure the score is on your transcript. But the admission officer, reading hundreds of pages a day in his busy season, expects to glance at a certain spot on a certain page to see an SAT score. He will become irked if it isn't there.

✔ **Don't write in longhand.** You know by now that most people's handwriting is difficult to read. Don't make an admission officer struggle to figure out what you're saying. He may give up and move on to the next application. If you don't have access to a computer or typewriter, print.

✔ **Don't leave any question blank unless it's labeled optional.** An unanswered question is a clear sign of carelessness. And carelessness produces negative reactions.

Now, the Wait

Congratulations! If you've read and completed the steps detailed in the preceding sections of this chapter, that's it. The only tasks left are to address an envelope, find some postage stamps, and put your carefully prepared documents (on paper or disk) in the mail. If you're dealing with a technologically enlightened college that accepts applications by modem, this final step is unnecessary. You're finished. Not all that tough, right?

The hard part starts now. The waiting. If your college asked for applications in mid-January and announces decisions April 1, you've got about 10 weeks in limbo. That's the max. Most waiting periods are shorter. But for those weeks, you'll be in the dark with no clue as to how well that lovingly created essay, fine-tuned activities list, and masterful meaningful experience statement are being received.

You're not alone. A couple of million other students are pacing and biting nails along with you. Sure, it would be nice if an admissions officer would call the day your application arrives and tell you how it fared. But it doesn't work that way. Get on with your life as a high school senior. Remember, if your college accepts you, it will want to see the rest of your senior year grades. That's the challenge you face as you wait.

Part IV
Paying for College

The 5th Wave — By Rich Tennant

"OH, HIM? HE'S SOME GUY FROM MUNCIE, INDIANA, LOOKING FOR A WAY TO PAY FOR HIS DAUGHTER'S COLLEGE EDUCATION."

In this part . . .

1 mention the nasty word: money. You need some to go to college. But the odds are good — say two to one in your favor — that you don't need as much as you think. In this part, you get a good idea of how much money you really need to have at Harvard, Yale, or anywhere else. The actual figures are probably a far cry from those five-digit numbers printed in directories. And, you get advice on how to find the money you do need.

Chapter 11 explains why most students don't pay the full sticker price and shows you how to figure out what colleges will expect you to pay. Chapters 12 and 13 describe the many types of financial aid available — the kind that you get because you need it, and the kind that you get because you're you. Chapter 14 tells you how to get the money. And Chapter 15 offers tips that you can use during your precollege years to plan for the day when you'll need college money.

Chapter 11
Shake Off the Sticker Shock

. . . .

In This Chapter

▶ Discovering what colleges don't tell you

▶ Defining financial aid

▶ Dispelling the myths and anxieties

▶ Knowing that you have a need

▶ Figuring out your need

▶ Figuring out how much you'll really pay

. . . .

Sometimes you have to wonder about colleges and what they do. For years, colleges have allowed the nation's media to report that their tuitions are soaring to the stratosphere, beyond the reach of the average family's bank account. But colleges have done little to tell the other half of the story.

So what's the other half? Few students pay those astronomical prices. The only students who pay the full price are students who can afford to do so.

How Many Students Pay Less?

Yes, Harvard and Yale, and a dozen or so other schools, are charging more than $28,000 a year for tuition and room and board. But as you read this, 78 percent of the freshmen at Harvard and 69 percent at Yale are paying less than $28,000. Some are paying considerably less. At Stanford, 68 percent are paying less than the advertised sticker price. At the University of Chicago, 75 percent pay less. Across the nation, at all colleges from Duke to Dakota Wesleyan, 63 percent of first-year students are paying less than the price you read in directories.

And here's one more fact. A College Board survey in the 1996-97 school year found that two-thirds of the students at private colleges were paying less than $12,000 a year in tuition.

Many colleges don't tell you this stuff. They're not trying to hide something. It just hasn't occurred to them that these facts would interest you. If you check the fine print for each school in those directory listings, you'll see something like "72 percent of freshmen receive financial aid." That means just 28 percent of the freshmen pay the full sticker price.

The price you pay depends mainly on two things:

1. The financial condition of you and your family

2. How much the college wants you (Don't underestimate this important factor.)

The more attractive you are to a college, the more eager it will be to have you on its campus, and the more likely it is to offer you a price you can afford. (Advice on making yourself attractive is in Part III.) Much of the aid based on your financial need will come in grants and loans, even campus jobs. But the aid based on your attractiveness is much easier to understand: It will be a good, old-fashioned discount off the sticker price.

Chapters 12 and 13 describe in detail both kinds of aid.

When Will You Know the Exact Price?

In Chapter 1, I suggest that you forget about money in the early stages of selecting a college because you don't know how much you'll have to pay. You still don't. The pages in this chapter can give you a good idea, but until you apply for admission and financial aid, until your applications are digested by computers, and until some human beings on campus study the computers' digestion and make you an offer, you really won't know for sure.

And, believe it or not, some colleges are getting smarter about telling you their real costs. A new process launched in 1995 allows colleges to collect financial information about you early in your senior year in high school. These colleges give you an early idea of how much you'll be expected to pay. Some colleges are "utilizing it as a marketing approach," says Barry McCarty, veteran financial aid director at Lafayette College. "They want to make you think in terms of the discount instead of the sticker price." Hey, Barry, ol' buddy, it's about time!

The new process and the new forms that go with it are called PROFILE. The people who invented this process trademarked its name in all capital letters so that it'll jump out at you on pages like this one. (What really happened is that they couldn't think of a name that would make a good acronym — like SAT — so they just used a word in all capital letters.) If you haven't heard about PROFILE yet, you will as you get into the application process. And I describe more about it later in this chapter.

Financial Aid — What's It All About?

You may think of financial aid as a government handout to the poor. In many cases, that's what it is; and 30 years ago, that's basically all it was. Now, though, financial aid is a lot more. The term *financial aid* has evolved to include anything that makes up the difference between what a student pays and a college's published price. Financial aid can be a government grant, a subsidized loan, a collection of private scholarships, or a tuition discount offered by a college. All of these items, taken together, are considered financial aid.

We're talking billions here

Last year, $40 billion came from various government programs to help students pay for college. Another $9 billion came from colleges themselves, usually in tuition discounts. That's a whole lot of aid out there! Some of it is waiting for you.

Are those horror stories and myths for real?

You may have heard horror stories from friends, or friends' parents, about the trauma of applying for financial aid, about the reams of forms to fill out that ask all kinds of personal information. You probably have also heard some myths about applying for financial aid. Some of the most popular myths are

- ✔ Obtaining financial aid is too difficult, so why waste time?
- ✔ My parents make too much money, so I won't get any aid.
- ✔ Getting financial aid is just another way to borrow money, and I don't want to go into debt.

The time to straighten out the rumors and shoot down the myths, one by one, is here.

The trauma myth

Yes, you need to fill out forms when you apply for financial aid. And, yes, those forms ask a lot of personal questions about your income, your bank accounts, and the stocks your parents own. But the colleges are asking for the same information — and less of it, by the way — that the IRS expects you and your parents to provide on your tax returns. The IRS wants the information to take your money. The colleges want it to give you money.

Plus, there's a bright side, if you look at it this way: When you dig out your financial records and apply for financial aid in January, you'll have much of the work done for your (and your parents') tax returns in April.

The too hard myth

Applying for financial aid takes time, true. But it takes much less time than applying to get into a college. The forms may seem intimidating when you first pick them up, but check out those questions. All they're asking for are numbers. No essays, no personal statements on meaningful experiences, and no lists of activities in order of their importance to you are required. None of that heavy-thinking stuff that confronts you on the college application is found on the financial aid forms. Just a few numbers that you and your parents have somewhere in your files. All you have to do is dig the numbers out and write them down.

Figuring out the aid you can get, based on your financial condition, is not an effort in graduate-level math (as some wimps would have you believe). Actually, the math involved boils down to finding two numbers and subtracting one from the other. I explain how this computation works later in this chapter, in the section "Let the Calculations Begin."

The too rich myth

This may be the most prevalent myth of all. Too many times have I heard otherwise intelligent adults say their kids aren't eligible for financial aid because they, the parents, make too much money. And these are parents with incomes in the $60,000 to $70,000 range. Boy, do they need this book!

You may be surprised to know that right now, as you read this book, students from families with six-figure incomes are receiving financial aid at many of the high-priced colleges in the country. This aid is based on financial need. And they're getting the money legitimately, without cheating.

How is this possible, you wonder? Because the formula that determines financial need considers enough other factors — besides income — that make some so-called rich kids eligible. Two years ago, Gettysburg College in Pennsylvania counted 81 freshmen on financial aid whose families had incomes of $100,000 plus. The same college had 611 aid recipients from families earning $50,000 or more.

The just another loan myth

One form of financial aid is, indeed, a loan. Any college student of the last 20 years knows what a student loan is. You borrow money at a low interest rate to pay for college and then spend 10 years repaying it. Such a loan is considered financial aid because someone else — usually the government — is paying interest on the borrowed money while you're in school and subsidizing the interest rate to below-market levels when you start repaying.

Last year, students borrowed $27 billion in subsidized loans — more than half of the $49 billion pot of financial aid ladled out by the government and colleges. Uncounted millions more are distributed each year in private scholarships. You may have to borrow some money to attend the college of your choice, but a lot of money is out there being given away.

Still, you won't get any money unless you ask for it. Asking means filling out forms.

If you're older

When it comes to money, adults are no different than students going to college directly from high school. The cost of attending is the same, and the available financial aid is the same. The rules and eligibility for aid programs apply to all students from age 18 to 88. (If you're over 88, you may have a problem getting a loan.)

When you, a student going to college in your mature years, read about financial aid in this book, everything you read applies to you if you have not yet earned a bachelor's degree. If you're an older student returning for a second degree, you'll find that some aid programs are limited to students pursuing Degree No. 1.

One thing is important to remember. In the "Dependent or Independent" section later in this chapter, I explain how to determine whether you are a dependent or independent for financial aid purposes. If you're 24 or older, don't worry about it. From age 24 on, you are automatically considered to be independent even if you live at home and your parents pay all your bills.

Need with a Capital N

If you haven't seen the word *need* yet, you haven't read any college litera-ture on financial aid. The vast majority of money given away is based on need. Need is the most important word in the financial aid process. It translates to a simple number with a dollar sign in front of it. And this number is the key to unlocking most financial aid vaults. You must have a need to start playing the financial aid game.

Usually, the size of your need is directly related to the amount of aid you'll get. And in this case, the larger your need, the better.

Your need is supposed to represent the amount of financial aid for which you're eligible. But rare is the student who gets exactly the amount of his or her need. Many students get less because, frankly, even $49 billion is not enough to meet every student's need. But if you're lucky, or you understand the process, or you're a student some college really wants, you can get more than your need.

Different needs for different schools

Rest assured, you will have a need. You will have a different need for every college to which you apply. You could have two different needs at the same college because some colleges play the game with more than one set of rules.

Your need could be zero, but zero-need people can get financial aid, too. As you can see in Chapter 12, some financial aid is available for every student, regardless of how wealthy she or he may be.

Fine-tuning the formulas

Your need will have little relation — perhaps no relation at all — to the amount of money you need to go to college. But it's a number that financial aid directors must have on their desks to begin the process of giving you money.

Back in the '60s, when almost all aid came from government programs to help low-income students, Congress wrote a formula to determine how much help each low-income student should get, and the term *financial need* was born. Over 30 years, the formula has undergone tinkering, pounding, revising, and massaging, but it's still a formula that determines need. It's the formula that triggers access to all federal aid programs.

Over the last 15 years, as colleges began giving away more and more of their own money, many decided that they didn't like the government formula. So they wrote their own. Thus on many campuses — particularly those of pricey private schools — students have one need for government programs and another for access to the college coffers. And then, when all the numbers are crunched and formulas calculated, financial aid directors have the option of ignoring all your needs and giving you money based on how they feel about you. Colleges call this option *professional judgment*. That option is used every year.

Go figure

Figuring your need is not difficult. You merely find two numbers and subtract one from the other. The first number is the cost of a college. That varies, of course, with the college. The second number is the amount a formula decides that you and your parents should pay. That's your *Expected Family Contribution*. This amount is the same regardless of the college. You simply subtract the amount you're expected to pay from the college's cost and, presto, you have your need. So, to understand why your need at Harvard will be greater than your need at Frostburg State is easy. Harvard costs more.

Your *Expected Family Contribution* — the number a formula somehow comes up with as the amount of money you're supposed to be able to afford for college — usually is shortened to EFC, sometimes just FC. In all financial aid explanations, including this one, EFC means Expected Family Contribution. When you see EFC in this book, I want you to know what I'm talking about.

Here's another term you don't have to remember, but you might hear it some time and wonder about it. This term is *need analysis*. That's how the financial aid people talk about the process of figuring your need. When two financial aid directors have a friendly discussion at a financial aid directors' convention, one might say, "You analyze need your way and we'll analyze need our way." Translated, he's saying, "I don't like your formula, I'm using my own."

You start the process of figuring your need when you fill out the forms that ask you and your parents to bare your financial souls. A computer eventually crunches those numbers to spit out your EFC. If you're applying to certain colleges, two computers will crunch your numbers and spit out two EFCs. Very likely these EFCs will not be identical.

The tools you'll need

But you don't have to wait for the computers. You can get a pretty good idea of your Need with a pencil, paper, pocket calculator, and those numbers from your financial aid application. If you know how to use a calculator to figure percentages, you can determine your need on your own. I show you how. But first, you must decide what kind of student you are. (See the following section.)

Dependent or Independent?

This question has nothing to do with your attitude toward life. It may have nothing to do with who pays your bills. But it's the question you must answer before you can calculate your Need. The computers need to know how to look at you before they massage your numbers. So, are you a dependent or independent student?

Your answer makes a difference

The answer is important. If you're dependent, your parents' income and assets get pushed into the equation. If you're independent, the formula looks only at you and any spouse you may have acquired. Being independent almost always gets you a better need, and thus more financial aid. Face it, parents almost always have money. If their money isn't considered in deciding how much you're expected to pay, logic says that you'll be expected to pay less.

Some yes/no questions

For years, the line between dependents and independents was fuzzy, left open to various interpretations. A few years ago, Congress drew the line more clearly. Now, no doubt remains. If you can answer yes to one of six questions, you are independent. Answer no to all six, and you're a dependent. The six questions are

1. **Are you 24 or older?**

   It doesn't matter whether you're living at home, with your parents paying all your bills. If you have reached your 24th birthday or will become 24 in the year you're applying, you're independent.

2. **Are you married?**

   You can be wed at 18, and you'll be independent. Your parents' income won't count against you, but that big money your spouse earns will.

3. **Are you a graduate or professional student?**

   If you've already earned a bachelor's degree and are working on a Ph.D. or going to law school, other factors won't matter. The law says you have earned independence.

4. **Do you have dependents you can claim on your tax return?**

   If you're an unmarried mother living at home, but can claim your child as a dependent, you are independent for financial aid purposes.

5. **Are you an orphan or ward of a court?**

   If so, don't worry about these other questions. You're independent.

6. **Are you a military veteran?**

   Ex-GIs get a real break. Join the Army at 18, serve two years, return home to live with your parents and go to college. You'll be a dependent of your parents for all other purposes. But their income and assets won't be factors in deciding how much financial aid you get. You're considered independent.

Those are the six questions. If you can answer yes once, you are independent. No six times makes you dependent. The difference will become clear as you calculate your need.

Let the Calculations Begin

You figure your need by simply finding two numbers and subtracting one from the other. Easy, right? The tough part is finding the numbers. But that's not really so difficult. The two numbers are the cost of attending a college and the amount you're expected to pay.

In the financial aid folks' jargon, those two numbers are called *Cost of Attendance* and *Expected Family Contribution,* often shortened to COA and EFC. Thus the simple subtraction can be looked at this way: COA – EFC = Need.

Cost of attendance

The first number, a college's Cost of Attendance, can be looked up in any directory or computer search program found in a library or high school counseling office. When you look it up, don't cheat yourself. The cost of a college for financial aid purposes is more than just its tuition. Cost includes every dollar you reasonably can expect to spend as a student. That's why the cost is called Cost of Attendance.

Start with the tuition. If you plan to live on campus, add room and board. Then add a reasonable amount for books, transportation to and from campus, and the cost of your daily living expenses, such as toothpaste and laundry.

Your financial need at a specific college is determined not by the tuition charged, but by the total cost of attending the college. Table 12-1 lists typical Costs of Attendance used at some colleges.

You don't have to make a wild guess at those numbers. Most colleges now give you pretty good estimates in their directory listings and their financial aid brochures. A typical directory listing will include tuition and fees, room and board, books and supplies, average transportation costs, and a number called *other expenses,* which means toothpaste and laundry. Those are the numbers financial aid officers at colleges will use to determine your need. So they're the numbers you should use. If you want to save some time, just call a college financial aid office and ask what number it's using this year for Cost of Attendance.

Table 11-1	**The Real Cost of College**			
	Yale	*Baylor*	*U. of Michigan*	*Frostburg State*
Tuition	$22,000	$8,806	$5,548	$3,280
Room/board	6,680	4,254	4,897	4,836
Books/supplies	655	650	510	700
Transportation	700	850	220	200
Personal expenses	1,480	1,390	1,210	865
Total	$31,515	$15,950	$12,385	$9,881
Out-of-state charge	$0	$0	11,524	3,710
Total for out-of-staters	$31,515	$15,950	$23,909	$13,591

The Cost of Attendance at any college must be more than its tuition. For students living on campus, COA must be more than tuition and room and board. If the number you get from a college is not higher, ask again.

Your contribution, a.k.a. EFC

Now comes the fun part, figuring how much of your and your parents' hard-earned cash must be subtracted from the Cost of Attendance to get your need. This number is called your Expected Family Contribution, or EFC. Your EFC will be generated by a computer. But you can make the same calculations (on the worksheet in this chapter) and come up with a pretty close estimate.

All students applying for financial aid get an EFC from government computers. That's because these students must file a government form, called the Free Application for Federal Student Aid (or FAFSA), to trigger eligibility for government aid programs. A majority of the nation's colleges keep it simple and use the government's EFC for their own aid programs.

But some picky colleges — about 500 at last count — don't like the government's formula and calculate their own EFCs to give away their own money. Those colleges will ask you to fill out a second form to give them additional information for their formulas. In most cases, that second form will be called a PROFILE.

What's a FAFSA?

The form that every student must file, the _Free Application for Federal Student Aid,_ usually is shortened to its acronym, FAFSA. That's pronounced like it looks: FAF-Suh.

Financial aid folks will toss around that word, FAFSA, like you should know what it means. Now you do.

The information you and your parents report on the FAFSA is fed into computers working for the government, which spit out an Expected Family Contribution, or EFC. A copy of the FAFSA appears in Chapter 15, where I talk about how to apply for aid. But the numbers you'll use also can be used on the worksheet later in this chapter to find your EFC and your need at the colleges you're considering.

Any well-equipped high school counseling office should have copies of the FAFSA for its students to pick up and take. If your school is not so well-equipped, the financial aid office at your college can give you one. The FAFSA, as its name clearly says, is free.

If you have a computer and a modem, you can download a FAFSA from the U.S. Department of Education Web site, www.ed.gov. Click the button labeled _Money Matters,_ then click the words _FAFSA Express,_ then click _Download Instructions._ Before you click the final link, _Initiate Download,_ make sure that your computer meets the system requirements spelled out on that Web page.

Can you use estimates?

Most of the numbers on your financial aid application will be numbers you'll use later on your income tax return. But the FAFSA should be submitted in January, and Form 1040 isn't due until April. If you don't have precise numbers when you apply for financial aid — maybe your W2s haven't arrived yet — estimates are acceptable. Indeed, most financial aid applicants use estimated numbers. If your estimates are way off, you'll have a chance to correct them later.

Filling Out the Worksheet

Now you can play computer. You can push your numbers through the government's formula, just as a computer eventually will, and come up with your EFC. You'll do our computing on the worksheet. With your records handy, completing the worksheet should take a snappy 15 minutes. If you are a dependent student, start at the top. If you are independent — that is, if you answered yes to one of the six questions mentioned earlier — skip the first eight sections of the worksheet and start where it says Student's Contribution. I discuss this section of the worksheet in the section "Wake-up call for independents," later in this chapter. I told you being independent gives you a break.

Worksheet to calculate how much you must pay

Relax. This worksheet is easier than it looks. The hard part will be finding all the financial records you need. When you have them at your side, just follow the simple instructions and fill in all the numbers. In 15 quick minutes, you will have your own personal Expected Family Contribution. (If you want to run this through a copier so you don't have to worry about the page flopping over, fine. This book loves copiers.)

Income and tax numbers are for the year before you need financial aid. If you're enrolling in college in 1996, the following numbers are for 1995.

Parents' Contribution

(Dependent students only)

1. Income

Parents' adjusted gross income	$	_____
Untaxed income (include IRA contribution)	+	_____
Total income		_____ **(A)**

2. Allowances

Federal income tax		_____
Social Security taxes (Table 11-2)	+	_____
State, other taxes (Table 11-3)	+	_____
Employment allowance (Table 11-4)	+	_____
Income protected (Table 11-5)	+	_____
Total allowances		_____ **(B)**

3. Available Income (Line A – Line B) _____ **(C)**

4. Assets

Cash in bank accounts		_____
Investment equity (excluding residence)	+	_____
Business net worth (Table 11-6)	+	_____
Net Worth		_____

5. Asset Protection Allowance (Table 11-7) − _____

Discretionary Net Worth (DNW) _____

6. Available Assets (12% of DNW) _____ **(D)**

7. Adjusted Available Income (Line C + Line D) _____

8. Parents' Total Contribution (Table 11-8) _____

I. Contribution to Student

      Parents' Contribution divided by
number of family members in college _____

Student's Contribution

(Independent and dependent students)

9. Income

      Student's adjusted gross income _____

      Untaxed income   + _____

Total Income _____ **(E)**

10. Allowances

      Federal income tax _____

      Social Security taxes   + _____

      State, other taxes   + _____

      Income protected   + $1,750

Total Allowances _____ **(F)**

11. Available Income (Line E – Line F) _____ **(G)**

12. Contribution from income (50% of Line G) _____ **(H)**

13. Assets (cash in banks, investment equity) _____ **(I)**

14. Contributions from assets (35% of Line I) _____ **(J)**

II. Contribution by Student

      (Line H + Line J) _____

Expected Family Contribution (I + II) $ _____

Okay, I'll walk through the worksheet, section by section:

Section 1: Report your parents' income just as it will be reported to the IRS. Add the two numbers and put the total on Line A.

The lines that have letters (Line A, Line B, and so on) are important because they have numbers you'll use later. Write these numbers clearly so that you can read them ten minutes from now.

If your parents are divorced, count the income only for the parent with whom you live. If you have acquired a stepparent, his or her income must be included. It doesn't matter that Stepdad signed an agreement saying he's not going to spend a buck on your education. Those agreements are meaningless in the face of this onrushing formula. All parents with whom you live — biological or otherwise — get their income counted.

Some colleges get picky and also want to know about the person they call your *noncustodial* parent. Those that do will send you a separate form for this information.

Section 2: This section lets you deduct a lot of stuff from your parents' income. Their federal income taxes that you deduct come from their tax return. For the other deductions in this section, just check the accompanying tables and see in which category your parents' financial situation belongs.

The deductible Social Security taxes depend on their income (Table 11-2), and their state taxes depend on the state where you live (Table 11-3). Your parents also get allowances for their expenses of going to work (Table 11-4). And your parents can exclude a certain portion of their income from the ravages of the formula, depending on the size of your family and how many of its members are in college (Table 11-5). Add all these allowances and write the total on Line B.

Table 11-2	Social Security Taxes
Earned Income	
$57,600 or less	7.65% of income earned by each person (max $4,406 per person)
Over $57,600	$4,406 + 1.45% of income over $57,600 (max $5,529 per person)

Table 11-3	State & Other Taxes
Apply the percentage below to the total income on the worksheet.	
Parents	
10%	New York
9%	District of Columbia, Oregon, Wisconsin
8%	Maine, Maryland, Massachusetts, Michigan, Minnesota, Rhode Island
7%	California, Delaware, Hawaii, Iowa, Montana, Nebraska, New Jersey, North Carolina, Ohio, South Carolina, Utah, Vermont, Virginia

Parents	
6%	Colorado, Georgia, Idaho, Kansas, Kentucky, New Hampshire, Pennsylvania
5%	Arizona, Arkansas, Connecticut, Illinois, Indiana, Missouri, New Mexico, North Dakota, Oklahoma, West Virginia
4%	Alabama, Mississippi
3%	Florida, Louisiana, South Dakota, Washington, Puerto Rico, Virgin Islands
2%	Alaska, Nevada, Tennessee, Texas, Wyoming
Students	
7%	District of Columbia, New York
6%	Hawaii, Maryland, Minnesota
5%	California, Delaware, Idaho, Iowa, Kentucky, Maine, Massachusetts, Montana, North Carolina, Ohio, Oregon, Oklahoma, South Carolina, Utah, Wisconsin
4%	Arkansas, Colorado, Georgia, Indiana, Kansas, Michigan, Nebraska, New Mexico, Rhode Island, Vermont, Virginia, West Virginia
3%	Alabama, Arizona, Mississippi, Missouri, New Jersey, Pennsylvania
2%	Connecticut, Illinois, Louisiana, North Dakota, Puerto Rico, Virgin Islands
1%	Florida, New Hampshire
0%	Alaska, Nevada, South Dakota, Tennessee, Texas, Washington, Wyoming

Table 11-4	Employment Allowance
Two parents:	35% of lower earned income; max $2,500
One parent:	35% of earned income; max $2,500

Table 11-5	Income Protection Allowance				
Family Size	*Family Members in College*				
	1	*2*	*3*	*4*	*5*
2	10,840	8,980			
3	13,490	11,650	9,800		
4	16,670	14,810	12,970	11,110	
5	19,660	17,810	15,970	14,110	12,270
6	23,000	21,250	19,300	17,450	15,600

For each additional family member in college add $2,600 to the number from the above table.

Section 3: Another simple subtraction. Subtract all the allowances in Section 2 from the income listed in Section 1. The difference is the amount of money the formula thinks your parents have available to pay your college bills. This difference is called, appropriately enough, Available Income. The number goes on Line C.

Section 4: This section is where the formula looks at the rest of your parents' wealth. The formula wants to know the cash they have in banks and the value of their investments. Notice that it says "investments excluding residence." That means don't include the value of your parents' home. (This is a key reason many colleges don't like the government's formula. These colleges think that home equity should be counted as an asset.) You also can exclude the value of any tax-deferred retirement accounts, such as an IRA. If either or both of your parents own a business, use Table 11-6 to figure its net worth. Enter the number. Then add the three numbers you've entered to produce your parents' total Net Worth. The net worth on this form is not what their accountant calls their net worth, but you're not dealing with accountants here. You're dealing with bureaucrats and their computers.

Table 11-6	Business Adjusted Net Worth
Net Worth	*Adjusted Net Worth*
Less than $1	0
$1 to $75,000	40% of net worth
$75,001 to $250,000	$30,000 + 50% of net worth over $75,000
$230,001 to $385,000	$107,500 + 60% of net worth over $230,000
Over $385,000	$200,500 + 100% of net worth over $385,000

Section 5: Not even bureaucrats expect your parents to spend all their assets on your education. They can protect some for their retirement. The amount depends on their age (the older, the better). Check out Table 11-7 to determine how much your parents can protect. Enter the number here and subtract it from their Net Worth. Guess what you've got? You've got a term invented by an ingenious bureaucrat: Discretionary Net Worth. Notice that like so many bureaucratic terms, it also can be known by its initials (DNW).

Table 11-7	Asset Protection Allowance	
Older Parent's Age	*Married*	*Single*
25 or younger	0	0
26	2,100	1,500
27	4,300	3,100
28	6,400	4,600
29	8,600	6,200
30	10,700	7,700
31	12,900	9,200
32	16,000	10,800
33	17,200	12,300
34	19,300	13,900
35	21,500	15,400
36	23,600	16,900
37	25,800	18,500
38	27,900	20,000
39	30,100	21,600
40	32,200	23,100
41	33,000	23,500
42	33,900	24,100
43	34,700	24,500
44	35,400	25,100
45	36,300	25,600
46	37,200	26,200
47	38,500	26,900
48	39,400	27,500

(continued)

Table 11-7 *(continued)*

Older Parent's Age	Married	Single
49	40,500	28,000
50	41,500	28,700
51	42,800	29,400
52	43,900	30,300
53	45,300	31,000
54	46,700	31,800
55	47,900	32,500
56	49,400	33,500
57	50,900	34,300
58	52,500	35,300
59	54,400	36,300
60	56,000	37,200
61	58,100	38,200
62	59,800	39,300
63	61,900	40,400
64	64,100	41,800
65 or older	66,300	42,900

Section 6: I told you that you'd have to calculate some percentages. Here's one. Figure 12 percent of that DNW, and you have the amount of your parents' assets that the formula decides is available to pay tuition. This number is called Available Assets. That makes sense. That number goes on Line D.

Section 7: Now some simple addition is needed. Add your parents' Available Income from Section 3 to their Available Assets that you just calculated. The total is (no drum roll necessary) their Adjusted Available Income. The Adjusted Available Income is also called AAI. Remember that. The next table you read will mention AAI. If you don't remember what AAI is, you won't know what the table is talking about.

Section 8: Another percentage must be calculated. But because you boned up on how to calculate percentages before you started this little exercise, it's no problem. Check Table 11-8. This table tells you what percentage of your parents' AAI goes here in Section 8. (I hope you remember what AAI is.) The number you write is the amount the formula figures your parents have to spend on colleges, for you and all your siblings.

Table 11-8	Parents' Contribution
Adjusted Available Income	*Parents' Contribution (from worksheet)*
$3,408 or less	$750
$3,409 to $9,700	22% of AAI
$9,701 to $12,200	$2,134 + 25% of AAI over $9,700
$12,201 to $14,600	$2,759 + 29% of AAI over $12,200
$14,601 to $17,100	$3,455 + 34% of AAI over $14,600
$17,101 to $19,600	$4,305 + 40% of AAI over $17,100
$19,601 or more	$5,305 + 47% of AAI over $19,600
Adjusted Available Income can be a negative number.	

Subtotal I: Making progress! You have moved from Sections and Lines to a Subtotal. This is one of two numbers that will make up your EFC. Count the number of family members who will be in college next year at least half-time. And half-time, according to the government's definition, means carrying at least six credits. If Mom takes a couple of classes at night, worth at least six credits, she counts. Divide your Parents' Contribution in Section 8 by the number of college students they must support. If you, Mom, and your older brother will be in college next year, divide by three. If you're the only lucky one, divide by one. The result is the amount your parents are expected to pay for you. It goes right there at "SUBTOTAL I, Contribution to Student."

States have aid, too

Every state offers some financial aid to its residents — often restricted to residents staying in-state for college. Last year, all state scholarships totaled $2.4 billion — a tiny fraction of the $34 billion in federal programs.

Some state aid is based on need, and some is awarded for academic ability. A little goes for other reasons. Maryland, for example, allows each state legislator to award a scholarship to whomever he or she selects.

Each of the 50 states has an agency that coordinates its student aid. Up-to-date high school counselors know how to contact the agency in their states and know what kind of aid is available. If your counselors aren't up-to-date, call the financial aid office of a college in your area and ask for the state agency's address. Then write for information.

Wake-up call for independents

It's time for you independent students to wake up. Section 9 is where you start. Parents are done. And dependent students, you're not finished yet. You must do this part, too.

Section 9: This is where you report your income for last year, just as you will on your tax return. If you're married, I have bad news. Student's income means student's income plus spouse's income. Add the two numbers and put the total on Line E.

Section 10: Just like your parents, you get to deduct stuff from your income. Your federal income tax is the number from your tax return. For the other taxes, check the appropriate tables in this book. And notice the line that says "Income Protected" with the number $1,750 printed on it. Every student, regardless of who you are, can deduct the first $1,750 of your income. Add up all your allowances and write the total on Line F.

Section 11: Now it's getting easier. There's just one line per section. Simply subtract your allowances from your income and put the result on Line G.

Section 12: The formula thinks you should spend half of your available income on college. So divide that Line G number by two and write the result on Line H.

Section 13: Add up all your assets. For most students, this will take a second or two. Your assets include money in the bank and any investments, like those mutual fund shares your grandmother buys you every birthday. Write your total assets on Line I.

Section 14: This formula is getting generous. It wants you to spend only 35 percent of your assets on your education. So figure 35 percent of Line I and put it on Line J.

Subtotal II: Combine your two *contributions* — half your available income and 35 percent of your assets. In other words, add Lines H and J. That's the amount the formula wants from you.

The Result: Put them together. The amount your parents are expected to pay for your year at college (Subtotal I), added to the amount you're expected to pay (Subtotal II) make up your Expected Family Contribution. That's your EFC. Congratulations! You've done it! Easy, wasn't it?

Good News: Your computer makes it easier.

If using a calculator is not one of your strong points, you can get a ballpark estimate of your EFC on the Web site operated by the National Association of Financial Aid Administrators. It asks you to enter a couple dozen facts about your family's financial condition and then estimates the EFC that you deserve. The site is at www.finaid.org. Click on the words *EFC Estimator* under *Tools.*

Finally, here's your need

Now to find your need at any college in the country, just check the college Cost of Attendance (remember, that's more than tuition) and subtract your EFC. That's it! You've determined your need.

Now those people who told you how hard the process would be look even more foolish, don't they?

When it pays not to marry

You sharp-eyed readers have already noticed it. The formula slaps you with a penalty for being married. It's not intentional. The wise folks in Congress who wrote the formula didn't intend to make marriage a more expensive route to college. But sometimes Congressional wisdom falls a little short of the ideal.

If you're living with the love of your life, but in an unmarried condition, your partner can make $100,000 a year, and it isn't counted against you for financial aid. Take the vows and suddenly that $100,000 is part of your income for calculating need. Unfair? Certainly. But it's the rule. Financial aid directors insist the law is not designed to encourage unwed cohabitation. That's just the way it works out.

And there's another marriage penalty on the books, as you probably noticed, for divorced parents. Mom can live with Boyfriend and not worry about how much he makes (at least for your financial aid). As soon as they get married, though, Stepdad's wealth counts against you.

What? You Need Another Need, Too?

Now that you've carefully calculated your need from the worksheet, it's time to face a fact of life: About one-third of the nation's colleges don't like your need. They're stuck with it for the federal government's aid programs because it's the need the law says they must use. But when colleges give away their own money, they want you to figure out a need on their own terms.

Almost all the colleges that require two needs are private, and most are in the high-price range of the private sector. Public colleges, which rely on state subsidies for most of their cash, usually don't have much of their own money to give away. And the lower-priced private schools figure that you don't need much help to pay their bills.

Why are they doing this?

The one big reason some colleges insist on two needs is your home. More precisely, your parents' home. Several years ago, Congress decided parents' home equity should not be considered part of their assets to calculate their kids' college needs. High-priced colleges rebelled and said home equity, by golly, is an asset and we're going to count it as an asset. So a second supplemental application form was born that tells colleges your parents' home equity — yours, too, if you own a home — and other information. That second form has evolved into PROFILE.

The good news and the bad news

If a college says it wants you to submit a PROFILE as well as a FAFSA, that's good news and bad news. The bad news is the college will count home equity in deciding how much of its money you deserve. The good news is that the college has money to give away. Numbers from your PROFILE will be crunched through a formula similar to the one you used on the worksheet. But this number-crunching method will produce a different EFC, very likely higher than the one you got.

How Much You Really Will Pay

The need you just calculated from the worksheet triggers your eligibility for the federal government's aid programs. (I explain those programs in Chapter 12.) If your need is large enough, you automatically will get some money to help pay your tuition. If you have any need at all — if your EFC is lower than the cost of your college — you'll probably get some aid. But all government aid, with the exception of one loan program, is based on your need figured from the government's formula.

Suppose that you have no need

If the cost of your college is less than your Expected Family Contribution, your need is zero. (This number can't be a negative number.) Some people will say you have no need. Technically, that's true. I like to say you have zero need. But even zero-need students can be needy. And even zero-need students can get financial aid.

And, still another formula

Need, as I said earlier, is just a starting point. And your Expected Family Contribution may have little relation to the amount your family eventually pays. They are numbers you use to get into the game. At most selective colleges, what you really will pay is determined by another formula. It's one I invented just for this book, but it works. The formula is HMTWY/HMTTYWP = $$$. You won't be able to calculate the formula because you'll never know the numbers that go in two of those variables. They can't be quantified.

Should you pay for help?

As you look for a college, you may hear from some people who are in the business of finding scholarship money. They'll offer to help you look — for a price. They might even guarantee that they'll find you a scholarship. A Web search for scholarships will bring you a list of dozens of companies charging anywhere from $25 to $1,000 to find you money.

Think carefully before buying the service. Consider these facts:

✔ **More than 80 percent of all aid is from government programs.** You'll find out how much you can get by sending in one form. Your total cost is 32 cents postage.

✔ **More than $9 billion of aid is awarded by the colleges themselves.** If they want you to have some, they'll let you know.

✔ **Millions of dollars in scholarships are awarded by private organizations.** A search service may be able to find some for which you are eligible. But you still have to apply and convince the organization you deserve the money. You will be paying the service for research you could perform free at a library.

Before you do business with a search service, make sure you understand exactly what it will provide. If it offers a guarantee, be clear in your mind what it's guaranteeing. Then decide if the cost is worth what you will receive. And if you have a computer, check out the National Association of Student Financial Aid Administrators' Scam Alert at www.finaid.org

---

HMTWY stands for How Much They Want You. *HMTTYWP* stands for How Much They Think You Will Pay. Someone at the college will mix those two intangibles and come up with $$$ — the amount they expect you to pay. It's your real Expected Family Contribution. A father who recently survived the financial aid process with his daughter compared it to buying a car. That's a good way to look at it. The number of cars for sale out there (places in college) is larger than the number of car buyers (you). A high-quality buyer can get a very good deal.

Chapter 12

Money You Get Because You Need It

. . . .

In This Chapter

▶ Detailing the plain and old, but attractive, grant

▶ Defining subsidized jobs as financial aid

▶ Exploring loans of all kinds

▶ Noting aid for special people

▶ Knowing that, yes, there really is aid for everyone

. . . .

*T*hink about the lottery. The one that sells tickets in almost every state and pays off in sums beyond your dreams. A college student in Idaho bought a lucky ticket and won $87 million.

You could win that lottery 40 times, and still you would not have the $40 billion that the government distributes every year in student financial aid. Each year, $4 of every $5 spent to help students through college comes from government programs.

Aid Based on Need

Most of that $40 billion goes to students who need it. Let me amend that. Most of it goes to students whose financial information — submitted on the proper forms — persuades the government's computers that they need it. (If you've read Chapter 11, you know how the computers determine what you need.) So, most of the government's aid programs fall into the category that financial aid folks call *need-based*. Other aid, from nongovernment sources, also can be need-based.

Need-based aid is any program for which your eligibility depends on the magic number that you calculate in Chapter 11, your *need*. For those who haven't read Chapter 11, your need is the difference between the cost of attending a college that you are considering and the amount that the computers think you can afford to pay.

Need-based aid can be a grant that you keep or a loan that you must repay. It can be a job with wages subsidized by the government. It can be money paid directly to you, or to your college, or to your parents. Each program is different. Each program was born and reared independently of all the others. The only place they come together is in a college financial aid office. This is where someone (yes, a human being) looks at all the computer-generated numbers and decides how much you deserve in grants, loans, jobs, and anything else that may be available.

Your need is determined by a computer. Your aid is determined by a real person. That's one break you get. You can talk to a real person.

What's in the Package?

The combination of grants, loans, and other stuff that you are offered is called your aid package. Some packages are a lot prettier than others. The best-looking packages give you all grants. You use them to pay your college bills and then you can forget about them. You don't have to pay them back. Less-attractive packages contain loans and jobs.

The relationship of grants to loans in your package is decided by that human being called a financial aid officer. The ratio depends, to a large extent, on how much the college likes you. The aid officer must play by the rules in giving away the government's money, but the rules give her a great deal of flexibility (which you can find out about in Chapter 14).

Now for some names. You may have heard students talk about Pells and Staffords, Perkinses and SOGs. You probably shrugged off the terms as gobbledygook because you didn't understand them. Well, that's about to end. After you read this chapter, you can throw Pells around in a conversation with the best of them. Here's a look at the faucets from which that need-based aid is flowing.

The most comprehensive information on all financial aid, including government progams and private scholarships, is at www.finaid.org, a Web site operated by the National Association of Student Financial Aid Administrators.

Free advice

A free service from your federal government is a handy booklet describing all federal financial aid programs in easy-to-understand words. The booklet even includes a few easy-to-understand charts and tables.

It's called *The Student Guide: Financial Aid from the U.S. Department of Education*. It can be ordered by calling 800-433-3243. *The Student Guide* is available online at www.ed.gov.

If anyone tries to sell you *The Student Guide,* call the preceeding number and complain. It's published for free distribution.

Grants: Where Plain and Old Look Pretty Good

Yes, grants are plain. Nothing about them is complicated. Someone sends you a check. You put it in your bank and then write a check for the same amount to the college. Or, better yet, someone sends a check to the college, and the school informs you that your tuition bill has been reduced.

And, yes, grants are old. One of the first financial aid endeavors, created back in the '60s, was a program of grants for low-income students. The program was begun for the most altruistic of reasons: to help kids who couldn't afford college to get there. The program was called Basic Opportunity Grants (immediately shortened to BOGs, of course).

Three decades later, the program still exists. It's been revised occasionally, and its eligibility formula rewritten several times. Along the way, it was renamed to honor a wealthy Rhode Island senator who chaired the Senate's education committee and usually murmured his approval when college lobbyists asked for something. His name is Claiborne Pell. And those basic opportunity grants are now called Pell Grants.

Pell Grants

Pell Grants are the only program in which a financial aid officer has no discretion. These grants are based strictly on a student's Expected Family Contribution as figured by a computer (the EFC from Chapter 11). Pell Grants come automatically to students who qualify.

If your EFC is low enough, you get a Pell Grant. If your EFC is above the cutoff line, you don't. The cutoff line changes each year, varying with the amount of money Congress puts into the program, but it's usually around $2,000. If the formula decides your family should spend less than $2,000 for a year for you at college, you'll probably get a Pell.

If you qualify for a Pell, guess what determines its size? Here's that magic number again: your need. Your Pell Grant is larger at higher-priced colleges because your need is greater at higher-priced colleges. (Remember: Need = College Cost – EFC.) A Pell Grant's size ranges downward from a maximum set every year by the amount of money the program has. The max grant is usually around $2,300. In 1996, the max was $2,340.

Usually Pell Grants are paid directly to your college, which credits your account. And then you can forget them. They are plain old grants. They do not have to be repaid. You do not have to work for them. It's money you get because you need it.

The Pell is often called the foundation on which a financial aid package is built. That's a good description because a Pell is given automatically to a student who qualifies. The financial aid officer starts with this grant then adds money from other sources over which he has some discretion.

Supplemental grants

Supplemental grants, too, are plain and old. Supplemental grants also come with no strings and are handed to students with a large need. They're almost as old as the Pells, born in the early '70s to supplement the Pells for the neediest of the needy. Thus, they're supplemental grants. That's their original name, and, surprisingly, it has survived all these years.

First, these were called Supplemental Opportunity Grants (SOGs, of course). Then, some smart bureaucrat decided to be more specific and made them Supplemental Educational Opportunity Grants. That's their official name today. You'll often see them in college literature as SEOGs. But some veteran financial aid officers still call them SOGs.

SEOGs or supplementals are *campus-based* aid programs. (They're also need-based, but you've already heard that story.) In a campus-based program, the government sends a lump sum to each college, which then distributes the money as it sees fit, following the government's rules. Every accredited college in the country, public and private, can have access to the government's campus-based programs.

The rules say SEOGs are for students with *exceptional financial need.* Then, they allow each college financial aid office to define exceptional. A logical mind would think that students who qualify for Pell Grants would have the most need, thus only Pell recipients would get SEOGs. Ah, but that's not true. You're not dealing with logic here. Pell people are supposed to get priority for SEOGs, but not necessarily all the SEOG money. An aid director can give it to whomever she thinks really needs it. Remember, I told you about human discretion.

By law, a SEOG must be at least $100 and no larger than $4,000. In 1996, the national average was about $600. Like the Pell, a supplemental grant usually is credited to the student's account.

Subsidized Jobs

Even while you're trying to find your right colleges, you can be helping other students get financial aid. The student who takes you on a guided tour of the campus is working for the admission office. His pay is very likely part of his aid package. The students who fill your plate in the campus cafeteria, offer advice in the library, and answer the phone when you call for an appointment are also probably earning some of their college costs from the federal government.

Some jobs are considered financial aid because the government gives a college money to pay the wages. And subsidized jobs have been around as part of the aid package for a quarter-century. Your parents may remember them as Work-Study, or College Work-Study, or CWS. It's now called Federal Work Study (FWS, of course), but it's the same campus-based, need-based aid program.

Here's how FWS works. Each college gets a lump sum from the government that it can use for 75 percent of working students' pay. The jobs can be on campus or with off-campus employers who have worked out a deal with the college. The rules say that you must be paid by the hour — no commission-type arrangements are permitted — and earn at least minimum wage.

No strings whatsoever

Here's the good news. The money you earn goes to you with no yo-yo strings attached. You can use it to pay tuition, buy books, do the laundry, eat at a high-class restaurant, or spring for a movie for your roommate. Nobody needs to know.

There's the rub

Oh, yes, there's a catch. It's not an unlimited money supply. When the college offers you a job as part of your aid package, it attaches a dollar limit. Say it's $1,200. This number means you can earn $1,200, but no more. Even if you and your boss like each other so well that you want to work there forever, it can't happen. That's the rule you must play by to get the job. Work-study jobs are assigned by the financial aid office, but they're supposed to go only to students who have a need — that is, those students whose EFC is lower than the college's cost. (For more on EFC, Expected Family Contribution, see Chapter 11.)

Low-Interest Loans

People are baffling to me sometimes. Many will borrow 80 percent of the cost of a car and take four or five years to pay it back, all without a word of complaint. Others will borrow 80 percent of the cost of a house and agree to repay it over 30 years, with perhaps only a slight shudder. Why then do so many people complain about borrowing money for a college degree? Is college not as important as a car or house? If you hear someone complain about a college loan, consider giving her this book. (You wouldn't think of loaning it to her.) Better still, suggest that she buy it.

What makes them ugly

Loans are part of financial aid. They help make up the difference between the cost of college and the amount you pay. But they're the ugliest part of the aid package because, unlike grants and jobs, it's your money being spent. Think of them as credit cards — you're still spending your money, you just haven't had to pay yet. Borrowing money for college is just delaying the inevitable.

Okay, I've said that. I had to put student loans in their proper context. They are one form of financial aid, but they're the least desirable. I don't want to get a reputation for bad-mouthing student loans, though. They really don't deserve to be knocked. Millions of college graduates who hold decent, well-paying jobs would not have a degree if low-interest, government-subsidized student loans did not exist.

It takes all kinds

Your parents may fondly remember Guaranteed Student Loans, or GSLs, which helped many students of their generation pay their way through college. They filled out a form, took it to a bank with a letter from the college saying that they were eligible, and, in a couple of days, they had enough money to cover tuition and room and board.

Hey, the GSLs are still there waiting for you. They haven't been called GSLs for years, but the concept is the same. Now, it's difficult to know what they're called. The names change every year. They could be Stafford Loans or Direct Loans or FFELs (pronounced fells), depending on whom you talk to and where the conversation occurs. I sort out these names for you as I discuss each loan program. But I start, as they like to say about the Rose Bowl, with the granddaddy of them all.

Perkins Loans

This one goes back to Sputnik. In case you haven't met Sputnik in your history classes yet, it was the first human-made satellite to orbit the Earth. The Soviet Union did it back in the '50s, and it scared everyone to think that another country was more technologically advanced than the good old USA. The U.S. leaders began clamoring for better-trained engineers and scientists.

Congress eventually decided that one way to encourage students to become better educated is to lend them government money for college. It was a radical idea at the time. But it was the birth of what is now known as student financial aid. That first loan program, called National Defense Loans, still exists. In the '70s, it was renamed for a Congressman named Perkins.

Table 12-1 shows a typical repayment schedule for money borrowed in the Perkins Loan program, where interest is 5 percent, courtesy of the experts at the U.S. Department of Education.

Table 12-1	Repaying a Perkins Loan			
Amount Borrowed	*Number of Payments*	*Monthly Payment*	*Total Interest*	*Total Repaid*
$3,000 (last payment)	119 1	$31.84 28.90	$817.36	$3,817.86
$5,000 (last payment)	119 1	$53.06 49.26	$1,363.40	$6,363.40
$15,000 (last payment)	119 1	$159.16 150.81	$4,090.85	$19,090.85

Perkins is one of those campus-based aid programs. The government gives a lump sum to each participating college, which then lends it to students. Notice that I said participating college. A few schools don't take part because they don't like the paperwork involved. But most colleges do have Perkins money, and they can include it as part of a student's aid package.

The rules say Perkins Loans go only to students with exceptional Need, but again each financial aid director can define exceptional. Also, the higher your need, the more likely you are to get a Perkins.

A Perkins Loan is the most attractive of all student loans because of its low interest rate — just 5 percent. However, this loan is also the smallest. Only about $900,000 is put into the Perkins Loan each year but billions more are recirculated as old loans are repaid.

The maximum you can borrow in Perkins is $3,000 for each undergraduate year, up to $15,000. For graduate or professional students, it's $5,000 per year, up to $30,000. The college has its choice of paying you the money or crediting it to your account.

You have nine months after you leave college to start repaying the loan. You can take up to ten years to pay it in full. Many colleges sell their loans to banks, to keep the money circulating faster. If you're at one of those colleges, you'll hear from the bank shortly after the college tells it you're no longer a student. You and the bank will then work out a repayment schedule.

Stafford Loans

Stafford is the big daddy of federal financial aid. It's the direct descendant of the old GSLs, and by far the largest program of financial help to college students. The Stafford Loan also has become one of the largest sources of confusion to students applying for aid because of all the other names that go with it. You may hear a Stafford described as a Direct Loan or a FFEL (pronounced *fell*) Loan or a Ford Loan, sometimes all in the same sentence.

Don't be confused. Forget all those other terms. A Stafford Loan is a Stafford Loan regardless of what capitalized adjectives are used to describe it. Those adjectives are the result of some longtime bickering among colleges, banks, and the government over the source of the money — where it comes from before it gets to you. That's not something you need to worry about. But if you're the type of person who likes to know these things, the simple explanation is that all money loaned in the name of Stafford comes from one of two places:

> ✔ **Banks:** You get a notice from your college saying that you're eligible, take it to a bank, and get the money. Loans from banks are called FFEL Loans. FFEL stands for Federal Family Education Loans, a name devised by government bureaucrats.
>
> ✔ **Colleges:** The loan comes directly to you from your college financial aid office. This is money that came directly to the college from the federal government with no banks getting in the way. Thus, it has a surprisingly obvious name: Direct Loan. (Officially, the Direct Loan is the William D. Ford Federal Direct Loan.)

Another reason not to worry about the difference is that you have no choice. A college offers either Direct Loans or FFEL Loans, but not both. Some colleges prefer to have more control over their loan money. Some feel more comfortable dealing with banks. For you, the difference is hardly monumental.

Now for another potential source of confusion. You'll often hear a Stafford Loan described as a *subsidized Stafford* or an *unsubsidized Stafford*. They are two entirely different things. I'm talking here about subsidized loans, the kind where interest payments are deferred until you are out of college. That's real financial aid.

Subsidized Stafford Loans are what most people in the work force mean when they talk about their student loans. They're what most people in the financial aid business mean when they talk about Staffords. Subsidized Staffords are the daddy of the financial aid family. Unsubsidized Staffords are the baby brother. They're nice to know about and can be nice to have around.

Subsidized Staffords

Subsidized Stafford Loans — Staffords, for short — usually are the topping on a typical package of financial aid. The aid director will gather all the other money he can find for a student from government programs and his own school's resources. If the student has any need remaining, she'll be offered the chance to obtain a Stafford. But need is essential. Subsidized Staffords can only be used to meet a student's need — the difference between the college's costs and the Expected Family Contribution.

As a freshman, you can borrow up to $2,625 in a Subsidized Stafford, and the ceiling rises as you move through college. (See Table 12-2.) You can borrow up to the max, so long as you have that much need.

Table 12-2	Stafford Loan Limits (1996-97)	
	Dependent	**Independent**
First Year	$2,625	$6,625
Second Year	$3,500	$7,500
Third/Later Years	$5,500	$10,500
Max/Undergrad	$23,000	$46,000

The interest rate is adjusted annually, but can go no higher than 8.25 percent. It's at about 7.5 percent now. Repayment starts six months after you graduate or drop out. You don't even worry about the interest until then. The government pays it for you.

You have ten years to repay your Stafford Loan, but that's flexible. The law allows you to negotiate with the bank for a longer period. You also have the option of making fixed monthly payments or income-sensitive payments that fluctuate with the amount of money you earn. The bank that holds your loan must offer you this option six months before your first payment is due.

Table 12-3 presents examples of repayment plans for Stafford Loans, calculated by experts at the U.S. Department of Education. The plans are figured at 8.25 percent interest, the highest rate permissible. The rate changes each year, but it's usually below 8 percent.

Table 12-3	Repaying a Stafford Loan			
Amount Borrowed	**Number of Monthly Payments**	**Total Monthly Payment**	**Total Interest**	**Amount Repaid**
$2,600 (last payment)	64 1	$50.00 $28.62	$628.42	$3,228.42
$4,000	120	$49.06	$1,887.20	$5,887.20
$7,500	120	$91.99	$3,538.80	$11,038.80
$10,000	120	$122.65	$4,718.00	$14,718.00
$15,000	120	$183.98	$7,077.60	$22,077.60

If your college offers FFEL Stafford Loans, you get the money just like your parents got the old GSL. First, pick up a loan application from your college financial aid office and a letter from the college saying that you're eligible. (Both documents probably will come with the letter notifying you of your aid package.) Then take them to a bank. The bank will send you the money.

(In most cases, checks are issued with you and your college as joint payees.) If your college offers Direct Loans, you sign a promissory note with the financial aid office and the money is credited to your account.

No credit check is necessary to obtain a Stafford. To qualify, you must be at least a half-time student with a financial need.

Unsubsidized Staffords — where you don't need a need

In Chapter 11, I tell you that some financial aid is available for everyone, even students with zero need. This is it. Any student attending college at least half-time is eligible. It's a loan you can go for if all the other aid you're offered leaves you still wondering where you'll get some money.

The Unsubsidized Stafford is a child of the '90s, conceived in response to middle-income families' complaints that they were being squeezed out of college by soaring tuitions. This type of a loan looks a lot like its better-known parent, the Subsidized Stafford. Interest rates and the flexible repayment options are the same. You use the same application form, available at your college financial aid office.

This Stafford is called *unsubsidized* because no one is paying the interest for you while you're in college. The responsibility is yours. You either can pay it as you go, or let it accumulate, adding to the principal until you leave school.

And here's a break for the independent student — that's you if you answer yes to one of the six questions in Chapter 11. You can borrow more. Loan maximums increase the longer you've been in college, but, at each step, independent students have ceilings more than twice as high as dependents. (Refer to Table 12-2.)

The Unsubsidized Stafford is the least attractive of all student loans, but it's still better looking than any loan you'll get in the open market. One reason is that you can have no payments while you're in college. Another is that the interest rate can go no higher than 8.25 percent, regardless of what the market does. And any bad debts in your past don't matter. You qualify just by being a student. You don't even need a need.

PLUS Loans

Here's something for Mom and Dad. The *P* in PLUS stands for Parents. (The full name is Parents' Loans for Undergraduate Students.) If your Expected Family Contribution is a little more money than your parents actually expect to contribute, PLUS is their chance to borrow some of it at below-market interest rate. The rate is adjusted each year, but it's now hovering around 8.3 percent. It cannot exceed 9 percent.

Your parents can borrow the difference between the cost of your college and the amount of financial aid you receive. Your need is not an issue. In other words, if the cost of a year at Flagship State is $7,500, and the school offers you $5,000 in aid, your parents can get a PLUS Loan for $2,500. The money goes directly to the college, copayable to the parent. There's no grace period. Repayment starts immediately.

If your financial aid package doesn't meet your full need, most colleges will send you information about applying for a PLUS loan. If you don't receive such information, ask your financial aid office.

All loans can be direct

In the section "Stafford Loans," earlier in this chapter, I explain the difference between Direct Loans and FFEL Loans. Direct Loans come from the government through your college. FFELs come from a bank. Now that you know about unsubsidized Staffords and PLUS loans, you should know that they, too, can be direct.

Except for the source of the money, Direct and FFEL loans are the same. The qualifications, interest rates, repayment plans, and other particulars are identical for every unsubsidized loan, whether it has the word Direct, FFEL, Ford, or Stafford in its title. The same goes for subsidized and PLUS loans. The only difference is the source of the money. And that's not a big difference for you.

I won't bore you with why some people thought a Direct Loan program was needed in the mid-'90s, except to say that a lot of college financial aid folks were tired of dealing with banks. So a handful of schools agreed to test a new (or is it very old?) campus-based program. In this program, the government sends the money to the colleges, and the colleges lend it to you. (Are you thinking what I'm thinking? Isn't this where this all came in, back in the Sputnik days?) They call the new program Direct Loans. The number of participating colleges is increasing every year.

Direct Loans are easier for you than the other kind because you don't have to go through the formality of applying to a bank. If a college offers an Unsubsidized Direct as part of your package, it has the money there waiting for you. Now, does that make you feel better?

If Your Credit Isn't Good

Okay, here's some good news. I know from experience that some of you will find the following statement hard to believe, but believe it: A bad credit rating doesn't hurt you in qualifying for most student loans. If you or your family has had trouble paying some bills, or even filed for bankruptcy, your spotty history won't be checked to decide whether you get a Stafford or Perkins Loan. The only credit problem that will disqualify you is defaulting on a previous student loan. If you're in default, you are ineligible for any future loans.

The only qualifications for a subsidized Stafford or Perkins is attendance (carrying at least six credits) at an accredited college and financial need. For an unsubsidized Stafford, even need isn't essential. You will not be asked for your credit history as part of a Perkins or Stafford application.

The only federal loan program in which poor credit can hurt is the PLUS loan for parents. A credit history is part of the PLUS loan application, and the borrower's credit will be checked.

Other Need-Based Goodies

If you're a special kind of student, you may find that Congress has created a very narrow aid program targeted to people just like you. If you qualify, your financial aid office will be happy to let you know. I mention a few of these programs just so that you're aware that they exist.

If a student qualifies for and does not get his full need covered from the other sources:

- ✔ **Veterans:** Government education benefits of up to $350 a month are available for military veterans who have three years active duty, or two years active duty and four years in the reserves.

- ✔ **Veterans' dependents:** Dependents of veterans killed or permanently disabled by a service-related injury can get $404 a month for education expenses until age 26.

- ✔ **Nurses:** Government-subsidized loans are available, at 5 percent interest, for nursing students with a need. Loan ceilings are $2,500 the first year and $4,000 each year thereafter. If a student qualifies and does not get her full need covered from other sources, financial aid officers at schools with nursing programs can include the loans as part of a student's aid package.

> ✔ **Pharmacists:** A government program called Health Education Assistance Loans is designed mainly for graduate and professional students, but this program also offers low-interest loans to undergraduates studying pharmacy.
>
> ✔ **Native Americans:** Grants from the U.S. Bureau of Indian Affairs are available to students with a need who are more than 25 percent Native American, Eskimo, or Aleut.

That's Not All, Folks

This chapter looks at financial aid based strictly on need. (The only big exception is the Unsubsidized Stafford Loan, which is included here because it is part of the Stafford family.) As you may have noticed, all these programs have ties to the government, which writes the eligibility rules. And the government's rules usually begin with need. You must need the money to get it.

But another $9 billion or so that doesn't come from the government flows to students each year. And the rules for the distribution of this money, when rules exist, are fuzzier. Some money is given away with no concern for need. Some is tied to need, but, well, need can be defined in many ways. And an interesting thing about this $9 billion or so is that the people giving it away are the people who make the rules. So, changing the rules as they write the checks is no problem. More often than you can imagine, this money is given away not because you need it, but because of who you are. That's what I look at in Chapter 13.

Chapter 13

Money You Get Because You're You

*B*elieve it or not, you are valuable. Yes, you, the person who picked up this book. You're discovering that this college planning business isn't really so tough. And you're about to find out something that many of your friends will never bother to figure out: One of your most valuable assets in finding money for college is the person reading this book (unless someone else is reading this book to you).

Too many students shrug off colleges that might be right for them after looking at the price tag. Price tags often are meaningless. Other students will give a quick glance to the financial aid formula, decide they won't qualify for much money, and shrug off colleges they think they can't afford. But not you.

Lots of Money Is Available

If you read Chapter 12, you can find out that most financial aid comes from the government. But each year, uncounted billions of dollars are available from other sources, just waiting to help deserving students pay tuitions. Yes, billions. (And $1 billion is equal to winning a $40 million lottery 25 times!) This extra money is uncounted because no one ever has been able to come up with a complete list of all the money and add up the sum.

Tuition discounts and scholarships

Some of that money may be offered to you by a college in your financial aid package. Colleges give away about $9 billion of their own funds in tuition discounts each year. Some of that money comes in the form of thousands of scholarships that are offered by private organizations, from service clubs to labor unions to big businesses. Much of the money from both sources is distributed not because your parents are poor, not because you have a financial need, but because you're you.

Still you won't get any of this money unless you ask for it and convince people that you deserve it.

Well, they don't exactly give the money to you

Right now is the time to make one fact clear. Colleges will talk about giving you grants and scholarships from their own funds. In this book, I say that they do that. But that's not precisely accurate. No college in the country is going to mail you a check or hand you a dollar bill. They don't give you anything.

College grants and scholarships come in the form of discounts off the published tuition prices. Colleges decide their published tuition prices and then decide how much of that tuition they want you to pay. They tell you the difference is an institutional grant. They're really saying, "This price is for the rest of the world, but you get a lower price, because you're you."

A Logical Look at Tuition Discounts

Now, because you have a clear, logical mind, look at these tuition discounts logically. Say Ivy U. announces its tuition next year will be $26,000. But in its budget, which it doesn't announce, is a $30 million expenditure for scholarships. That means Ivy U.'s financial aid office can give tuition discounts totaling $30 million to next year's students.

If Ivy didn't offer discounts, it could spread that $30 million among all 6,000 students on its campus and, presto, tuition would be down to $21,000 for everyone. But Ivy U. won't do that because it doesn't think that all its students should pay $21,000. Ivy U. thinks that some should pay $26,000 and some should pay much less.

Who pays full price?

I'm sure by now that your logical mind has figured out what's going on. At Ivy U., as at every high-priced college in the country, the published tuition is the maximum tuition. In reality, tuitions range downward from the sticker price. If you've concluded that Ivy's $26,000 is just for students who can afford it, you're not too far off. It's the price for

- ✔ Students who can afford maximum tuition.
- ✔ Students who have been accepted, but about whom Ivy is not too thrilled.
- ✔ Students who don't apply for financial aid. (Ivy figures students who don't apply for aid can afford the sticker price.)

The tuition discount is a relatively new major player on the financial aid stage. It began to appear regularly in the early '80s, as tuitions were soaring and Ronald Reagan's budget cutters were slashing government aid programs. Many fine students were caught in the squeeze, facing college costs beyond their reach. To keep those students on their campuses, colleges began to move toward multilevel tuitions: pushing the sticker price even higher and then offering substantial discounts.

Which schools offer discounts?

Discounts are used chiefly by private colleges in the upper half of the cost spectrum ($14,000 and up). Discounts occur less frequently at less expensive private schools. And they're even more rare at state colleges and universities, many of which have tuitions prescribed by state law.

What you read in this chapter as *discounts* is described in college literature as scholarships and grants. Often, these discounts are called institutional scholarships or institutional grants. But these scholarships and grants are no different from the discount off the sticker price that you get on a new car.

A need for this, a need for that

Colleges will tell you that most discounts they offer are based on that old friend, your financial need. (If you haven't read Chapter 11, your need is the cost of your college minus the amount that a formula decides you're expected to pay.) Some colleges insist that every dollar they award is need-based. If that's what they say, of course, that's what they mean. But when colleges talk about money, need can mean many things.

For government aid programs, your need is clear. The government's formula is written into law, and the only variable is the cost of a college. When colleges distribute their own money, they can make their own rules. Several hundred schools will ask you to fill out a supplemental financial aid form called PROFILE, to get information about you that the government doesn't ask. Other schools will send you their own in-house form for the same purpose. If your parents are divorced, you may get yet another form for the parent who's not in your household.

Not one of those supplemental forms is required to tap into the $40 billion in government aid. These forms are used only by colleges to decide how much tuition they'll ask you to pay. But if a college of your choice asks you for a PROFILE, don't dillydally. Fill out the PROFILE and put it in the mail. Otherwise, the college will think that you don't need the money. You can be certain of one thing: Any college that requests a PROFILE is offering tuition discounts.

The colleges that want more information about you will use the PROFILE to calculate your Expected Family Contribution — the money they expect you to pay toward your year in college — on their own terms. (See Chapter 11.) Then they'll subtract the EFC from the college's cost to come up with your need. This number will be different than the need you calculate in Chapter 11 with the government's formula. The college's figure will be your second need, based on whatever rules the college is using that year. The college's number very likely will be lower than your original need.

I hate to clutter your head with this terminology, but the following is something that you should know. You'll hear people in financial aid offices talk about *federal methodology* and *institutional methodology.* Those who like to talk in abbreviations will say FM and IM.

Federal methodology is the way the government formula figures your need. Institutional methodology is the way the institution — the college — figures your need. The two are never identical. If you ask a financial aid officer to explain his institutional methodology (how he figures your second need), you may get lucky, and he'll explain it in words you can understand. Most students aren't that lucky. But ask, anyway, because you're doing so will show him that you know what you're talking about.

How colleges meet your need

If a college proclaims that it meets every student's need, it's usually talking about the second need that it calculated using its own rules. The college will give you as much aid as it can from the government programs by using your government need, and then the college will plug in a discount to meet your second need.

How some need is met

Topnotch Tech's Cost of Attendance is $15,000. Your Expected Family Contribution, figured the government's way, is $2,000. So your need is $13,000. But when Topnotch Tech collects more information about you (including your parents' home equity) and runs this info through its own formula, your EFC rises to $5,000. And your second need is only $10,000.

The Topnotch financial aid office assembles a package of $6,500 in grants and loans from federal programs and adds a $3,500 tuition discount (which it calls an Institutional Grant), which brings your total aid to $10,000. Your second, but lower, need has been met. You still must find $5,000 to enroll at Topnotch.

What's the difference?

The two main reasons that some colleges figure your need their own way are the reasons I mention in Chapter 11: home equity and noncustodial divorced parents. The government's form doesn't ask about the value of your parents' home, and it doesn't ask about the financial condition of a divorced parent who isn't living with you. Many colleges think both those items should be considered in determining your family's contribution to your education. As some financial aid people like to put it, "We want to know your ability to pay, not your willingness to pay."

Need versus merit

At a 1996 college fair in Minneapolis, I talked to a student who had the credentials to get into any Ivy League school. He told me what was important to him in selecting a college. Near the top of his list was "merit money."

The student was speaking the language of the college financial aid folks. He was asking, "How much can I get off the sticker price without any regard to my financial need?" His question is a question any good student should ask at any high-priced college. The answer may be surprisingly pleasant.

In the last few years, as competition among colleges for good students has become more intense, colleges are increasingly ready to deal. To avoid being confused with auto dealers, colleges don't use the word discount. They offer discounts as *merit scholarships.*

In financial aid conversations, merit has become almost a generic term, meaning any aid that is not based on need. In the minds of financial aid officers, need and merit are the only two reasons for giving away money. Thus, aid that is not need-based must be merit-based.

Merit comes in many forms. Merit can be academic merit, athletic merit, musical merit, dramatic merit, artistic merit, geographic merit, economic merit, ethnic merit, or the merit of being born to an alumnus. Merit money is the aid you get because you're you.

Every year more colleges say they're giving discounts based on merit. That means they're no longer bothering with the ritual of calculating a second need for students they really want. They're just making an offer. Forget this need thing.

At all colleges giving discounts, the line between need and merit is fuzzy. Ron Shunk, financial aid director at Gettysburg College, was the first person that I heard saying he awards aid on "need-based merit." Or was it "merit-based need"? Whatever his words were, Shunk was saying that he is spending Gettysburg's money on students Gettysburg really likes, and who also need some financial help.

Regardless of what catchy phrases and assorted euphemisms others may utter, the bottom line is this: Colleges are using their money to attract the students they want. There's nothing wrong with that. It's good old American free enterprise. The colleges will play the government's need game to give away the government's money and then use their own funds to build the college community they want. To try to lure you away from Topnotch Tech, they'll give you money because you're you.

Private Scholarships

Angel Ragins of Macon, Georgia, raised $400,000 in scholarships during her high school senior year. Meta Jones of Washington, D.C., won $29,000 in private grants that paid for a year at Princeton, with a little left over. Neither had to worry about FAFSAs or PROFILEs or calculating their financial need or asking their parents for tuition money.

Their feats are so rare, however, that it brought them national publicity. Ragins's photo appeared on the cover of *Parade* magazine. Both were featured, three years apart, in *USA Today.* The messages they sent in their national media interviews were the same. If they can do it, anyone can. Ragins repeats her message in a book telling how she did it, *Winning Scholarships for College,* on bookstore shelves.

Where the lists are

Directories of private scholarships are published by the dozen. They typically provide a description of the scholarship, its eligibility rules, and a contact address. That should be enough for you to identify money for which you may qualify and to start seeking more information. Here are some of the better-known directories, likely to be at your neighborhood bookstore, your public library, or perhaps even your high school counseling office:

✔ *The Scholarship Book* by Daniel Cassidy, president of National Scholarship Research Service, a private organization — with 50,000 scholarship listings, it's probably the most comprehensive on the market. This directory includes advice on going after the private money.

✔ **Need A Lift?** — the scholarship list most often recommended by financial aid directors themselves. This list is published by the American Legion, updated annually, and distributed by the Legion's Emblem Sales office, PO Box 1050, Indianapolis, IN 46206.

✔ *The Financial Aid Book* — from Student Financial Services, also a private organization — lists more than 3,000 scholarships by academic major, religious affiliation, organization membership, ethnic background, parental affiliation, and other categories.

✔ *Paying Le$$ for College* — from the Peterson's publishing empire — is a financial aid guidebook, accompanied by a list of private scholarships.

✔ **Foundation Grants to Individuals** — a list of scholarships offered by the nation's thousands of private foundations. This list is available from the Foundation Center, 79 Fifth Ave., New York, NY 10003.

✔ *Free Money for College* by Laurie Blum — more than 1,000 scholarships are listed by state, not subject area.

✔ *Don't Miss Out: The Ambitious Student's Guide to Financial Aid* by Robert and Anna Leider — focusing on financing college, the book lists hundreds of scholarship, grant, and loan sources, including federal and state governments, college aid programs, private sources, and employers.

✔ *A's & B's of Academic Scholarships* by Debra Wexler — a guide for "good" students whose family's income prevents them from receiving other kinds of aid — describes 100,000 awards, ranging in value from $200 to $18,000, and provides all the details on the requirements.

✔ *ARCO College Financial Aid,* by the publishers of the ARCO college directory — it's another guidebook with scholarship lists.

✔ *Winning Money for College* by Alan Deutschman — one of Peterson's thin little books devoted exclusively to finding private money.

✔ *Directory of Financial Aids* by Gail Ann Schlachter and R. David Weber — a super-compendium of all aid, including scholarships. Schlachter has produced a companion volume, *Directory of Financial Aids for Women.*

✔ *Free College Money, Term Papers & Sex (ed),* by Matthew Lesko — despite the provocative title, it's basically a directory of scholarships.

✔ *College Blue Book* — one of its five volumes is devoted exclusively to financial aid sources for college students at all levels. This monster is usually found only in library reference sections.

(continued)

(continued)

Some fairly thorough lists also are available — free — through Web sites operated by The College Board and the National Association of Student Financial Aid Administrators. Check out www.collegeboard.org and www.finaid.org.

But be careful when you're seeking scholarships on the Web. Distinguishing the legitimate from the con is not easy. If you enter the words scholarship and search into any Web search engine, you'll get lists of dozens of companies offering to find you scholarships for a fee. And you'll notice that those fees can run up to $1,000 or more. You don't know which companies are even capable of performing the service they advertise.

To be safe, stick with the Web lists offered — free — by the two reputable national organizations that I mention. Each is a membership association of college officials. Neither is in business to make a buck finding you a scholarship.

The successful scholarship search

Ragins's and Jones's stories are remarkably similar. They began their scholarship searches in a public library, with a large supply of patience. Each started with a directory — one of those thick books that contains nothing but listings of scholarships and their eligibility rules. They made lists. Oh, did they make lists. They wrote down every scholarship for which they could possibly qualify. They sent hundreds of letters to organizations granting those scholarships. They bugged their guidance offices for scholarship notices. They followed up with phone calls. They worked their home towns, knocking on doors of clubs and churches asking whether they gave money to deserving college students.

Ragins and Jones both say it was hard work. But both say it was worth the effort. Ragins said she was motivated by the fact that she had to work at Wendy's to get spending money during high school. She was determined to have no Wendy's in her college life. And Jones said this: "The money is out there, but most students don't have the energy to get it."

The money's there, go look for it

You don't need $400,000 for a year at college. You probably don't need $29,000. But the money Ragins and Jones found, and millions more, is given away by private organizations every year. You sure could use some of the money. Even without the outstanding academic records that Ragins and Jones brought to their searches, you can find some scholarships. But the scholarships won't come to you. You have to look for them.

One way to start is in a library making lists from a directory. Dozens of such books are out there listing thousands of private scholarships and their qualifications. Your high school counseling office could have a few. (Some are listed in the sidebar "Where the lists are," in this chapter.)

A faster way is at a computer. Some directory publishers put the same information on software, selling it to schools and libraries. The computer asks 20 or so questions to compile a profile of you and your parents and then churns out a list of scholarships for which you might qualify, with addresses and phone numbers of the folks giving the money away.

Aid searching is really pretty easy

The rest is up to you. Write to every organization on the list, asking for information and application materials. Some offer Web addresses at which you can electronically apply. When the applications arrive, apply. The process is what a politician might call a win-win situation. The worst thing that can happen, from where you sit, is that your application will be denied. And then you're no worse off than you were before.

Some scholarships are awarded just for academic excellence. Others have different criteria. Some go to students of certain religious or ethnic backgrounds, or to those who intend to specialize in certain fields. Some are targeted to children of veterans, or students whose parents are members of organizations, such as labor unions and service clubs. Some go to kids of company employees.

Some have even narrower restrictions. If you're a female in York, Pennsylvania, thinking about being an architect, wouldn't you like to know that a scholarship exists for red-haired females from York, Pennsylvania, majoring in architecture? (Calm down, red-haired Yorkies. I just made that one up.)

Some colleges have scholarships for students with certain surnames. Amherst College has one for a student who can't get any other scholarship. Most of those offbeat awards come from the money left to specific colleges through rich people's wills. If you qualify, a college will let you know because it usually doesn't find many takers. Lafayette College in Easton, Pennsylvania, has never used a scholarship restricted to residents of West Palm Beach, Florida.

Private scholarships, as well as tuition discounts, are money you get because you're you. But nobody will be waving the money in your face. If you want a tuition discount, you must apply for financial aid. If you want a private scholarship, you must apply to the organization that awards it.

Military money

Some fine sources of college money — if you don't mind tying up some of your life in exchange for it (and keep in mind that you'll be expected to defend your country in exchange for it, too) — are the U.S. military services. The Army, Navy, and Air Force pay students who join their Reserve Officers' Training Corps programs (usually shortened to ROTC). These programs are available at more than 600 four-year colleges.

ROTC applicants must meet physical and academic qualifications. And they must agree to commit six years of their postcollege lives to the service, usually split between four years of active duty and two years in the reserves.

Some full-ride, four-year scholarships, giving students a college degree at no cost, are awarded each year by all three ROTC programs. These scholarships are competitive, with different rules for each branch of the service.

The best guide to all military money, including the tuition-free service academies, is written by Princeton University's financial aid director, Don Betterton. His guide is called *How the Military Will Help You Pay for College,* available at bookstores and libraries. Information on ROTC can be obtained from:

Air Force
HQ AFROTC
551 E. Maxwell Blvd.
Maxwell Air Force Base
Montgomery, AL 36116

Army
Army ROTC Scholarship Program
Building 56
Fort Monroe, VA 23651

Navy
NROTC Scholarship Program
Naval Air Station
250 Dallas St.
Pensacola, FL 32508

Chapter 14

Getting Financial Aid

● ●

In This Chapter

▶ Ask or you won't receive

▶ One way to kick off the New Year

▶ Not only is this form one-size-fits-all, it's free!

▶ But picky colleges' forms aren't free

▶ What if your parents split up?

▶ Sometimes you can make a better deal

▶ Audits happen

● ●

*I*n all the talk about all the money that's available to help you pay for college, one simple fact remains. You won't get one dollar of it unless you ask for it. And asking for the money means filling out forms.

One Form for All

If the thought of more forms in your form-filled life makes you shudder, I have some good news. The overwhelming majority of the nation's college students deal with only one form to trigger all the financial aid that's coming to them. This form is an uncomplicated, four-page form, produced by the federal government that asks questions about your money and your parents' money.

Even more good news: You fill out the form only once. Then you send it to the government's computers, along with a list of the colleges to which you're applying, and the computers take it from there. The proper people at your colleges will get all the information they need to give you some money.

And, are you ready for this? This financial aid form is free. It doesn't cost a cent to apply or to have the form processed, regardless of how many colleges are on your list. That's why it has the word free in its name. It's called the Free Application for Federal Student Aid and is usually identified by its acronym, FAFSA.

This Won't Hurt a Bit

True, facing the task of filling out a FAFSA can be a little traumatic — disclosing your financial condition to total strangers usually is. And you may need time to find all the records that you must use to answer the form's questions.

But after you've found your records, the form is a relative piece of cake. Just fill in numbers, sign your name, put it in the mail, and wait for the news about the financial aid you'll receive. The whole process is far less demanding than filling out college admission applications. There are no essays, prioritized lists of activities, or other heavy-thinking stuff.

Want to take the trauma out of baring your financial soul? To keep the process in perspective, look at this comparison: If you buy a car, the financing agency wants much of the same information to give you a loan. When your parents buy a house, the bank wants the same information, and more, to approve a mortgage. And every April, the IRS wants to know all the same stuff on your tax return.

The overwhelming majority of college students fill out one form. That's because most colleges — including almost all public colleges — are satisfied with the government's form for all their financial aid programs. But those schools I talk about in Chapter 13, the private colleges that give away a lot of their own money in tuition discounts, usually want more information than the government requires. They'll insist that you fill out a second form, perhaps even a third. I look at those forms later in this chapter.

The number of financial aid forms a college requires usually is directly related to the college's cost. More expensive schools want more forms. At expensive schools, your need is greater, and you're likely to get more aid. Following these facts to their logical conclusion: The more forms you submit, the more aid you're likely to receive.

When to Apply

How about Christmas Eve? Nah! Just kidding. That's not a good time to fill out applications. But it is a good deadline — for more than finishing off a shopping list.

The ideal time to fill out financial aid applications is the last week of December. It's ideal for at least two reasons, which I'm about to explain. But before you can fill out the forms, you must find all your necessary financial records: your income, bank balances, investment interest, and other stuff that tells how much you're worth.

What you need to apply

The basic financial aid application takes about 15 to 20 minutes to complete, if all your records are at hand when you start. The records you need are for the full year *before* the year in which you want aid. For example, if you're applying for the fall of 1998, your financial records are needed for 1997.

Dependent students need the records for themselves and their parents, including a custodial stepparent. Independent students need records only for themselves and their spouses.

If you fill out the application before you have W2 forms from your employer (and you should), estimates from check stubs or other sources are perfectly okay.

The following are the records that you need:

- ✔ Earned income for the year
- ✔ Federal taxes paid for the year
- ✔ Untaxed income received (Social Security benefits, child support, for example)
- ✔ Money in checking, savings accounts
- ✔ Value of investments
- ✔ Value of any business or farm owned

If you find all those records by December 24, put them in a safe, convenient desk drawer. Then you'll be ready to roll soon after Christmas, when you have a few hours to kill. If you don't have precise numbers for, say, your annual income, estimates are permitted. You'll have a chance to change them if you guess wrong.

Start the New Year right

Why is the last week of December the ideal time to fill out your financial aid applications? Because school is out, and you're temporarily free of its distractions and demands on your time. More importantly, it's ideal because your basic government form, the FAFSA, cannot be submitted before January 1 of the year you're applying for aid. That's the law. And that means the early birds will be at their post offices, FAFSAs in hand, on the morning of January 2.

Get to the money before it runs out

Join the early birds. The pot of financial aid for which you're applying has limits. The pot will run out. If you apply early, you'll be assured your application is considered on its merits, and you won't lose money you deserve because a college has spent all its cash. Every year, financial aid directors tell sad tales of good students who received no aid because they applied too late.

If one of your colleges requires a second, supplemental application, it will tell you its deadline. In most cases, the deadline will be later than January 1. So a good idea — to avoid the dry-well scenario — is to fill out both forms at the same time and get them both in the mail on January 2.

A few colleges want their supplemental form earlier — perhaps even in the fall of your senior year. Those colleges that do will let you know.

The One-Size-Fits-All Form

One of the few actions Congress has taken the last few years that draws unanimous applause from college students is to wipe out the cost of applying for financial aid. In the early '90s, the people who processed your application would charge you a fee. The more schools on your list, the more you paid. In 1993, Congress said no. It decreed that no one shall pay to apply for government aid. To underscore its message, Congress told federal bureaucrats to design an application with the word free in its title. Thus came the Free Application for Federal Student Aid, or FAFSA. It's a one-size-fits-all financial aid form.

The FAFSA should be available at any well-equipped high school counseling office. If your school is not so well-equipped, any college financial aid office can send you a copy.

If you have a computer and a modem, you can download the FAFSA — and instructions for filing it electronically — directly from the U.S. Department of Education's computers in Washington. Go to the department's Web site, www.ed.gov. Then click on Money and FAFSA Express. But even if you submit the form via modem, the law says you must wait until after January 1.

How the application process works

You fill out the FAFSA once and mail it or send it electronically to the government's computers. A computer crunches your information and churns out a report. This report gets back to you within a month — only via snail mail, not through your computer — announcing your Expected Family Contribution. (You can walk through the computer's formula for arriving at your EFC in Chapter 11.)

If you subtract your EFC from the cost of the colleges you're considering, you'll come up with your financial need at each college. The computer, meanwhile, sends the same information to the colleges on your list. The colleges then calculate your need and decide how much money to offer you.

You may not need to know this but, just in case, here it is. The notification you get from a computer about your Expected Family Contribution is called a *Student Aid Report*. It should not surprise you that it's known throughout the land as a SAR. The SAR will tell you whether you're eligible for a Pell Grant (see Chapter 12) and, if so, for how much. Unless the computer owners bought a new supply of paper, your SAR will be light blue.

From estimates to actuals

Also in the SAR will be a recapitulation of all the information you submitted on your FAFSA. If some numbers were estimates that turned out to be inaccurate, this is your chance to correct them. Change the numbers on the SAR and send it back to the computer. The computer's address is on the form.

The SAR's arrival is a good time to check all the numbers you submitted, estimates or otherwise just to make sure they're accurate. If you find one you wrote incorrectly, you can change it on the SAR. No harm done.

Filling Out the FAFSA

In this section, I stroll through the FAFSA line by line. You see how easy it really is.

Your vital statistics

Section A is a quickie. Take a look at Figure 14-1. Your name, address, birth date, Social Security number, and a few other vital statistics are needed here. No problem.

Beware! Be sure to answer every question, except those that say an answer is optional. If the answer is zero, write zero. Any unanswered question will cause the computer to kick out your application and return it as incomplete. You'll have to resubmit it with the question answered. The process of figuring your need will be delayed by about a month.

Your education

Section B, in Figure 14-2, collects information to be used by social scientists years from now, when they're doing demographic research. It asks questions regarding the date you received your diploma and your parent's educational background.

Section A: You (the student)

1–3. Your name

1. Last name   2. First name   3. M.I.

Your title (optional)   Mr. ◯ 1   Miss, Mrs., or Ms. ◯ 2

4–7. Your permanent mailing address *(All mail will be sent to this address. See Instructions, page 2 for state/country abbreviations.)*

4. Number and street (Include apt. no.)

5. City   6. State   7. ZIP code

8. Your social security number (SSN) *(Don't leave blank. See Instructions, page 2.)*

9. Your date of birth

Month   Day   Year
1 9

10. Your permanent home telephone number

Area code

11. Your state of legal residence

State

12. Date you became a legal resident of the state in question 11 *(See Instructions, page 2.)*

Month   Day   Year
1 9

13–14. Your driver's license number *(Include the state abbreviation. If you don't have a license, write in "None.")*

State   License number

15–16. Are you a U.S. citizen? *(See Instructions, pages 2–3.)*

Yes, I am a U.S. citizen.   ◯ 1
No, but I am an eligible noncitizen.   ◯ 2

A

No, neither of the above.   ◯ 3

17. As of today, are you married? *(Fill in only one oval.)*

I am not married. (I am single, widowed, or divorced.)   ◯ 1
I am married.   ◯ 2
I am separated from my spouse.   ◯ 3

18. Date you were married, separated, divorced, or widowed. If divorced, use date of divorce or separation, whichever is earlier. *(If never married, leave blank.)*   Month   Year
1 9

19. Will you have your first bachelor's degree before July 1, 1997?   Yes ◯ 1   No ◯ 2

Figure 14-1: Section A.

Section B: Education Background

20–21. Date that you (the student) received, or will receive, your high school diploma, either— *(Enter one date. Leave blank if the question does not apply to you.)*

• by graduating from high school   20.   Month   Year   1 9

OR

• by earning a GED   21.   Month   Year   1 9

22–23. Highest educational level or grade level your father and your mother completed. *(Fill in one oval for each parent. See Instructions, page 3.)*

	22. Father	23. Mother
elementary school (K–8)	◯ 1	◯ 1
high school (9–12)	◯ 2	◯ 2
college or beyond	◯ 3	◯ 3
unknown	◯ 4	◯ 4

If you (and your family) have **unusual circumstances**, complete this form and then check with your financial aid administrator. Examples:
• tuition expenses at an elementary or secondary school,
• unusual medical or dental expenses not covered by insurance,
• a family member who recently became unemployed, or
• other unusual circumstances such as changes in income or assets that might affect your eligibility for student financial aid.

Figure 14-2: Section B.

Your plans

Section C, in Figure 14-3, looks like more of the same vital statistics, except that it focuses on the future. Questions 24 through 39 are self-explanatory, merely asking for information about you.

You might pause for thought at Questions 33 through 35, where you're asked what types of financial aid you'd like to receive. Don't pause for long. Check *all* the boxes. This is no time to worry about whether you want to borrow money or work on campus. You'll have time to consider those decisions after you find out whether anyone is offering you loans or jobs. At this point, you want to remain eligible for as many types of aid as you can get. Don't rule out anything.

Section C: Your Plans *Answer these questions about your college plans.* *Page 2*

24–28. Your expected enrollment status for the 1997–98 school year
(See Instructions, page 3.)

School term	Full time	3/4 time	1/2 time	Less than 1/2 time	Not enrolled
24. Summer term '97	○ 1	○ 2	○ 3	○ 4	○ 5
25. Fall semester/qtr. '97	○ 1	○ 2	○ 3	○ 4	○ 5
26. Winter quarter '97-98	○ 1	○ 2	○ 3	○ 4	○ 5
27. Spring semester/qtr. '98	○ 1	○ 2	○ 3	○ 4	○ 5
28. Summer term '98	○ 1	○ 2	○ 3	○ 4	○ 5

29. Your course of study *(See Instructions for code, page 3.)* Code ☐

30. College degree/certificate you expect to receive
(See Instructions for code, page 3.) ☐

31. Date you expect to receive your degree/certificate Month Day Year ☐

32. Your grade level during the 1997–98 school year *(Fill in only one.)*

1st yr./never attended college	○ 1	5th year/other undergraduate	○ 6
1st yr./attended college before	○ 2	1st year graduate/professional	○ 7
2nd year/sophomore	○ 3	2nd year graduate/professional	○ 8
3rd year/junior	○ 4	3rd year graduate/professional	○ 9
4th year/senior	○ 5	Beyond 3rd year graduate/professional	○ 10

33–35. In addition to grants, what other types of financial aid are you (and your parents) interested in? *(See Instructions, page 3.)*

33. Student employment Yes ○ 1 No ○ 2
34. Student loans Yes ○ 1 No ○ 2
35. Parent loans for students Yes ○ 1 No ○ 2

36. If you are (or were) in college, do you plan to attend **that same college** in 1997–98? *(If this doesn't apply to you, leave blank.)* Yes ○ 1 No ○ 2

37. For how many dependents will you (the student) pay child care or elder care expenses in 1997–98? ☐

38–39. Veterans education benefits you expect to receive from July 1, 1997 through June 30, 1998

38. Amount per month $ ☐ .00
39. Number of months ☐

Figure 14-3: Section C.

Your status

Section D, in Figure 14-4, determines whether you're dependent or independent for financial aid purposes. This section asks the six magic questions listed in Chapter 11. Answer one of the six *yes,* and you are independent. Answer all six *no,* and you're dependent. Being independent usually is better for your financial aid prospects.

Again, answer all the questions. Even the questions that don't apply to you (about dependent children or veterans' benefits, for example) should be answered with zeroes. Leaving them blank will produce a *request for more information* and a delay in the process.

Section D: Student Status

40. Were you born **before** January 1, 1974? .... Yes ○ 1 No ○ 2
41. Are you a veteran of the U.S. Armed Forces? .... Yes ○ 1 No ○ 2
42. Will you be enrolled in a graduate or professional program (beyond a bachelor's degree) in 1997-98? .... Yes ○ 1 No ○ 2
43. Are you married? .... Yes ○ 1 No ○ 2
44. Are you an orphan or a ward of the court, or **were** you a ward of the court until age 18? .... Yes ○ 1 No ○ 2
45. Do you have legal dependents (**other than a spouse**) that fit the definition in Instructions, page 4? .... Yes ○ 1 No ○ 2

If you answered **"Yes"** to **any** question in Section D, go to Section E and fill out **both the GRAY and the WHITE** areas on the rest of this form.

If you answered **"No"** to **every** question in Section D, go to Section E and fill out **both the GREEN and the WHITE** areas on the rest of this form.

Figure 14-4: Section D.

Your household

Be alert! One question in Section E, in Figure 14-5, could mean the difference between hundreds or thousands of financial aid dollars. If you read Chapter 11, and work through the formula for your Expected Family Contribution, the final step is to divide the total available money by the number of family members in college. This is where you tell the computer that number.

If you're dependent, you'll answer Questions 48 through 52. Number 52 is the key. This question asks how many family members will be in college "at least half-time." The instructions (which aren't printed here) tell you half-time means at least six credits. Any member of your family — Mom, Dad, or siblings — who is thinking about taking six credits next year should be counted. There is no law against changing one's mind.

Independent students provide the same information in Question 47. They should count a spouse and any children who plan to take at least six credits next year.

Your money

Okay, this form was easy until now. Here's the traumatic part. In Section F of the FAFSA, in Figure 14-6, starts asking about your money and, if you're dependent, your parents' money.

Regardless of your status, dependent or independent, you must answer questions about your income and taxes. If you're married, your spouse's income is combined with yours to produce one total. All numbers are for the year before you expect to receive financial aid. For example, if you're applying for aid for the fall of 1996, you must report your income for 1995.

Section E: Household Information

> **Remember:**
> **At least one "Yes" answer in Section D means fill out the GRAY and WHITE areas.**
>
> **All "No" answers in Section D means fill out the GREEN and WHITE areas.**

STUDENT (& SPOUSE)

46. Number in your household in 1997–98
(Include yourself and your spouse. Do not include your children and other people unless they meet the definition in Instructions, page 4.)

47. Number of college students in household in 1997–98
(Of the number in 46, how many will be in college at least half-time at least one term in an eligible program? Include yourself. See Instructions, page 4.)

PARENT(S)

48. Your parent(s)' **current** marital status:

single ◯ 1   separated ◯ 3   widowed ◯ 5
married ◯ 2   divorced ◯ 4
State

49. Your parent(s)' state of legal residence

50. Date your parent(s) became legal resident(s) of the state in question 49 *(See Instructions, page 5.)*
Month   Day   Year
1 9

51. Number in your parent(s) household in 1997–98
(Include yourself and your parents. Do not include your parents' other children and other people unless they meet the definition in Instructions, page 5.)

52. Number of college students in household in 1997–98
(Of the number in 51, how many will be in college at least half-time at least one term in an eligible program? Include yourself. See Instructions, page 5.)

Figure 14-5:
Section E.

Section F: 1996 Income, Earnings, and Benefits *You must see Instructions, pages 5 and 6, for information about* Page 3
tax forms and tax filing status, especially if you are estimating taxes or filing electronically or by telephone. These instructions will
tell you what income and benefits should be reported in this section.

	STUDENT (& SPOUSE)	PARENT(S)

Everyone must fill out this column.

The following 1996 U.S. income tax figures are from: **53.** *(Fill in one oval.)* **65.** *(Fill in one oval.)*

A—a completed 1996 IRS Form 1040A, 1040EZ, or 1040TEL .... ○ 1 A .... ○ 1

B—a completed 1996 IRS Form 1040 .... ○ 2 B .... ○ 2

C—an estimated 1996 IRS Form 1040A, 1040EZ, or 1040TEL .... ○ 3 C .... ○ 3

D—an estimated 1996 IRS Form 1040 .... ○ 4 D .... ○ 4

E—will not file a 1996 U.S. income tax return ....*(Skip to question 57.)*.......... ○ 5 E ......*(Skip to 69.)*.......... ○ 5

1996 Total number of exemptions (Form 1040–line 6d,
or 1040A–line 6d; 1040EZ filers— *see Instructions, page 6.*) **54.** ☐ **66.** ☐

1996 Adjusted Gross Income (AGI: Form 1040–line 31, **55.** $ |_____| .00 **67.** $ |_____| .00
1040A–line 16, or 1040EZ–line 4—*see Instructions, page 6.*)

TAX FILERS ONLY

1996 U.S. income tax **paid** (Form 1040–line 44, **56.** $ |_____| .00 **68.** $ |_____| .00
1040A–line 25, or 1040EZ–line 10

1996 Income earned from work (Student) **57.** $ |_____| .00 (Father) **69.** $ |_____| .00

1996 Income earned from work (Spouse) **58.** $ |_____| .00 (Mother) **70.** $ |_____| .00

1996 Untaxed income and benefits (yearly totals only):

Earned Income Credit (Form 1040–line 54, **59.** $ |_____| .00 **71.** $ |_____| .00
Form 1040A–line 29c, or Form 1040EZ–line 8)

Untaxed Social Security Benefits **60.** $ |_____| .00 **72.** $ |_____| .00

Aid to Families with Dependent Children (AFDC/ADC) **61.** $ |_____| .00 **73.** $ |_____| .00

Child support received for all children **62.** $ |_____| .00 **74.** $ |_____| .00

Other untaxed income and benefits from Worksheet #2, **63.** $ |_____| .00 **75.** $ |_____| .00
page 11

1996 Amount from Line 5, Worksheet #3, page 12 **64.** $ |_____| .00 **76.** $ |_____| .00
(See Instructions.)

Figure 14-6:
Section F.

But if you're following my earlier good advice and completing your form the last week of December, you don't have final numbers for 1995 income and taxes. Your W2s won't arrive for a month. However, you do have good estimates. You can use a couple of paycheck stubs and a calculator to get a ballpark total of how much you've earned and the taxes you've paid. That's good enough. Check the box in Question 53 that says estimated and estimate away. If your estimates are far off, you can correct them without penalty when your SAR arrives.

And you'll be in good company. Every early bird who shows up at the post office January 2 will be mailing estimated income and tax numbers.

I'm repeating an earlier warning because it's very important. If you have zero as an answer, write 0 on each line. Don't leave a single line blank. A blank line will trigger a computer's dreaded request for more information rather than an EFC, and that's an alternative you don't need. It delays the process unnecessarily. When the answer is zero, write a zero.

Questions 65 through 76, down the right side of page 3, are answered only by parents of dependent students. (You, the student, can answer them if your parents will share the information.) It's the same income and tax information that you reported about yourself on the other side of the page. And estimates are just as allowable.

No need to mention your home

Section G, shown in Figure 14-7, is where you, your spouse, and your parents report your investments. There's one notable exception. You do not mention your home. The equity you or your parents have built up in your principal residence is not considered an asset in determining your need and your eligibility for government financial aid programs. Many colleges disagree with this approach, and that's the key reason they'll ask you to submit another form.

Another exception to the investments your parents must list is retirement savings. All the money stashed in IRAs in the past doesn't count. The money going into retirement funds during the last 12 months was reported as income.

As you complete Section G, notice Question 84. If you have calculated your EFC in Chapter 11, you already know why it's asking the age of your older parent. That determines how much of your parents' assets are shielded from the formula that figures EFC. The older your parents, the more assets they can protect, because Congress assumes they'll need the money sooner for retirement.

Section G: Asset Information **ATTENTION!**

Fill out Worksheet A or Worksheet B in Instructions, page 7. *If you meet the tax filing and income conditions on Worksheets A and B, you do not have to complete Section G to apply for Federal student aid. Some states and colleges, however, require Section G information for their own aid programs. Check with your financial aid administrator and/or State Agency.*

Age of your older parent **84.**

	STUDENT (& SPOUSE)	PARENT(S)
Cash, savings, and checking accounts	77. $ .00	85. $ .00
Other real estate and investments value *(Don't include the home.)*	78. $ .00	86. $ .00
Other real estate and investments debt *(Don't include the home.)*	79. $ .00	87. $ .00
Business value	80. $ .00	88. $ .00
Business debt	81. $ .00	89. $ .00
Investment farm value *(See Instructions, page 8.)* *(Don't include a family farm.)*	82. $ .00	90. $ .00
Investment farm debt *(See Instructions, page 8.)* *(Don't include a family farm.)*	83. $ .00	91. $ .00

Figure 14-7: Section G.

Where the information all goes

Section H, in Figure 14-8, tells the computer where to send your information. Enter the name of up to six colleges where you think you'll apply. Six is the max because the form only has six lines. Don't list more on an attached sheet because the computer won't read attached sheets.

Section H: Releases and Signatures   *Page 4*

92–103. What college(s) do you plan to attend in 1997–98?
(*Note: The colleges you list below will have access to your application information. See Instructions, page 8.*)

Housing codes	1—on-campus	3—with parent(s)
	2—off-campus	4—with relative(s) other than parent(s)

Title IV School Code	College Name	College Street Address and City	State	Housing Code
XX. 0 5 4 3 2 1	EXAMPLE UNIVERSITY	14930 NORTH SOMEWHERE BLVD. ANYWHERE CITY	S T XX.	2
92. 001537			93.	
94.			95.	
96.			97.	
98.			99.	
100.			101.	
102.			103.	

104. The U.S. Department of Education will send information from this form to your state financial aid agency and the state agencies of the colleges listed above so they can consider you for state aid. Answer **"No"** if you **don't** want information released to the state. (*See Instructions, page 9 and "Deadlines for State Student Aid," page 10.*) .... **104. No** ○ 2

105. Males not yet registered for Selective Service (SS): Do you want SS to register you? (*See Instructions, page 9.*) .... **105. Yes** ○ 1

Figure 14-8: Section H.

This form is produced by bureaucrats. If you want more than six colleges to get your information, you must do it the bureaucratic way. Wait until the computer sends you a SAR, about a month after you submit your application. On the SAR, in addition to opportunities to correct estimated information, is a place to list more colleges that should get your data. Send the SAR back with the rest of the names, and those colleges will also hear from the computer.

Don't fall into the signature trap

By far, the most common reason the computers reject a FAFSA is the lack of a signature. The signature section is easy to miss. Shown in Figure 14-9, this section doesn't even have a label, such as Section M or whatever. It's just up there daring you to overlook it. And if you do overlook this section, guess what? A request for additional information will arrive in the mail when you were expecting an EFC. Your financial aid process gets pushed back a month.

106–107. Read, Sign, and Date Below

All of the information provided by me or any other person on this form is true and complete to the best of my knowledge. I understand that this application is being filed jointly by all signatories. If asked by an authorized official, I agree to give proof of the information that I have given on this form. I realize that this proof may include a copy of my U.S. or state income tax return. I also realize that if I do not give proof when asked, the student may be denied aid.

Statement of Educational Purpose. I certify that I will use any Federal Title IV, HEA funds I receive during the award year covered by this application solely for expenses related to my attendance at the institution of higher education that determined or certified my eligibility for those funds.

Certification Statement on Overpayments and Defaults. I understand that I may not receive any Federal Title IV, HEA funds if I owe an overpayment on any Title IV educational grant or loan or am in default on a Title IV educational loan unless I have made satisfactory arrangements to repay or otherwise resolve the overpayment or default. I also understand that I must notify my school if I do owe an overpayment or am in default.

Everyone whose information is given on this form should sign below. The student (and at least one parent, if parental information is given) must sign below or this form will be returned unprocessed.

106. Signatures   *(Sign in the boxes below.)*

¹ Student

² Student's Spouse

³ Father/Stepfather

⁴ Mother/Stepmother

107. Date completed   Month   Day   Year
                                               1997 ◯
                                               1998 ◯

Figure 14-9: Don't forget to sign your form.

Easy, wasn't it? Nothing at all like that Common Application to get into college. You now have completed the only form you're likely to need to get the financial aid you deserve — unless, of course, you're applying to one of those picky colleges that wants more information.

Picky Colleges Want More

All colleges must use the FAFSA, the government's financial aid application, to determine your eligibility for government programs. Many also use your FAFSA information to give away their own money. But several hundred picky colleges figure their own Estimated Family Contribution (EFC) with additional information from you. Almost all the picky colleges are high-priced private schools that have budgeted millions to offer in tuition discounts. They want more information to fine-tune the process of giving discounts to the students they feel most deserve them.

They want a PROFILE

Most schools that want more data will ask you to submit a PROFILE, a new form introduced in 1995, now used by more than 800 colleges. This form replaces the old, venerable Financial Aid Form (FAF), which has been phased into oblivion after three decades of valiant service. And PROFILE is hardly free. You will pay $5 to request the form and $14.50 for each college that gets your information.

And you have to apply for it

That's right, you have to apply for it. The people who developed PROFILE say they're making the application process easier on you. Well, before 1995, you could walk into your counseling office and pick up a FAF (the form picky colleges wanted) along with a FAFSA. Now, getting the forms is not that easy. You must apply to get a PROFILE.

Yes, you read that right. You must send an application to The College Board to get an application on which you can apply for financial aid. Another step has been added to the process. This is easier? And you must pay that $5 fee just to obtain the application to apply.

What next?

The one-page application for an application officially is called a *PROFILE Registration Form.* All high school counseling officers are supposed to have copies, and a college that wants a PROFILE probably will send you one. You also can apply to get a PROFILE through the College Board Web site, www.collegeboard.org, with the fee charged to a credit card. You fill in your vital statistics, mail it or send it electronically to The College Board, and back to you comes your personalized PROFILE with your name, address, Social Security number, and other pertinent data already in place.

The purpose of the two steps is to help the colleges, not you. Every college using PROFILE can customize it to its own taste. If College X, for example, wants to know about the IRAs your parents have stashed away over the years, it can ask for that information on your PROFILE. Colleges W, Y, and Z, which don't want to know about IRAs, won't get the information. When you submit a registration form, you will list the colleges to which you want the information sent. The College Board then sends you a customized PROFILE that includes the questions those colleges want you to answer.

If you get a PROFILE, you'll notice it duplicates every question on the FAFSA, then asks more. That's because some schools are using your PROFILE to get a head start on your need-finding process. They don't want to wait for the government's data after January 1. They'll ask you to submit a PROFILE in the fall of your senior year and then give you an estimated EFC and financial need. That will give you a good idea of the money you'll get, at least at that college. But you still must file a FAFSA after January 1 to get the government's money.

I've said it before and this is a good time to say it again. If a college asks you to submit a PROFILE, spend the $14.50 and do it. A college requesting a PROFILE is almost certainly giving away a lot of its own money in tuition discounts. You won't get any if you don't play the game.

Some schools want their own form

Some picky colleges don't mess with PROFILE. They have their own in-house financial aid form that they'll send directly to you. Fill it out and send it back.

If you encounter a college using PROFILE, here's some good advice. Smile and accept the extra work and the additional forms. They probably mean extra money. A college using PROFILE has a lot of its own money to give away; otherwise it wouldn't be so picky. The only way you'll get some of the money is by playing the game by the college's rules. Play the game. It may be long, but it'll be profitable.

If Your Parents Are Split

If your parents are divorced or separated, most colleges in the country ignore the parent with whom you don't live. The government's financial aid form, the FAFSA, asks only about members of your household. So, in a divorce situation, this means your custodial parent and a stepparent (if one has been acquired) must report their financial information. This is necessary if you're officially dependent.

Stepparents

A stepparent's income and assets are included in calculating your need, whether or not the stepparent likes it. If your stepfather signed a prenuptial agreement saying he's not responsible for your education, he should have saved the energy it took to sign his name. Congress, in writing the financial aid law, decreed that if Stepdad has custody of you, his money counts. Prenuptial agreements cannot overturn federal law, as some unhappy stepparents with poor legal advice have learned.

Lafayette's Barry McCarty puts it this way: "If you just married someone who has a child, even if you didn't know that child a month ago, the law says that you must contribute to the child's college costs."

Noncustodial parents

A divorced parent with whom you don't live is called your *noncustodial* parent. When you think about the term noncustodial, it makes sense. What else should that parent be called? But that term is tossed around financial aid offices so frequently, often in rancor-filled situations involving noncustodial parents, that it's evolving into the realm of jargon.

Even some picky colleges don't bother with a noncustodial parent. They want financial information for the adults with whom you live, and that's all. But a couple hundred of the pickiest colleges have the attitude that the two people who produced you — your natural parents — have a responsibility to educate you. Even if you haven't talked to your natural father in ten years, some colleges want to know where he works, how much money he makes, and how many mutual funds he owns. They want to include the noncustodial parent's income and assets in determining your financial need.

They get another form

Because of this demand by the pickiest colleges, The College Board has produced a separate form: the Divorced/Separated Parents' Statement. This form is a simple little two-page form that asks the noncustodial parent for the same information other parents report on the FAFSA and PROFILE. The registration form you submit to get a PROFILE asks whether your natural parents are divorced or separated. If you answer yes, a college that wants noncustodial parents' information will go after it. Some will send you a divorced/separated form and ask you to deliver it. Others will ask for the noncustodial parent's address and send it directly.

Some noncustodial parents willingly provide the information. Others adamantly refuse. And, of course, that's when things get sticky. A college has no law on the books to enforce its request for the information. All the school can do is ask. Some colleges have been known to ask repeatedly, and in unfriendly tones, if their initial polite request is ignored.

What if they don't want to fill out the form?

What can you do if one of your colleges and your noncustodial parent are in a standoff over financial disclosure? Frankly, nothing — unless you can persuade your parent to cooperate.

What will the consequence be? A college that doesn't get the information it asks for will frown disapprovingly, but do little else. It's true, you don't want financial aid directors frowning over your application, but that result may be out of your hands. When decision time comes, though, it's highly unlikely that a financial aid director will penalize a student because she has a stubborn parent.

Only the pickiest of picky colleges vigorously go after noncustodial parents. Even if you're dealing with a college that requests PROFILE information, it does not necessarily want information about your noncustodial parent. The ones that do will let you know early in the process.

Negotiating a Better Deal the First Time

Twice, when you're dealing with financial aid people, the opportunity can arise for you to take the initiative and try to get yourself a better deal. The first time is after you've submitted your applications and then something changes in your life. The second time is after the colleges make you an offer. I discuss the first chance here and the second chance in Chapter 15.

Professional judgment plays a part

Here's a term to commit firmly to your memory: *professional judgment.* Those two words appear in the federal law governing financial aid. What they mean is "nothing in this law is carved in stone." A financial aid director may use her professional judgment to change anything her judgment decides needs changing. That's right. Any financial aid director can use professional judgment to raise or lower your need, without regard to your Expected Family Contribution.

Professional judgment is used most often when something significantly changes the student's or parents' financial condition, and that significant something isn't reflected on the application forms. Professional judgment was used extensively at Midwest colleges after the 1993 floods. Parents whose businesses were wiped out were allowed to estimate next year's earnings instead of reporting the previous year's incomes. Nothing in the law permitted that change, except the clause allowing professional judgment.

When to ask for financial aid

If your financial situation changes after you've mailed your FAFSA, let your colleges' financial aid offices know about it. If a parent loses a job or takes a new job with lower pay, your need will be higher. If you decide to quit work and concentrate on AP chemistry, you'll probably be congratulated by the college for an astute decision, and it will judge your need to be higher. Write a letter to each financial aid office with which you're dealing and explain the circumstances.

To change your need, your Expected Family Contribution, and your financial aid package through professional judgment, a college needs a good reason. The school won't go looking for good reasons. You must bring the reasons to its attention. A serious illness in your family, a divorce, or severe damage to your home could all be good reasons.

When you inform a college financial aid office about changes in your life, be persuasive. Explain in specific terms how the change has affected your finances and be sure that any hardship your family experiences is spelled out clearly. After a professional judgment decision is made, there is no appeal.

If You're Thinking of Lying, Know This

It happens. Just as taxpayers can be audited by the IRS, financial aid recipients can be audited by the colleges giving them money. There's one big difference, though. The IRS audits to see whether you paid enough. Colleges audit to see whether you're getting too much.

In the world of financial aid, they don't call this process an audit. The audit process is called _verification_. A student who must submit to verification is being _verified_. But it's the same thing to some tax payers. Audit is to taxes as verification is to financial aid.

One-third randomly get verified

One-third of all financial aid applicants are verified, whether they need it or not. They're selected randomly by the government's computers. If you're among the unlucky one-third, the bad news will come on that light blue Student Aid Report that announces your EFC. The report will advise you to collect all the records that support the numbers on your FAFSA and be prepared to bring them to your college financial aid office. A financial aid officer will check them against the numbers you submitted. And if your original numbers are wrong, they'll be changed and a new EFC computed.

The college has no choice but to verify the applications that the computers tell it to verify or lose its eligibility for government aid programs. And whether you're a high school senior applying for the first time or a third-year college student and a veteran of the process makes no difference. The computer can select you randomly from the vast pool of applicants in its memory.

And some are checked for good reason

Colleges also can ask for verification on their own. Some colleges will ask if they see numbers that raise questions, such as $100,000 in the bank on a $20,000 annual income. Some colleges use their own random process to select students for verification. And some very picky colleges want to verify every student awarded aid, before the money is distributed.

If you're verified, the burden is on you to prove that the numbers you submitted are real numbers. Your tax return is the easiest proof. If you give the IRS the same numbers you give FAFSA, colleges will take your word that the numbers are good.

If you took my good advice and mailed your FAFSA by January 2 with estimated tax and income numbers, be sure that you check your estimates when the real numbers are available. You can amend your estimates, as I described, when you receive your Student Aid Report.

Chapter 15

Easing the Pain

• •

In This Chapter

▶ Deciding whether to save or to borrow

▶ Forecasting how much you'll need

▶ Saving: Ideas to help you

▶ Making the most of what you have

• •

*W*hen you talk about money for college, two inescapable facts leap out. Fact 1: Your chances of getting financial aid to help pay the bills are good. Fact 2: Some bills must be paid by you, or your parents (unless you're lucky enough to get a full free ride to a certain college). I have discussed Fact 1 at length in Chapters 11 through 14. Now it's time to talk about Fact 2. Where will you get the money to pay your share of the bill?

Planning Is Key

If you're now in eleventh grade or older, this chapter is not for you. If you don't already have the money for your share of the costs, now is the time to start cultivating a friendship with a banker.

This chapter is for the folks — students and parents — who will face bill-paying time 2, 4, 10, or 20 years down the road. When the time comes, wouldn't it be great if you could simply write a check to cover each year at Bigbucks U. as you enroll? With some careful planning, you might be able to swing it.

Planning, in this case, means that boring word, saving. Face facts: The more money you put away in a bank account or other investments, and the earlier you start stashing your money, the better your chance of being able to write those pay-as-you-go checks. That seems obvious. And to most people, it is. The problem is that too many people just don't do it. A recent survey by *Money* magazine shows that half of all parents don't save for college at all, and only 25 percent are saving by the time their child is eight-years-old.

Save or Borrow?

Ah, you sharp-eyed readers think you got me. If you've already worked out the formula in Chapter 11 to determine your financial need, you think you see a giant contradiction in the savings message I just mentioned. You know that the more you have in savings and investments, the higher the Expected Family Contribution (EFC) will be churned out by the formula. And, therefore, the more you'll have to pay for college from your own pocket. So why bother with savings, you ask.

The less you have, the more your need, but . . .

Well, sharp-eyed reader, you're absolutely right, to a point. The less you have saved, the greater your need, true. If you have nothing stashed away, you'll be eligible for more financial aid than the diligent saver. But if you've read the earlier chapters, you should also remember something else that you found out. Much of your financial aid package will likely be in loans. They may be low-interest loans with repayment deferred until after college, but they are loans nonetheless. Eventually, you must come up with the money.

So the decision you need to make, if you're thinking about it several years in advance, is should you earn interest now on money you save or pay interest later on money you borrow? That's your choice. And your decision must be dictated by your financial condition.

There are other considerations, too

You need to take into account certain considerations when you make your decision. Keep in mind that the relationship between the amount you save and the amount you must borrow is not precise. You can't say that $10,000 in savings will eliminate $10,000 in loans because too many other factors are involved. Not the least of those factors is a student's attractiveness to a college. A very desirable student likely will have his entire need, and perhaps more, covered by grants and discounts. Borrowing will be unnecessary. Planning in advance academically could be more profitable than financial planning. (See Chapter 9 for more on becoming attractive.)

A dollar saved means a dollar not borrowed

As a general rule, however, you can figure that a dollar saved plus interest will eliminate the need to borrow a dollar or two somewhere down the road. Look at an example. Suppose that you and your best friend are accepted by Bigbucks U., where a year's cost is $21,000. Your parents and your friend's parents earn the same income and pay the same taxes. But your parents have $20,000 in savings. Your friend's parents never save.

When the computer digests your financial information, it says your Expected Family Contribution is $9,000. Your friend's EFC, without savings in the formula, is $7,000. At Bigbucks U., your need is $12,000 ($21,000 – $9,000). Your friend's need is $14,000. You're both excellent students with musical talent. Bigbucks offers both of you packages of grants and tuition discounts to cover your full need.

Your friend still must come up with $7,000. With nothing in the bank, his choices are to borrow the money or find another college. You must come up with $9,000. If you want, you can take that amount from savings and borrow nothing. Or you can take, say, $5,000 from savings (reserve $15,000 for your next three years at Bigbucks), and borrow $4,000. Either way, your debt will be smaller than your friend's because your family saved for your college years.

And, you sharp-eyed readers who have memorized the Chapter 11 formula, guess what? In your sophomore year at Bigbucks, your need will be greater because you'll have less savings. You just spent some of it on college.

How Much Money Will You Need?

Nobody really knows how much money you'll really need. A lot of people make guesses, some of them educated guesses. But even the people who set tuitions at colleges every year have no idea what they'll be charging two years from now. To plan ahead, the best you can do is make some educated guesses, along with the rest of us.

There is good news

Believe it or not, something about the cost of college is going down in the '90s. It's the rate at which tuitions are going up. I don't mean to confuse you, but you have to take good news wherever you can find it.

I'll put it more simply: Every year since 1991, the average increase in college tuitions has been less than the year before. If this trend continues, by the time you're ready for college, the annual increase could be minuscule. Just don't count on it. As long as inflation stays low, the annual tuition increases may continue to get smaller. But not even the most optimistic forecaster predicts that colleges will let a year go by without bumping up the costs a bit.

The dire predictions of college costs 20 years from now that you see in magazines and newspapers — and even in some planning books — show tuitions at the most expensive schools pushing close to $100,000 a year. That could happen if the assumptions made by those dire predictors are accurate. But assumptions are merely assumptions. Nobody knows for sure. And the trend I just mentioned suggests that maybe those assumptions are too dire.

The forecast formula

An often-used forecast of college costs — the one that shows how much you'll have to spend a year for the next two decades — is based on an annual increase of 7 percent. If anything increases 7 percent a year, it will just about quadruple in 20 years. At Harvard and Yale, the cost of tuition and room and board is now in the $28,000 neighborhood. Annual bumps of 7 percent will put it in the $112,000 neighborhood in the year 2018.

Are 7 percent increases likely? In the immediate future, probably not. For one thing, the nation's inflation rate is less than half of 7 percent. For another thing, not too long ago colleges were severely burned by negative publicity when they were raising costs 10 and 12 percent a year. College presidents, who have the final say on tuitions, don't like negative publicity. They try desperately to avoid it.

That's a big reason the annual rate of increase is steadily going down. The average increase for four-year private colleges in 1996 – 97 was 5 percent. In 1997 – 98, if inflation remains barely noticeable, the increase is not likely to be more than 5 percent. If the trend continues a few more years, a $100,000 tuition will be nowhere in sight 20 years from now.

By the way, when I talk about a $28,000 tuition today becoming $112,000 in the future, this is at the most expensive colleges — the high-prestige places that can charge that kind of money and still get four times as many applicants as they need. Most colleges aren't that expensive.

Which colleges charge what today

The College Board, which performs other valuable services in addition to giving us SATs I and II, recently put college costs into a better perspective with a little statistical exercise. It ranked all colleges by tuition charged for the 1994 – 95 school year. This is what it found:

- ✔ One-fourth of all private four-year colleges charge more than $12,751; one-fourth charge less than $6,840. That means half the private colleges in the country are between those two numbers.

- ✔ One-fourth of all public four-year colleges charge more than $3,068; one-fourth charge less than $1,818. So half the nation's public colleges are between those two numbers for residents of their states.

Remember, that's just tuition. Add another $4,000 or so for room and board to get the annual basic cost of on-campus college life. The College Board did that, too. This is what it found the average student was paying for tuition and room and board in 1996 – 97:

- ✔ At a four-year private college, $18,184
- ✔ At a four-year public college, $7,118
- ✔ At a two-year public college, $1,394

These, of course, are the sticker prices. Discounts, Pell Grants, and other goodies in the financial aid pot make the out-of-pocket average costs much lower.

What they'll charge ten years from now

What does this mean to you with college in your future? At 7 percent inflation, ten years from now, those average annual costs will be up to about $35,000 (four-year private), $14,000 (four-year public), and $2,600 (two-year public).

But pretend we don't have 7 percent inflation because, right now, we don't. Then those average prices will be lower. How much lower? I, along with the rest of the world, don't know. But for the sake of offering an educated guess, say the average increase for the next decade is the same as the increase for 1997 — 5 percent. When a child now in second grade enters college, the average annual cost of tuition and room and board will be

- ✔ At a four-year private college, $31,000
- ✔ At a four-year public college, $13,000
- ✔ At a two-year public college, $2,350

Remember also that you'll still be able to find hundreds of colleges below the average (and hundreds above, as well), just as you can today.

How Much Must You Save?

There is no ideal savings plan for college. Just as each student must find her own right colleges based on her own priorities, each family must determine its own savings plan based on its own financial condition. But here are some questions to consider:

- ✔ How much can you afford to put away each week, each month, each year?
- ✔ How much time do you have until the first tuition bill arrives?
- ✔ How receptive are you to the idea of borrowing money to pay for college? Are you more amenable to saving now and earning interest, or spending now and paying interest later? You have a choice.

Some mulling numbers

Mull over these questions and decide what's best for you and your family. But here are some guidelines to help you reach a decision as you mull:

- ✔ **Set aside $4 every working day, starting the day your child is born.** Invest the money where it earns 8 percent, and by the time your child is 18, you'll have $44,000. That should cover four years at Flagship State without even filling out a FAFSA. And it could be all you need for four years at Bigbucks U., if you get enough financial aid. If $4 each working day (or $80 a month) is too steep, make it $2. You'll still have a nice $22,000 nest egg at college time.

- ✔ **If your child is in second grade, put away $230 a month.** By the time he walks across the stage for his high school diploma, you'll have $50,000 tucked away. (That's $12,500 to cover each year's Expected Family Contribution.) Stash aside only $115 a month and you'll have a total of $25,000.

- ✔ **If Junior is in eighth grade, $680 a month will produce $50,000 by tuition time.** A mere $270 a month will add up to $20,000.

- ✔ **If college is two years away, you can still build up a $25,000 savings account by putting away $1,000 a month.** All these calculations assume that you're earning 8 percent on your savings. If you have an astute broker who can get you a better return, you won't have to save as much.

A work-free income source

Regular monthly savings is the simplest, but probably the most painful, method of planning to meet college costs. Nobody likes to save. Human instinct is to spend a dollar as soon as it enters your pocket. Humans need some discipline to repress that instinct and put away some money to make more money.

I don't like to call it saving because saving is such a boring activity. But boring as it may be, saving money requires less energy than anything else we do to make a buck. Saving is a way to get paid for doing nothing. It's a work-free source of income.

Two excellent volumes of advice on work-free income sources can be found on a bookstore shelf near this book. They are *Personal Finance For Dummies* and *Mutual Funds For Dummies,* both by Eric Tyson (IDG Books Worldwide, Inc.).

Juggling for Money

Saving isn't the only way to have more money available at college time. You also can plan ahead for the FAFSA, the form every student files (or should file) to qualify for financial aid. Sharp-eyed readers who have read Chapter 11 probably have already figured out ways to handle their money in the years before college to make their need — and their financial aid eligibility — greater when the time comes. In other words, you can juggle your own money so that you can get more aid.

If you're skeptical about this idea, you should know that nothing I am about to suggest is illegal, unethical, immoral, or frowned upon by picky financial aid directors. Some of the pickiest directors who have written their own advice books suggest some of the same steps. Just as careful tax planners take advantage of the tax laws to pay the minimum required by law, careful college planners can take advantage of the financial aid rules to get the maximum allowed by law.

Put the money in the right place

As you save $4 a day to build up that $44,000 I suggest in the section "Some mulling numbers" in this chapter, where are you putting it? I'm not asking if you're into Fidelity or Vanguard mutual funds. I'm asking in whose name is the money.

If you think you're being nice to your eight-year-old son by putting his college money in his name, think again. You're hurting him.

If you haven't read Chapter 11, or have forgotten it, I'm about to mention a key point that I discuss there. It's the formula to calculate assets in relation to college costs. The formula takes about 5 percent of parents' assets as part of the Expected Family Contribution to college costs. But it takes 35 percent of the student's assets. That's a huge difference! If the $44,000 savings is in Junior's name, a computer will tell him to spend $15,400 of it on his first year at Bigbucks U. If it's in his parents' name, only about $2,200 will go to the Expected Family Contribution. You increase your financial need by about $13,000 simply by changing the name on the savings account.

This asset-shifting tactic, from kids' names to parents' names, is the exact opposite of what you would do to save taxes. Kids' interest income is usually taxed at a lower rate than parents' money because kids usually have less of it. And for kids under 14, the first $600 of interest income is tax-free. So you'll have to do some strategic planning to balance your tax needs with your college cost needs.

Say no thanks to gifts

If Grandma or Aunt Cathy wants to give Stephanie Student a $1,000 savings bond for a college nest egg, don't reject their generosity, but ask them to please wait a while. Suggest that Grandma write Stephanie a nice note (grandmothers are good at nice notes) saying she has a $1,000 bond squirreled away for her college education, and when the time comes Grandma will write Stephanie a check. Meanwhile, the bond stays in Grandma's name. No formula yet has asked about grandparents' assets.

Tell the family to go to class

If Mom or Dad — or anyone else in the family — has been thinking about going to school for a class or two at night, wait until Steve and Stephanie are ready to be full-time college students.

Everyone enrolled for at least six credits is considered a student by the financial aid formula. Each family member who counts as a student substantially reduces the Expected Family Contribution for all other members.

Sell stocks early

If you plan to sell some investments — stocks, bonds, mutual funds — to raise college money, do it early in the student's high school junior year. Capital gains earned the year before you apply for financial aid (from January of eleventh grade to December of twelfth grade) count as income in determining financial need. Gains realized earlier don't count.

Pay the doctor early

Large medical and dental expenses not covered by insurance are deducted from your income by most of the high-priced colleges using PROFILE as a supplemental financial aid form. (See Chapter 14 for more on PROFILE.) Pay all the medical bills you can by December of the student's senior year.

Pay extra on the mortgage

The more money you can put into your home equity, the fewer dollars you'll show the government's computers that figure your Expected Family Contribution. Home equity is an asset the government's financial aid formula specifically ignores.

Give the max to IRAs

The same government computers that ignore home equity want to know about the money you put into retirement plans — IRA, 401(k), SEP, Keogh — but only in the calendar year before you apply for aid. All the retirement savings you have accumulated in the past are ignored. Fund your retirement plan to the maximum until January of eleventh grade, then slow down.

And get some good advice

All these suggestions are legal and can increase your eligibility for college financial aid. Some might fit with your other financial planning goals and strategies. Some might not. I mention them to give you food for thought.

As you plan for college, while at the same time planning for retirement and planning to save on taxes, your best-laid plans can contradict each other. A wise idea is to seek advice from an expert financial planner. I don't know enough about expert financial planners to recommend any, but *Personal Finance For Dummies* by Eric Tyson (published by IDG Books Worldwide, Inc.) is a good place to start. You also should check out *College Financial Aid For Dummies* by Dr. Herm Davis and Joyce Lain Kennedy (IDG Books Worldwide, Inc.).

You can lock in today's price

Yes, you can lock in today's tuition for your child even if she's not yet home from the maternity ward. Several plans — some public, some private — exist across the country allowing you to pay now and be assured of today's tuition even 18 years down the road. They're known generically as prepaid tuition plans, but no two are identical. And each of the plans has a downside that you should consider carefully before leaping into a commitment.

Public plans

Several states allow you to lock in tuition at current prices for their state colleges by paying the full cost now or in installments over the years. When your child is ready, the tuition is prepaid regardless of how much it has increased in the intervening years. At last count, 14 states offered such a plan and at least 20 were seriously considering one.

The advantages:

✔ You're making an investment for your child's education with very little risk. Unless your state government goes bankrupt, your money is safe.

✔ The minimum payments usually are less than required by other forms of investment such as mutual funds.

✔ Federal taxes on the money you earn from the investment are deferred until the student uses the money, and most states exempt the earnings from their state and local taxes.

The disadvantages:

✔ Most state plans require you to use the money at a public college in your state. This will be a severe restraint on a student's flexibility as she looks for a right college.

✔ The amount you earn on your investment is the amount tuitions increase. If tuitions in your state climb 4 percent a year, that's all you get. By assuming a little risk, you probably can find more profitable investments.

✔ If you move from the state before your child is in college, the plan still covers only the tuition for state residents. You will have to pay the difference between the in-state rate and the higher out-of-state tuition.

Private plans

The idea sprung a few years ago from the College Savings Bank of Princeton, N.J., and other financial institutions have come up with similar plans. These plans works like this: You deposit the cost of a year — or two, or three, or four — at Bigbucks U, all in a lump sum or in installments. When college time arrives, you'll get whatever a year at Bigbucks costs then. The downside: If Bigbucks' tuition increases 5 percent a year, that's all your money will be earning. And while you're waiting for your child to go to college, your interest earnings are subject to taxation. Check with your local banker for information. If a bank in your area offers such a plan, other bankers probably have heard about it.

Every lock-in plan has its own rules about what happens to your money if you don't go to the college for which you prepaid. Most will return your cash with interest. Some might make you forfeit it. Be sure you understand those rules before you make a commitment.

Part V
The Rest of the Story

In this part . . .

_T_his is the rest of the story. This part is where all the plots mentioned in Chapters 1–15 come together for a happy ending. In this part, I assume that you've chosen a college, you've made yourself attractive, and you've found the money. Here is where you pull all your work together to become a college student.

Chapter 16 helps you decide what to do after all those colleges accept you. Chapter 17 looks at your financial aid packages and helps you evaluate them to make your final decision. Chapter 18 is the rest of the story for students from abroad who are thinking about coming to the United States for college.

Chapter 16

You're Accepted, Now What?

· ·

· ·

The work is over. Now, you've reached fun time. Five of the six colleges to which you applied — including the two you like best — have accepted you. The sixth put you on a Wait List. After a few weeks of nervousness waiting for the mail, you're basking in the glow that comes with knowing you're really wanted. Now, you get to decide which of the five colleges you'll favor with your presence next fall.

And Now the Fun Begins

Once again, you're in control. It's just like the old days, back in your junior year, when colleges were filling your mailbox with pretty brochures pleading with you to apply. For a while there, you relinquished control of the process to the people who were considering your applications. Now you're the buyer again. Five colleges want you, but you can only enroll at one. Within days of their acceptance letters' arrival, all five probably will be in touch reminding you how wonderful they are.

For some of your friends, getting letters is not so much fun. A few of their top-choice colleges said no. They opened the mail to find the dreaded one-page letter that begins, "We regret to inform you . . . ."

Some of your friends have only themselves to blame. They didn't do the work you did. They didn't prepare their applications with tender loving care. They didn't bother following the simple instructions for reporting information about themselves. They didn't carefully polish their essays. They didn't seek out special teachers to write recommendations. They didn't read this book.

You think you're luckier than your friends. Well, maybe luck played a tiny role in your success. Much more important, though, was the record you compiled through four years of high school — the good grades, the tough courses, the commitment to activities. Without your solid record, luck would have been meaningless.

Okay, savor the glow for a day or two. Then sit down and start thinking again. You need to decide where you'll go to college.

The News Starts to Arrive

In Chapter 4, I assume some things about you to help illustrate the process of finding your right colleges. You start with the vast field of 3,500 degree-awarding colleges in the country. Eventually you find two you really like, plus two more where you think that you can be happy and thrive as a student. You apply to all four. Then you follow this book's good advice and apply to two more — a *reach* school, where your academic credentials are close but marginal, and a *safety valve* school that will be there if all else fails.

You are aware, in January when you mail your six applications, that it will be a long wait for the news. The schools at the head of your list, Topchoice U. and Equal College, announce their admission decisions in late March and early April. You really want to go to Topchoice or Equal — if you can get in and afford it. So regardless of when you hear from the other four, you know that your final decision will not be made until spring.

The safety valve works

The first college you hear from is Safety State, your backup school. In the middle of February, a few weeks after sending your application, you receive a letter from Safety saying you're in. Not a surprise, but at least a relief. You're now certain you won't be taking burger orders next fall.

A good news flash

A few weeks later comes the word from Threebie Tech, one of the colleges where you could be happy if your top two choices turn you down. Threebie uses rolling admissions — deciding on applications as they arrive. Threebie decided that you would be a fine addition to its campus. That's two out of two. Not bad.

In the last week of March, two more letters arrive. The first is from Fourmost U., the other college on your list in case the top two say no. Fourmost wants you. Then comes the same great news from Equal College, one of your top two choices. Your glow starts to spread.

One you didn't make . . . yet

You're not surprised that you haven't heard yet from the other two colleges. You know that Topchoice U. and Long Reach U. are among the selective group that announces all their decisions on April 1. By April 4, you've heard nothing. Your fingernails are getting a little frayed around the edges, and you think about calling the post office to ask whether it's delivering your mail. Then comes the letter from Long Reach, the school where your credentials are borderline, but you applied just in case.

The news isn't ideal. Long Reach cannot accept you for admission at this time. But if you're interested, the school will put you on a Wait List in case any vacancies occur. Enclosed is a card you must sign and return to get on the Wait List. (I'm using Wait List with capital letters because that's how most colleges use it. It's an entity with an official name: The Wait List.) You're disappointed but not shocked. You knew getting into Long Reach would be tough. You're pleased that it didn't reject you outright but said, "Maybe later."

At last! Hooray!

At this point, you're also a little worried. Long Reach is the first college that didn't say, "Please come." Could Topchoice also turn you down? You find out the next day when the Topchoice letter arrives. Your eyes start to sparkle a bit when you see how thick the envelope is. It has to contain more than a one-page rejection letter. You rip open the envelope, pull out the first page, and start to read: "I am delighted to inform you that Topchoice University is offering you admission to its freshman class in September. . . ." Your first reaction is "Whew!" Then the little sparkle becomes a golden glow that spreads all over. And you say to yourself, "Congratulations."

When will the news come?

One thing that's no secret about the college admission process is when you learn your fate. Every college admission office can give you either a precise date, or a pretty good estimate, of when a letter will be in the mail saying yes, no, or maybe.

The most selective colleges announce all their decisions — admissions, denials, and Wait Lists — on the same day. The eight Ivy League colleges, and many that compete for students with the Ivies, use April 1. Each April 1, cartons full of mail — a letter to every student who has applied — are trucked to a nearby post office. They arrive in students' homes a few days later.

Many selective colleges use earlier dates, usually in mid- to late March. They want to get their acceptance letters into students' hands

before the Ivy League letters arrive. Very few announce decisions after April 1. An admission officer will tell you what date the college makes its announcements.

All colleges with firm notification dates want a response from you by May 1. That has become the traditional deadline for students to decide where they'll enroll. If a college has not heard from you by May 1, it will offer your spot to someone else.

Colleges that use rolling admissions — considering each application as it arrives — typically take four to six weeks to let you know. Again, an admission officer at each school can give you a good estimate. The earlier you apply, when fewer applications are clamoring for the staff's attention, the less time it takes to give you a decision.

The Missing Piece

You have your choice of five colleges. You can become a freshman at any one of them merely by filling out an enrollment form, signing your name, and putting it in the mail. You rush to your collection of catalogs, brochures, and notes to remind yourself what you specifically liked about each college.

Whoa! Back up a minute. A key piece to the puzzle is still missing. If you haven't thought about it yet, one of your parents is probably reminding you right now. It's that nasty word again: money.

When you hear about financial aid

Three colleges say they want you, but they haven't said how much they want you to pay. You got a financial aid offer from Threebie Tech a month ago, after your acceptance letter arrived. And you know you can afford Safety State without aid. But you've heard nothing about money from Fourmost U., Equal College, or Topchoice U. And there's no way your parents can pay the tab at those places by simply writing a check.

You go back to your letter from Topchoice and read it carefully. Down near the bottom it tells you a financial aid offer will follow in a week to ten days. Equal and Fourmost also say their aid packages will soon be in the mail. You sigh and resign yourself to another wait.

Why the aid letter takes so long

If colleges could tell you how much money you'll get at the same time that they tell you that you're accepted, you would have an ideal situation. But it doesn't work that way. The financial aid office has been figuring how much aid you deserve to get ever since your application arrived. But it won't offer you a dime unless the admission office decides you're in. The aid folks can't make their final, precise money decisions until they get the final word on who has been accepted. Even then, many schools want to decide how valuable you are to them — compared to everyone else they've accepted — before they assemble your financial aid package. That's why there is a notification gap. (I look at financial aid packages and how to evaluate them in the next chapter.)

Recheck Your Choices

While you're waiting for your money offers, you can do things to start the final decision-making process. If you don't think of these items, the colleges that want you will remind you. You can check out those five schools to remember clearly their pluses and minuses — and to recall all the factors that put those five on your application list.

Start with your files. Review the catalogs and brochures you got in the mail. Check the notes you made from your research in the directories and from your campus visits. Ask yourself again:

- How strong is the program in the field you want to study?
- How closely does the campus fit your desires for size, location, and distance from home?
- What vibes did you get from the students?
- Are the professors and staff the kind of people you enjoy dealing with?

You already answered those questions once, when you decided Topchoice and Equal are where you would like to be. But in a busy senior year, some things slip out of your mind. Review them so that you remember how you felt when you applied.

Accept the invitations

High school seniors admitted by the Harvards, Yales, and Princetons aren't home many weekends in April. All the highly selective schools want decisions by May 1, and they use April to persuade you to accept their offers. They'll invite you to spend a few days on their campuses, talking at length with professors, living in their dorms, and meeting students — those now in college and others like you who have just been accepted.

Recruiting time starts all over again. Yale knows that if it wants a student, Harvard and Princeton likely want her, too. Each tries to sell her the glories of its campus during a personal visit.

The concept has spread below the Harvard-Yale level. If you're accepted by a college, it's a good bet that you'll be invited to some sort of campus event during the time that you're mulling its offer. You may be invited for a weekend visit or a reception on campus to meet students and faculty. If you live some distance away, you may be invited to a reception in your area attended by an assortment of deans, professors, and bright, articulate students.

When you receive an invitation, accept it if at all possible. Although you visited each campus before you applied, now it's time to return. You'll get a new sense of what you felt before. You may discover some things you missed the first time. Even if it's just a reception in a local hotel meeting room, be there. Talking to college officials as an accepted student will be different than when you visited as a potential applicant. You'll get more respect. You're now serious about each other. You've had several dates. Now you're talking marriage.

Even if you're not invited, go

All colleges don't have the marketing budgets to handle receptions for students they accept. They let you know they want you and hope you like them well enough to enroll. Don't let the lack of an invitation keep you away. Return to those campuses, also.

You don't need a formal agenda for a second campus visit. Just go back to see whether you feel the same way you felt a year earlier. Look for things you may have missed that can be important in your decisions. If you have lingering questions about something, perhaps courses in your field of study, ask for an appointment with someone who has answers. If you didn't stay in a dorm the first time, ask whether you can spend a night there now. The admission office will be eager to accommodate your requests. The college knows that you likely have more than one suitor, but it wants to be the one you choose for the walk to the altar.

The Wait List

Long Reach U., the place where you least expected to be successful, did not accept you. But it didn't reject you either. The school offered you a compromise called the Wait List.

What Wait List means

What Long Reach is saying is, "You're not among the best we got this year; then again, you're not among the worst. If you want to take your chances that some of those better people won't enroll, we'll keep your application alive."

The decision is up to you. If you'd like to stay in consideration, sign the card that says so and return it. If the college doesn't hear from you, its Wait List won't include your name.

The Wait List is a common phenomenon at colleges that have more applications than they need. Each year, these colleges try to guess precisely how many students they must accept to fill their freshman classes, but their guesses frequently are wrong. If year after year Old Siwash gets one-third of the students it accepts, it will send out 1,800 acceptance letters to fill its 600 freshman spots. But, whoops, this year only 500 of those 1,800 enroll by May 1. Old Siwash suddenly needs 100 more freshman bodies. Out comes the Wait List.

Why they use the Wait List

A Wait List generally is used for one of three purposes, depending on the college:

1. **As a supplemental acceptance list.** A college intentionally will accept fewer students than necessary to fill its class, as a hedge in case more enroll than anticipated. For example, an all-residential college with 600 available dorm beds and a historical one-third enrollment rate logically should accept 1,800 applicants to get 600 freshmen. But if 700 of those 1,800 show up, the school will have a very red face. It will have nowhere to put 100 of them. So the college takes fewer than 1,800. And when its one-third yield occurs again, it will fill the remaining slots from its Wait List. The school does the same thing every year.

Ah, you noticed — that word yield I tossed into the next to last sentence in the preceding paragraph. This word is jargon that occasionally slips into admission officers' everyday conversation. A college's *yield* is the percentage of accepted students who enroll. Harvard's yield usually is around 75 percent. Stanford's is about 55 percent. At some colleges, the yield is as low as 25 percent.

2. **As a hedge against a bad year.** A college will accept the students it thinks it needs, but keep a Wait List against events beyond its control. One such event would be fewer students enrolling than it expects. Another would be fewer students than expected enrolling at another college, say — because I'm using its name a lot here — Harvard. If Harvard takes 50 students off its Wait List, ten of them may have already signed up for Old Siwash. Suddenly ten students on the Old Siwash Wait List get word that they're in. And those ten create ten new vacancies at Flagship State. This has a domino effect.

3. **As a consolation prize.** Some colleges rarely admit anyone off a Wait List. They use the list to make many of their rejected applicants feel better.

How do you know which way your college uses a Wait List? You don't. If you ask, you'll probably be told that it's used to fill vacancies if enough students don't enroll. That will be true. Some candid admission officers may tell you — if you ask — how many Wait Listed students eventually were accepted in the past. But it's unlikely that anyone on campus will offer a forecast of how many vacancies will occur this year. They don't want to get your hopes up. Or down.

An astute high school counselor, who has dealt with the college for years, will have a good idea how often the Wait List is used. If you're lucky enough to have an astute counselor, seek his advice. And your friends at that college may have heard others' experiences with the Wait List, or even have been on the list themselves. Ask them, too.

The Deposit Dilemma

Back in February, you got the good news of being accepted from the one rolling admissions school to which you applied. But it came with some bad news. Threebie Tech accepted you for admission, but said it needed a $200 deposit to hold your spot. Deposit requests are common, and they vary in size with the college. Colleges feel a cash deposit is very clear evidence that you are serious about enrolling.

You had a problem. You knew your top two choices would not give you a decision for a few weeks. But you wanted to be sure you had a spot at Threebie, in case the others turned you down. You called a Threebie admission officer — the same one you interviewed a year earlier. She said they needed the $200, or they'd give your place to someone else. But she assured you that if you change your mind later, the deposit would be refunded. So you sent Threebie its money.

The same dilemma faces thousands of students every spring. One college wants a deposit before another college makes a decision. Most colleges understand the spot you're in and will refund your money if you go elsewhere. But ask to be sure.

Call the admission officer that you know and explain candidly that you can't make a firm decision until you hear from every college. The odds are high that the deposit will be refundable. If the admission office gets hard-nosed and says you lose your money if you change your mind, that might be a good reason for dumping the college from your list. It's not a customer-oriented attitude.

Wait for the Other Shoe

Now that you have revisited the campuses that want you, checked all your old records, and sought more advice from friends, teachers, and counselors, you still need the missing piece before you can decide where to go. You must find out how much each college expects you to pay and how it expects you to pay it. I take look at how to handle your money offers in Chapter 17.

Chapter 17
Evaluating the Money Offers

· ·

In This Chapter

▶ Looking at five colleges and their costs

▶ Examining four financial aid offers

▶ Comparing the packages

▶ Making your final decision

· ·

*W*hen you applied to five colleges, you didn't think about money. You knew that their costs, published in directories and catalogs, range all over the place. One school's advertised tab is over $26,000 a year. The least expensive, your safety valve school, costs just $7,200.

But the reason you didn't think about money was because you didn't know how much of those sticker prices you would have to pay. Now, in the spring of your high school senior year, you're about to find out.

Five Colleges, Five Costs

Early in the game, in Chapter 11, you can figure the total Cost of Attendance for each college on your application list — if you didn't, you need to get this piece of information now. The Cost of Attendance is more than just tuition and room and board. Cost of Attendance includes books and supplies, transportation costs of going to and from college, and personal expenses while you're there (the toothpaste and laundry factor).

You can get some good estimates of those expenses from financial aid officers when you visit the campuses. And they can tell you the total Cost of Attendance they use to determine your financial need. For the five colleges that accepted you, these are the total Costs of Attendance (figured with their input):

> ✔ Topchoice U. $25,380
>
> ✔ Equal College $17,950
>
> ✔ Threebie Tech $14,360

> ✔ Fourmost U. $24,350
>
> ✔ Safety State $7,200

From these totals, deduct your Expected Family Contribution to come up with that magic number, your financial need at each college.

Your Contribution

Your Expected Family Contribution for a year at college — also known as your EFC — is the amount a government computer expects you to pay after crunching your family's financial information through a complicated formula. Often your EFC has no relation to the amount that you're willing to pay. But that's another story. Most colleges take the computer's word for your EFC. Some colleges calculate their own EFC after asking you for more information on another form. (The formula and related information are described in Chapter 11.)

You use the worksheet in Chapter 11 to calculate your Expected Family Contribution. Your EFC comes to about $9,000. You can live with that amount. After all, your parents have $30,000 stashed away for your college bills and, with a little effort, you and they can handle $9,000 a year.

Then, a month after you submitted your financial aid application, you received a blue printout from the computer titled *Student Aid Report*. This printout announced that your official EFC is $9,100. Not bad. You must have understood the worksheet to come so close.

Your Need Five Ways

Your financial need is the number used to play the financial aid game. Most colleges say that they try to meet your need. Some do a better job than others. Your need differs at every college because it's determined by subtracting your Expected Family Contribution ($9,100 in this example) from each college's Cost of Attendance. Thus, at the five colleges accepting you, your need is

> ✔ Topchoice U. $16,280
>
> ✔ Equal College $8,850
>
> ✔ Threebie Tech $5,260
>
> ✔ Fourmost U. $15,250
>
> ✔ Safety State $0 (Your EFC is greater than the Cost of Attendance)

The numbers are your need figured five times by the government's computers using the government's formula. All colleges must use that need to determine your eligibility for federal aid programs. Colleges can figure a different need for giving away their own money — and many of them do. (See Chapter 11.)

Each college on your list finds out your need at the same time you do. They receive a report, similar to your blue printout, from the computer. The financial aid offices then begin assembling a package of grants, loans, and subsidized jobs that will come close to meeting your need. After you're accepted by the colleges, those packages are fine-tuned and massaged into the money offers that wind up in your mailbox.

The Jargon of Award Letters

To better understand what's in the letters you get from financial aid officers, you should know some terms that the officers use as they prepare your packages. You probably won't see many of these terms in your letters. But knowing what these terms mean can help when you call the financial aid office with questions. If you can toss the word *gap* casually into a conversation with a financial aid officer, she might pay more attention.

There will be no quiz. The following translations are for your information only.

Award letter: This is the letter that comes to you describing the financial aid a college is offering you. Everyone who applies for aid eventually gets an award letter. Some award letters contain no awards at all. They say, "Sorry, you get nothing." These letters are really rejection letters.

Package: This term refers to what's offered in your award letter — the combination of grants, loans, jobs, discounts, and other stuff that's in your financial aid package. This offer is known on campuses far and wide simply as your package.

Institutional grant: A major component of many aid packages, the Institutional grant designates money that the college itself (the institution) is giving you to supplement what you get from other aid programs. But this is not really a grant. No money changes hands. Institutional grant is an official term for a discount off the published sticker price.

Preferential packaging: Any good financial aid director seeking to improve the quality of his school's student body uses preferential packaging. Some even will tell you up front that they do it. Preferential packaging means the best students get the best packages. A student high on a college's desirability list will get a package with a larger ratio of grants to loans — maybe no loans at all — than a student who is marginally attractive. The aid package thus is used as one more recruiting tool. If you don't have to borrow money to go to College X, you're likely to prefer it over other colleges where you must get loans to enroll.

Gapping: This means that your aid package doesn't meet your full need as calculated by the formula. If your need at College X is $10,000 and it offers you $8,000 in aid, you've been gapped. Being gapped is not very pleasant. You know that a college isn't all that concerned whether you enroll there or go somewhere else when it gaps you.

Is This an Offer You Can't Refuse?

Now comes the moment — or moments — of truth. The day the mail carrier delivers your financial aid award letter is just as crucial to your college future as the acceptance letters from admission offices. The award letters tell you how much you'll pay. (By the way, descriptions of all the financial aid programs mentioned here are in Chapter 13.)

Safety State

The first school you hear from is your safety valve, nearby Safety State. It's no surprise when the letter arrives saying that you don't qualify for financial aid. You know your Expected Family Contribution is about $9,000. And you know Safety State's cost, even with books and personal expenses, is about $7,200. You have no need at Safety, and you never expected any aid from there.

Like almost all small state colleges, Safety State doesn't have any money of its own to give away to students it likes. But that's no problem at this point. After all, Safety is still your backup, in case all else fails. You picked Safety because you were certain that you could get accepted and afford the cost.

Threebie Tech

In early March, Threebie accepts you as a freshman. Then, two weeks later comes the rest of the good news: Threebie is offering you money. At last, you get an idea of what one of your top four colleges will cost.

Threebie's award letter gives you a fairly simple package. The school offers a campus job in the Work-Study program at which you can earn $800; a subsidized Stafford Loan, repayable after you leave college, for $2,625 — the maximum a freshman can borrow in the program; and an institutional grant (discount) of $1,835.

The letter says that the total aid offer is $5,260. Just to be sure, you get out your calculator and add up the package. They're right: $5,260. Then you pull out your records for Threebie. The school's total cost is $14,360. Your EFC is $9,100. Subtract one from the other and, hey, you get $5,260.

Threebie Tech has met your full need. You can go there for an out-of-pocket cost of about $9,000, which is what you were planning. You think, "Hey, this financial aid stuff isn't so bad." Now you decide to forget Safety State. Even if everyone else says no, Threebie Tech has accepted you and given you a price you can afford.

Fourmost U.

By the end of March, two more colleges accept you, and shortly thereafter they check in with award letters. The first comes from Fourmost U., one of the two colleges on your list where the cost is over $20,000. You open Fourmost's letter and look quickly at the bottom line: $13,785.

Your immediate reaction is "Wow! Thirteen grand! Almost three times as much as Threebie offers." Now you're starting to enjoy this. Then you look at the elements in the package. Fourmost offers a Work-Study job for $1,200; two loans — a Perkins for $2,460 (5 percent interest) and a Stafford for $2,625 (7.4 percent); and an institutional grant — a discount off the sticker price — of $7,500. You add up the numbers and, sure enough, the total is $13,785.

You pull out your records on Fourmost. The cost is $24,350. Subtracting $9,100 makes your need $15,250. Whoa! Wait a minute! Your excitement is fading fast. Fourmost's package that looked so impressive initially does not meet your need. The package is almost $1,500 short. You are expected to come up with about $10,500 from your own funds to spend a year at Fourmost. Yikes! You've been gapped.

Being gapped is not pleasant. Fourmost has accepted you, but you're not on the priority list of students that it would like to see in September. Your ego feels a little deflated. Fourmost is dropping fast from the list of places that you'd like to attend. You still have Threebie Tech though, and you haven't heard yet from your top two choices.

Equal College

Finally comes the news from Equal, one of the two schools at the top of your list. Your first preference has always been Topchoice U., but Equal, in your mind, is just as good. You think that you can be very happy at either college.

After your Fourmost experience, you decide to prepare yourself in advance of opening Equal's letter. So you check your need. Equal's cost is $17,950. Subtract $9,100 and your need is $8,850. Okay, what does Equal say? You open the letter and check the bottom line: $8,825. Hmmm. Interesting number. Equal has not met your full need, and technically you've been gapped. But the difference is just $25, such a small gap (you might call it a tiny slit). Your out-of-pocket cost at Equal would be $9,125, or $25 more than at Threebie. You figure you could save that $25 by not going to four movies.

Now you look at the pieces of the package. Equal offers you $2,000 in a Work-Study job, which means that you would be working about twice as much time as at Threebie. The package also includes two loans — a $1,500 Perkins and a $2,625 Stafford. And the school tosses in a discount of $2,700. Why, you wonder, couldn't they make it $2,725 and meet your need? Maybe they only give institutional grants in round numbers. Anyway, you figure that Equal's package is close enough. The school stays on your list as you await the word from Topchoice.

Topchoice U.

Topchoice is the last to check in because the school announces all its admission decisions April 1, later than any other school to which you applied. But Topchoice is still your first preference, even though it's the most expensive school on your list. The total cost at Topchoice, including books and transportation, is $25,380. But if everything else were equal, it's where you would like to be next fall.

You remember the feeling of euphoria when you found out that you were accepted by Topchoice. You remember fretting for ten days as you were waiting for the financial aid letter. In the meantime, you checked your need: $16,280 ($25,380 minus $9,100).

Now the award letter has finally arrived. You open the envelope. And suddenly that same feeling of euphoria comes over you. Can this be for real?

The total package is $17,280. Your first-choice college is meeting all your need — plus $1,000! Topchoice is offering you some merit money, above your need, just because it likes you. You are on its priority list. You are one of the students the school hopes will enroll, so you get a financial incentive. You can go to Topchoice U. for $8,100. Who needs to think about it any more?

Fortunately, your parents do. (I told you parents are wise. And they should be allowed to give input here because they're paying most of the bills.) Mom suggests that maybe you should read the whole letter from Topchoice to see how that 17 grand breaks down. And Dad quickly chimes in with, "Yeah. And how much do they want us to borrow?" So you read on.

You can pick and choose

A financial aid offer is not a take-it-or-leave-it proposition. When your award letter comes from a college listing the components of your financial aid package, you're allowed to pick and choose the items that you like.

At least that's the way it works at the over-whelming majority of colleges. A few fussy colleges will insist that you take the whole thing. Those that do will let you know in their award letters. But typically, the choices are yours.

If you have a phobia against going into debt, you can accept the grants and subsidized jobs offered by the college, but decline the low-interest loans. If you'd rather not work at school, you can decline the job and keep the rest.

Each award letter must be signed and returned to the financial aid office, indicating whether you accept or decline the package. Most letters will include instructions on how to accept some items and reject others. If your letter comes with no such instructions, call the financial aid office and ask.

But if you call, be patient. Busy signals are extremely common on financial aid office phones during the two to three weeks after award letters go out.

Topchoice offers a $1,000 campus job, a $2,955 Perkins Loan, a $2,625 Stafford Loan, and an institutional grant (discount) of $10,700. That's $17,280, or $8,100 short of Topchoice's total Cost of Attendance. Your need, indeed, is met and then some.

Comparing the Offers

Despite your strong inclination to pick up the Topchoice offer and sign it, I suggest you wait. Take a look at your four offers side by side to compare them.

When you list them together, here's how your packages compare:

	Topchoice	*Equal*	*Threebie*	*Fourmost*
Total Cost	$25,380	$17,950	$14,360	$24,350
Aid Offered				
Campus job	1,000	2,000	800	1,200
Perkins Loan	2,955	1,500	0	2,460
Stafford Loan	2,625	2,625	2,625	2,625
Grant (discount)	10,700	2,700	1,835	7,500
Total Aid	17,280	8,825	5,260	13,785
Cost to You	8,100	9,125	9,100	10,565

Now, to answer the question "How much will you have to borrow?" look at them another way.

	Topchoice	Equal	Threebie	Fourmost
Current Cost to You	$8,100	$9,125	$9,100	$10,565
Loans	5,580	4,125	2,625	5,085
Total Cost to You	13,680	13,250	11,725	15,650

And the totals don't include interest on those loans that starts accumulating after you leave college.

Selecting the One That's Best

Which of the four aid packages is best for you? You can answer this question in many ways, depending on how you define best. If you're looking for the least expense while you're in college *(Current Cost to You),* Topchoice wins. If you look at total debt, Threebie is best and Topchoice is a poor fourth. If you're looking for lowest cost over the long run, Threebie wins with Topchoice and Equal virtually tied for second. But Equal wants you to work your first year in college — probably at minimum wage — to earn $2,000. Topchoice will give you a job for $1,000. Threebie asks you to earn only $800. Does that make Threebie better?

There are no clear-cut answers. Just as you're the only one who can decide on your right colleges, now again only you — and your parents, if they're paying — can decide which aid package is best. You must ask yourself these questions:

- ✔ How much do you want to borrow?
- ✔ How much do you want to work at college?
- ✔ And, of course, how strongly do you feel about attending each college?

Find answers to those questions, put them in a bowl, and stir well. Out of the mix will pop your decision. The bowl, as you probably have figured out, is your mind.

Consider the cost of loans

When it comes to borrowing money, your parents have experience. They've probably borrowed large sums for their house and their cars.

The marriage penalty

Are the financial aid rules fair? Government and college officials who deal with aid programs insist they're as fair as they can be. But the rules do come with one particular inequity — a marriage penalty.

One blatant example is an adult who lives with a boyfriend or girlfriend. The unmarried mate's income is not considered for financial aid eligibility. If they get married, however, the spouse's income is counted. An adult college student stands to lose considerable financial aid by tying the knot.

Then consider two separate cases, those of Brian and Karen. Although their names aren't real, their financial aid applications are very real. They both applied for aid to the same $20,000-plus college. Brian's parents earn $112,000 a year. Karen's parents make $48,000. Brian got an aid package totaling $18,675. Karen's package was $14,125.

Doesn't seem fair, does it? The reason for the difference is Brian's parents are divorced. He lives with his mother, who is scraping by on a $27,000 salary. Most of his parents' six-figure income is earned by his father, whom he hasn't seen in several years. Only his mother's earnings are counted by the government formula.

Karen lives with her happily married parents. Both parents' incomes are counted toward Karen's need. Thus her financial aid is less than Brian's.

Some colleges would insist that Brian's father disclose his financial information and count it in determining his eligibility for their own college money. But other colleges simply ignore the noncustodial divorced parent, as does the government.

Brian's parents neither live with each other nor speak to one another. But they're still Brian's parents. If they were still married, he would get very little aid. Is Brian being rewarded because his parents are divorced? Or is Karen being penalized because her parents are married? Financial aid officers have been debating these questions for years. And they still don't have answers.

When you lay out the side-by-side comparison of each school's package, you or your parents should do some quick arithmetic. If your packages stay roughly the same for four years, you'll borrow more than $22,000 to earn a degree at Topchoice, but just over $16,000 at Equal. Pull out a calculator and a loan amortization booklet that tells you monthly payments on loans of various sizes and interest rates (you can buy one at an office supply store for $3.95) and start punching buttons to figure what you would pay — based on each loan program's interest rate — for those debts.

The best guess, which is a good one, is that you'd pay about $240 a month if you take the full ten years to repay your Topchoice debt. For a degree at Equal, your monthly payment would be about $175. That's a difference of $65 a month, or $7,800 over ten years. It's another ingredient to be stirred into the bowl.

Should you borrow?

This question rages in households across the country every year: Should a student, or a student's parents, go into heavy debt to pay for a college degree? Arguments are strong on both sides.

Some parents adamantly say, "No!" I have talked to students who say they had to pass up their first-choice colleges because their parents would not seek loans. A few parents even refuse to fill out the financial aid forms — and so cut off their kids from any form of help — because they don't want to disclose their financial information. A woman at a Midwest college said her father told her, "I'll do anything in the world for you except borrow money."

Are these parents being wise? That's a question each family must answer for itself. But as you wrestle with it, consider these facts. Your parents probably have borrowed 75 percent of the cost of a new car without blinking an eye. They've probably borrowed 90 percent of the cost of a house (it's called a mortgage) without a serious second thought. Yet they shudder and balk at the thought of borrowing one-third of the cost of a college degree.

Is college less important than a home or a car? Given today's stagnant real estate market, it certainly gives you the best return of those three investments. People with degrees earn more than people without them. And banks don't repossess or foreclose on degrees. Think about it.

Negotiating a Better Deal the Second Time

In Chapter 14, I talk about negotiating a better deal if your financial circumstances change after you apply for aid. Now you have a second chance to negotiate something better, after the award letters arrive.

That extra $1,000 that Topchoice U. tossed into your pot (see the aid package comparisons) gives you leverage. Now you can get on the phone to financial aid officers at Equal College and Threebie Tech and inform them of the Topchoice offer. (You're forgetting Fourmost. You haven't forgiven it for the insult of gapping you.) You tell Equal and Threebie that it looks like you'll have to take the Topchoice offer. But if they could match it, you'd certainly give them equal consideration. Depending on how attractive you are to the other two schools, a financial aid officer may suddenly find another $1,000 or more to offer as a tuition discount.

Financial aid directors won't like the fact that I'm telling you all this. But there's no reason why you shouldn't know it because hundreds of other students are negotiating better deals every year. One father who just went through the process compared it to buying a car: "You take the best offer, go to a dealer down the street, and ask him to top it." Hundreds of students wouldn't try it every year if it doesn't work.

The only colleges that can negotiate deals with you are colleges that give away their own money, usually in tuition discounts. The government's aid programs have rules that each college must follow. A financial aid director can waive the government rules through professional judgment (see Chapter 14); however, such a waiver is not a common occurrence. But when an aid director deals with his own money, he can use it at whim to meet his school's priorities. If enrolling you is a priority, you have a fine chance of negotiating for more.

The Choice Is Up to You

Go back to the key question still left unanswered. Where will you go to college?

You have narrowed your decision to two schools. You threw out Fourmost because it gapped you, and you eliminated Threebie because, well, you like the other two better. Threebie would cost — including debt — about $2,000 a year less, but you figure you'll handle the extra loans to get a college you really want. The two colleges that led your list when you applied, Topchoice U. and Equal College, are the two left in your race.

You're certain, from your campus visits and your second visits, that you can be happy at either school. Each has a strong program in your major. You feel comfortable with the students on each campus. You felt a rapport with the professors with whom you talked. Only one factor is tilting your feelings toward Topchoice, and that's the quieter social life at Equal. But in your big picture, that's a very minor problem.

When you look at the money, the big difference is debt. You'll spend less at Topchoice while you're there, but you'll owe much more when you leave. The difference is $65 a month in payments for the first ten years of your working career. Is it worth $65 a month to go to the college at the top of your list?

That's the last question you must answer. I can't help you with this one. The choice is up to you.

Chapter 18

What If You're Coming to the U.S.?

In This Chapter

▶ Realizing that the welcome mat is out

▶ Starting at square one

▶ Collecting information

▶ Discovering the three musts

▶ Getting financial aid

*A*merican colleges must be doing something right if so many students from other countries find them attractive. About 400,000 foreigners are enrolled at four-year colleges in the United States, and thousands of new students from other nations arrive at American airports every year. This chapter is for non-U.S. students thinking about attending college in the United States. Tips for Americans thinking about college in another country are in Chapter 1.

Okay, I've called you foreigners once, but that's the last time. You are foreign by definition because you come from other countries. But that word can have a negative connotation in the United States. People often use the word to mean residents of other countries that they don't like. So for the rest of this chapter, I will use *noncitizens.* That's because I am talking about U.S. colleges, and you are not citizens of the U.S. Noncitizens is also more politically correct. If you don't know what *politically correct* means, don't worry about it. You'll find out soon enough after you get here.

This is Chapter 18, near the back of the book, for a reason. The title of this part is The Rest of the Story. This is the rest of the story for noncitizens. Almost everything in Chapters 1 through 17 applies to you. This chapter tells you what doesn't, and what else does.

Canadians Read This, Too

Canadians may not feel like they're going abroad when they travel to the United States, but this chapter is for them, too. This is advice for all students who are not U.S. citizens — including citizens of Canada. But some requirements that I mention later don't apply to people coming to the U.S. from Canada. Canadians, of course, don't need a visa to enter the U.S. And all except those from Quebec don't have to worry about proving they know English.

You're Welcome

Be assured that United States colleges want you. All noncitizens who want to attend college in the United States and who are qualified to enroll will find colleges ready to welcome them with open arms. The basic rule of supply and demand is at work, and it applies to everyone. Colleges are not getting enough students from their traditional source — American high schools. So they're actively looking elsewhere to fill their classes. And elsewhere includes the other countries of the world. Your francs, lire, and yen are just as good as dollars in a college bank account.

Some colleges send representatives to other countries to seek out promising students and help them with the task of applying and enrolling. Almost all colleges have programs on their campuses to make students from other countries feel welcome. Most have special departments to deal with the needs of international students.

Now that I've told you how much you're wanted, here's the bad news. You can't just pick a college you like, apply, and get in. The process doesn't work that way. Everything I say in Chapters 9 and 10, about how colleges look at students and how students can make themselves more attractive, goes for noncitizens as well. If you apply to Harvard, you'll be one of 14,000 applicants. Harvard accepts about 2,000 students each year. You'll be competing with everyone else in the pool for one of 2,000 acceptance letters.

Harvard, of course, is an extreme. Most U.S. colleges are not so competitive. But the vast majority of colleges have minimum academic criteria and accept only those students who meet their standards. Applying to a college in most cases does not mean automatic acceptance.

Where Do You Start?

Noncitizens considering college in the U.S. should start at the same place as everyone else. Make a list. Identify the reasons you want to go to college and what you want from a college. Then pick up a directory of U.S. colleges and look for those schools that meet your needs.

Read the advice this book offers in Chapters 1 through 8 about finding the colleges that are right for you. The advice is for students everywhere.

Information Sources

You may not have access to the wide variety of directories and reference books that Americans find on the shelves of their neighborhood bookstores and libraries. Some directories are sold internationally, but you may have to search, or ask in a bookstore, to find them.

One excellent information source comes from The College Board, the most prolific purveyor of material to help students get into college. *The College Handbook Foreign Student Supplement* is a condensed version of The College Board's huge directory of all U.S. colleges. This supplement comes with a 30-page, clearly written explanation of many things you'll need to know about becoming a U.S. student. If you can't find it for sale where you live, write to College Board Publications, Box 886, New York, NY 10101-6992.

Other good sources of information include

✔ **American schools abroad.** Two large groups of schools exist to serve American children living in other countries. One is operated by the U.S. government for military dependents. The other is a private network of schools for Americans, usually staffed by Americans. These high schools send many of their graduates to U.S. colleges. Their counselors and teachers can be fine sources of advice.

✔ **U.S. embassies.** The U.S. government, through its embassies, operates advising centers in countries from Albania to Zimbabwe for noncitizens seeking information about the United States. The centers know much about U.S. colleges and regularly deal with requests for college information. Check with a U.S. embassy or consulate for the location of an advising center near you. The embassies also are aware of U.S. college representatives visiting their countries to recruit students.

✔ **Your universities.** Colleges and universities in other countries have close relationships with U.S. colleges. All universities are part of the worldwide higher education community. The likelihood is that a university in your country will have information on U.S. colleges, probably in its library.

✓ **Visiting professors.** U.S. college professors love to travel abroad. They love to do research in other countries. And they love to talk. (They earn much of their incomes by talking.) If you know of U.S. professors working or traveling near you, ask for some of their time to talk about U.S. colleges. Chances are good that your request will be enthusiastically granted.

✓ **Your friends.** This is the same advice I offered earlier to all students. Trust your friends, especially those whose opinions you respect. If you have friends who have been to the United States, ask them about U.S. colleges. These friends are fine information sources.

Your Three Musts

Before you get too far into the college-searching process, you should be aware of some things you absolutely will need. There are three musts for a noncitizen to become a U.S. college student. These musts are required either by the U.S. government or by the colleges themselves. You may already have them. If not, one or two may take a little work. These three musts are

✓ **Documents to enter the United States.** In other words, a passport and a visa.

✓ **The ability to communicate in a college environment.** In other words, use English well enough to understand lectures and be able to write papers with a high level of proficiency.

✓ **Proof that you can pay a college for educating you.** In other words, money.

Take a look at the reasons they're required for you.

Documents

This one is easy but essential. Noncitizens in the U.S. without valid documents are known as illegal aliens and are not welcome at U.S. colleges. To enter the United States legally, you must obtain a passport from your government and a visa from the U.S. government. Getting a student visa, good for the duration of your college career, usually is a routine procedure. A college that has accepted you will send you the necessary forms and advise you on how to apply. The college will also certify to the government that you are a student.

English

U.S. colleges conduct their business and transmit their knowledge in English. To function as a college student, the ability to use English is essential. And that ability is necessary in four areas:

- ✔ **Reading.** As a student, you must read textbooks, articles, and other written material. If you can read and understand this book, you're okay. If you need a dictionary to help with some words, fine. Bring one along.

- ✔ **Writing.** Almost every college class requires written assignments. The assignments must be written in English. You must be able to write in English so that those who read your words will understand what you say.

- ✔ **Speaking.** Can you communicate to others in spoken English so that you are understood? If so, you'll make it as an English-speaking college student.

- ✔ **Understanding.** Can you listen to someone speak English for 30 minutes and understand what is being said? If you don't know what a professor is saying in her lecture, you won't be able to cope as a student.

Before a college accepts you, it will want to know how good your English is. If you're from a country where English is not the principal language, most colleges will require you to take an English proficiency test. The most common is the Test of English as a Foreign Language, usually called TOEFL (pronounced *TOE-full*).

The TOEFL comes in three parts and tests your ability to understand written and spoken English and to write in English that others can understand. A college that requires the TOEFL will have a minimum score that you must obtain to qualify. Those minimums are listed in the directories marketed abroad. And any college will tell you its cutoff score.

Money

With very few exceptions, U.S. colleges are nonprofit institutions. But they still need money to survive. Tuitions paid by students are a principal source of colleges' incomes. If you're living on campus, the cost of housing and meals (usually called room and board) is added. The cost of tuition and room and board per year ranges from over $26,000 at some private colleges to under $5,000 at some small state-operated colleges. (The different kinds of colleges are described in Chapter 1.) Be aware that every state-operated college in the U.S. has two tuition prices — one for residents of its state and one for everyone else. You will have to pay the higher price.

For you, I have good news and bad news. The bad news is that most U.S. colleges won't accept you unless you tell them where you're getting the money to pay its bills. The good news is that some of the money may come from the college itself as tuition discounts. (See Chapter 14.)

When a college sends you an application, it will also send you a document on which you must identify your financial support. If your parents are providing you money, the form requests their financial information. If you are being sponsored by an American family, your hosts must supply the data. If you've earned scholarships, you must report them. A college does not want to allow you in the country as its student — and it must certify that you are a student so that you can get a visa — unless it's convinced that you can pay the bills.

Financial Aid Is Available

Does the name Hakeem Olajuwon mean anything to you? He's one of the best-known professional basketball players in the United States. He came to the U.S. on a student visa 15 years ago. And the entire cost of his college education was paid by the college he attended, the University of Houston. Olajuwon received what's known as a *free ride* — four years of college free — because even then he was an outstanding basketball player.

Athletics is one way of getting a tuition discount, or having tuition waived altogether. Good basketball players from other countries are in demand by those U.S. colleges where winning basketball games is a high priority. Discounts (also called scholarships) are available for other sports as well. Many Canadian students, for example, are riding free at U.S. colleges because they're excellent hockey players.

But you don't have to be an athlete to get financial aid, as you can see in Chapter 14. Everything in that chapter applies equally to U.S. citizens and non-citizens. If you're an attractive student — that is, someone a college would like very much to have in its student body — the college will offer you some of its own money in the form of a tuition discount. Just like American students, you won't have to pay the full sticker price.

Many colleges also offer aid to noncitizens based on their financial need. They have special forms for you, different from the financial aid applications used by U.S. citizens, because they want different information about you. In addition to requesting information about your family's income and assets, the form will ask such things as the source of your emergency funds in the United States, and the restrictions your country imposes on currency exchange. If you ask for a financial aid form, a college will send you one. Some send it automatically along with your application for admission.

One part of this book you can ignore, however, is the discussion of U.S. government financial aid programs. Noncitizens are not eligible for U.S. government aid — Pell Grants, Stafford Loans, SEOGs, and the other stuff I mention in Chapter 12. These programs are only for U.S. citizens.

A good source of financial aid information is *Funding for U.S. Study: A Guide for Foreign Nationals*, from the Institute of International Education, 809 UN Plaza, New York, NY 10017-3580.

Other Different Stuff

Just about everything you read in the rest of this book — except the parts on government financial aid — pertains to you. Like everyone else, you should ask questions. Make lists. Ask more questions. Make more lists. Prepare your college application just as a U.S. citizen would. (See Chapter 10.) A college will read an essay to find out the same things about a student in Iran as a student in Indiana. But you should get a little extra advice about a few things.

Questions

In addition to all the questions a U.S. student asks about a college — size, location, housing — you might have a few more:

- ✓ **What percentage of the student body is from outside the United States?** If the number is high, it indicates a campus on which you will be welcome.

- ✓ **What organizations exist specifically for international students?** If there are none, it's probably not a right college for you.

- ✓ **What level of English-language proficiency is required?**

- ✓ **Is there an opportunity to improve in English?** Some colleges have classes in English as a Second Language (commonly called ESL). They generally are state-supported universities that have large non-English-speaking populations in their states.

- ✓ **Is financial aid available to noncitizens?**

Tests

Most colleges require a standard admission test — the SAT or ACT — of all students who apply. Some waive the requirement for noncitizens with solid academic records. If a college wants you to take one of the tests, it will tell you when and where the test is administered in your country.

If your native language is not English, most colleges will require you to take the Test of English as a Foreign Language.

Recommendations

The letters of recommendation that accompany your application are just as important for you — maybe even more important — as for U.S. residents. Colleges that are unfamiliar with the schools in your country may not find out as much about you from your academic record as they would like. They'll look to the recommendations to tell them more.

It is essential that you get recommendations from people who know you well and can write persuasive letters about you. But beware. Gushing praise is meaningless. It tells a college nothing about you. Find someone who can write objectively and clearly about your strengths and, if you have any, your weaknesses. (More about recommendations in Chapter 9.)

If you know someone at a college in the United States who might be willing to write a recommendation for you, ask him to do it. He'll have a good idea of what a college admission office wants to know about you.

Tests are close to home

You'll likely have to take a test — maybe more than one — to get into a U.S. college. But the good news is that you won't have to travel far to take it.

Every college has its own test requirements for non-U.S. citizens and will let you know what it wants in its application materials. If your native tongue is not English, you'll probably have to take the Test of English as a Foreign Language (TOEFL). Some colleges may require the SAT I or ACT — admission tests used widely in the United States.

All these tests are given several times a year at testing centers around the world. Typically, you must register four to six weeks before the testing date.

Information on the TOEFL, SAT, and ACT is available at the U.S. government advising centers in other countries and at some U.S. embassies and consulates. You can also find this information at high schools operated for American children. And a college requiring a test very likely will send you information about it.

If you can't find test information anywhere else, you can write to the following addresses:

TOEFL   TOEFL Services
PO Box 6151
Princeton NJ 08541-6151

SAT   College Board SAT Program
PO Box 6200
Princeton NJ 08541-6200

ACT   ACT Test Information
PO Box 414
Iowa City, Iowa 52243

Transcripts

Even if your country's schools operate very differently than U.S. schools, a college will want some evidence of your academic record. In the U.S., such a record is called a high school transcript. The transcript lists the courses you took, the grades you earned, and your scores on standard tests. Your school undoubtedly has such a record about you. A copy of this record must be included with your application.

And with that advice, you're ready to go. On with your search. Turn to whatever subject in this book interests you most and start reading.

Part VI
The Part of Tens

The 5th Wave — By Rich Tennant

"Believe me, Miss Wilcox, this isn't the type of school you can just waltz in to, pick up a degree, and waltz out of again."

In this part . . .

Here come some lists. This list-filled part has become a tradition in ...*For Dummies* books. The books end with lists.

This part is called The Part of Tens because the lists are supposed to be lists of ten things. Some of my lists are. Some aren't because I couldn't think of ten things to include. But regardless of their length, they're good lists for you to have. They tell you important things in a neat little package. They're good for quick reading. Or ignoring. Whatever. This is your book.

Chapter 19

Ten Essays Heading for the Circular File

Relax. No one is going to toss your carefully prepared essay into a trash can. I am using a figure of speech, or a state of mind, used by admission officers to describe essays they don't even need to bother reading. After the first sentence or two, they can tell whether the essay is doing its job.

During the busy season, in February and March, an admission officer reads 40 to 50 essays a day. She longs for the essay she can savor, that makes her appreciate every carefully selected word, that makes her walk to a colleague's desk and say, "You really should read this." She doesn't get too many of this kind. The other kind can be read very quickly. She probably does so 40 times a day.

I'm about to give you a list of essay topics almost guaranteed to produce the glazed-eye effect for an admission officer. The following are topics that provoke her to drop the essay — somewhere — and move on. This list is not an all-inclusive list. Many other essays fill the same role. But you'll get the idea.

I Learned Self-Confidence as Homecoming Queen

Homecoming queen — or king — is a nice thing to be. The title shows that you're very popular among your peers. And popularity is a desirable trait in a college student, but it's not the first thing an admission officer looks for. And she definitely is not reading your essay to find out how popular you are. Homecoming queen is a school-related activity. List the title in the section meant for activities.

An attempt to make your royal reign a meaningful experience by describing how it built your self-confidence is not likely to grab the reader's attention and earn your essay a high score. An admission officer will have already read at least 73 essays on the confidence-building theme — probably five that same day. Some of them will be truly good essays because they will show self-confidence springing from a crucial point in the writer's life. Homecoming queen, however, won't make the cut.

I Knew I Would Get a 4.0 GPA

By the time an admission officer picks up your essay, he knows you have a 4.0 grade point average. The GPA is the first thing he looks for on an application. And he suspects your 4.0 was a struggle. Earning all *A*s in a college prep high school curriculum is not an easy task. Telling him the details of your struggle and how you finally conquered the odds to come home with a perfect report card doesn't add a thing to his knowledge about you.

The admission officer is reading your essay to find out about you. Don't tell him something he already knows.

My Busy High School Life

This essay falls into the category known as *regurgitation*. Regurgitation is not a nice word, and it's not meant to be. Many, many students (who haven't read this book) try to impress a reader by describing the many, many things that they have done during four years of high school. These students fail. They've done nothing but regurgitate information found in other places on their application.

Regurgitators lose points for several reasons. These individuals show an absence of imagination by writing a catch-all autobiography that covers many points, but focuses on none. They display an inability to follow instructions because this type of essay fits none of the commonly suggested categories. And they commit the cardinal sin of telling an admission officer things he already knows.

I Made Who's Who as a Sophomore

An admission officer won't be impressed if you made *Who's Who* as a sophomore. Many commercial enterprises, such as *Who's Who,* solicit good students for the purposes of making profits. (In this case, profits come from selling books.) If this is the most meaningful experience you can come up with for an essay, it doesn't say much about the rest of your life.

My advice? Don't even list these commercial operations on your application as awards. Very few admission officers look at them that way.

My Trip to Europe

These essays are known in the business as *travelogues.* They usually don't score many points. A veteran Ivy League dean of admission once said that essays about summer trips tell more about the parents' taste in vacations than about the student.

However, if an event occurred during your summer in Europe that you can relate as a significant experience, it could be the subject of a fine essay that ranks high on the scorecards. If you encountered a person who had a profound influence on you, that would work. But a mere description of your trip will be among dozens of such trip descriptions that won't get a second glance in the admission office.

I Learned Leadership as a Drum Major

Leadership is a valuable quality. Colleges covet such a quality and reward it in the admission process. And they know drum majors are leaders, responsible for 100 or more peers as they try to march and play music at the same time.

When an admission officer reads your list of activities, she sees that you were in the band four years and made drum major as a junior. She's impressed. She gives you points for commitment to an activity and leadership. If this was your most meaningful high school activity, say so down there where the application asks about your most meaningful high school activity. And explain why you feel that way.

But when the admission officer picks up your essay, she doesn't want to read about your band leadership again. She wants to read something new. You're regurgitating. Stop it. Fast.

My Struggle to Be Valedictorian

See all the other items in this list. Struggling to become a valedictorian is akin to overcoming odds to get a 4.0 GPA. Making valedictorian is a fine accomplishment. The work involved is a great struggle. But is your honor something a person reading your college application would know before he gets to your essay? Darn right. It's the R-word. Again.

My Summer at the Beach

A travelogue is a travelogue, regardless of the traveler's destination. See "My Trip to Europe" in this list, and look at the suggestions about discovering something during your summer travels that will work nicely as an essay topic.

I Don't Know What to Write About, So . . .

Believe it or not, some students try the following approach: They begin an essay with a list of notable accomplishments — similar to a regurgitation — and then ask the reader to pick one. What follows is a brief description of each accomplishment — giving the admission officer the opportunity to read the one that interests him most.

If you're thinking about writing such an essay, forget it. This method is what used to be known as a cop-out. If you're unable to pick one experience to write about, don't expect the admission officer to do it. That's not his job.

Your essay's role is to convey information about you — how you think, how you write, how you set priorities. A pick one essay does none of these things. This type of essay is a waste of your energy and time. An admission officer will not waste much time on it.

I Won't Tell You about My . . .

Come on. Do you think that an admission officer is a fool? Of course not. So you wouldn't think about writing an essay that starts with the words "I won't tell you about my . . . ." Although some of your friends might.

Some ill-advised students begin an essay by enumerating things they're not covering. They list all the achievements they could have written about — but didn't. Then they announce "The Topic They Chose."

This is a not-too-subtle way of reminding the reader of all the things the student has accomplished in a short but brilliant life. The reader does not need to be reminded. He does not want to be reminded. He takes off points if he has to be reminded. Intentional regurgitation is the worst kind.

Okay, Now What?

Now that I've shot down your ten best ideas for an application essay, I guess I ought to give you some suggestions about what you should write. Better yet, I'll let an expert do the suggesting. Gary Ripple is dean of admission at Lafayette College, a fairly selective school in Easton, Pennsylvania. I recently asked him THE question: "What are you looking for when you read an essay?" Then I turned on a tape recorder to capture his answer. His answer is very similar to the answer I've received from many of his colleagues in the admission business. The following are Ripple's words (the emphasis is mine):

"We're looking for *insights*. We're looking for glimpses of one's individual *characteristics*. We're looking for what they might *bring* — what they might *contribute* — to our institution. Grammar and basic writing style are essential."

Chapter 20

Ten Terms Colleges Hope You Never Know

*T*he information in this chapter is not really secret stuff, although it may sound like a secret code to you. The following are words and phrases that college officials use when they talk to each other. Officials try their best not to use these terms around you, but occasionally they slip and you hear one. Now when that happens, you'll know what the officials mean.

Admit-Deny

Admit-deny is one of their favorites. Officials say *admit-deny* all the time to each other. The term is shorthand jargon to describe the process of setting priorities on students who have been accepted to a college.

Say a college needs 500 freshmen. Every year, about one-third of the students who the school accepts eventually enroll. So every year the school must accept 1,500 applicants to get 500 freshmen. After this college notifies the 1,500 that they're accepted, it uses financial aid packages to try to entice the 500 that it wants most. The most attractive students get the most generous money offers. The lowest on the priority list get the dregs, not even their full need.

The bottom one-third likely includes some students who can afford the college without aid. But many students can't. The bottom one-third also includes students who have been admitted, but not offered enough money to be able to enroll. In effect, they've been denied admission. Thus, you might hear an admission officer saying to a coworker, "This kid's an admit-deny."

Application Score

All colleges use some kind of scorecard to rate their applicants. This scoring is the only way that the schools can keep a record of how the thousands of applications they receive each year compare to each other. Every college has its own scoring system. Some use a numbered scale, say 1 to 6. Others use letter grades, such as A to E. Some colleges may use numbers to rate students' academic records, and letters for other parts of the application. A student then becomes a 2B, or a 3A, or whatever.

The important thing for you to know is not how colleges keep score but that they do keep score. Each component of an application gets its own rating. Then the scores are combined for a total that often determines a candidate's fate. Typically scores are assigned for

- ✔ **Grade point average** (using the college's weighting system)
- ✔ **Rigor of high school curriculum**
- ✔ **SAT or ACT results**
- ✔ **Activities** (with emphasis on leadership)
- ✔ **Teacher/counselor recommendations**
- ✔ **The essay** (the essay often gets two scores, for writing and content)

Customary practice is for an application to be read and scored by two admission officers. If your total score is above a certain level, you're automatically in. If your total is too low, you're gone. Most students are in the middle, between the two cutoffs. These middle students' applications go to the admission committee for a decision.

Bidding War

A *bidding war* is similar to trying to get the best deal when you buy a new car. You take your best financial aid offer to another college and ask if it can do better. Financial aid officers don't like to encourage bidding wars, but admit they exist. And because good students are in such high demand, this tactic often works.

Building a Class

Building a class is a term for maintaining diversity in the student body. The diversity can take many forms — racial, ethnic, geographic, economic — depending on a college's priorities. The diversity often takes forms that can't be labeled. For example, a college may want to diversify among high schools in its area, making sure that it has students from each. Or a college may have a gender-balance policy that says that neither sex can be more than 52 percent of the student body. (More on diversity in Chapter 9.)

As the final decisions are made on who gets in, all these policies and priorities come into play. The freshman class is built to reflect these policies/priorities. Decisions sometimes are made, reversed, and then reversed again to build the proper class.

Buying Freshmen

The term *buying freshmen* represents the corollary to admit-deny. A college that gives its best financial aid packages to the students it wants the most is sometimes said to be buying freshmen. The term often comes as an accusation from officials of other colleges that would like to have the same students. But some financial aid folks use the term to describe their own activities.

At a recent convention of financial aid officers, the director at a prestigious southern university described his system of giving the best aid packages to the best students. Then he said, with a tone of pride, "Let's face it. I'm buying freshmen."

Flag

When an admission officer says "flag," she could be talking about the stars and stripes fluttering above the campus. Or she could mean something that affects her job. A *flag* is a mark on a piece of paper (maybe it's just a colored dot) added to an application to indicate that the application is special. Children of alumni get flags. Students with special talents get flags. Underrepresented minorities get flags. A flagged application is removed from the common pool and considered separately.

Gender Balance

Many colleges want a sexually balanced campus. These schools don't want a preponderance of either males or females. Some admission offices work under rules that come down from the president's office requiring each sex to be, say, at least 48.5 percent of the student body.

Gender-balance policies occasionally can cause some scrambling. If an admission office has carefully built a class of what it considers the college's best applicants and then counts and finds that it has 12 too many men, the admission office suddenly must toss out 12 men and accept 12 more women. Or vice versa.

Legacy Rating

Children of a college's alumni are called legacies. Legacies get an advantage at the admission office of their parent's college because of their parent's affiliation with the school. The size of the advantage usually is determined by the *legacy rating*. This is a rating of the parent's generosity in alumni fund drives.

An application from a legacy is flagged and sent to the alumni office, which returns the application with a score on whatever scale the college uses. Applicants with the highest legacy ratings often are admitted without regard to the rest of their application. Lowest legacy ratings take their chances with the rest of the applicants.

Need-Based Admission

Many colleges say they consider a student's wealth in the admission process. Others do it without saying so. When the financial aid well starts to run dry, colleges consider students' ability to pay in determining who gets in. The colleges try to avoid an admit-deny situation, in which they'll accept a student who has no chance of paying the bills.

So, procrastinators who apply late in the process run the risk of having their family wealth considered along with their grades and essay. (You don't have to worry about ending up in such a situation because you're taking this book's advice and mailing your application early in January. Plenty of financial aid will be available for you.) Ability to pay also can be a factor in taking students from a Wait List because, by then, all of the college's aid money could be gone.

The use of money as an ingredient in the admission recipe is often referred to as *need-based admission* or *need-conscious admission.* More accurately, the term should be need-based denial. Those who have a financial need don't make the cut.

A few years ago, Wesleyan University in Connecticut became the first to announce publicly that it would consider money in some admission decisions. Others soon took the same public step. In a 1994 survey by the National Association for College Admission Counseling, 19 percent of the 584 colleges responding said that they make some need-conscious decisions. Of this 19 percent, nine out of ten are private colleges.

Preferential Packaging

Preferential packaging is a more polite — and more common — term for buying freshmen. The students who are most attractive to a college get the best financial aid packages. The difference could be a better split between grants and loans, a larger discount off the sticker price, or more aid than students need to meet their financial need.

Any way that financial aid is packaged, the better students get more money. In that same 1994 survey by the National Association for College Admission Counseling, 54 percent of the colleges responding said that they use preferential packaging.

Chapter 21

Ten Abbreviations You Wish You Never Saw

- ▶ ACT
- ▶ CSS
- ▶ EFC
- ▶ ETS
- ▶ FAFSA
- ▶ FFEL
- ▶ FWS
- ▶ PLUS
- ▶ SAR
- ▶ SAT
- ▶ TOEFL

*W*hen you're happily ensconced as a freshman in the college of your choice, you'll be ready to push the college-finding process out of your mind and get on with the rest of your life. Among the stuff you'll quickly try to forget are a bunch of letters that run together in your head as unintelligible gibberish.

When you're thriving as a college student, you won't remember whether EFC is a need-based grant or that test you took on a Saturday morning. But before you get to that point, keeping all the abbreviations sorted out is a good idea. Here's a list to help you remember. (You can forget this list later.)

ACT

ACT stands for *American College Test*. Owned, appropriately enough, by the American College Testing Program in Iowa City, the ACT is one of the two major college admission exams administered nationally. This exam tests students' knowledge in specific subjects and then combines the subject scores into a composite score. A perfect score on the ACT is 36. The national average each year hovers around 19.

Almost all colleges require applicants to take either the ACT or its competitor, the SAT. And although most colleges prefer one or the other, they will accept either. The ACT is the test of preference for most colleges in the Midwest and South and is especially big in Iowa.

CSS

You'll read the initials CSS often while you're looking for money. They stand for *College Scholarship Service.* The CSS is a division of The College Board that deals with scholarships and all other financial aid.

You're most likely to encounter CSS — several times — if you apply to one of those picky colleges that wants more information to determine your financial aid eligibility. You'll be required to ask CSS for a copy of its new form, called PROFILE. Then CSS will send you a customized copy of PROFILE with your name, address, and Social Security number printed at the top. (Despite the fancy appearance, PROFILE is just another application form.) You will be required to fill out PROFILE and return it to CSS, along with $14.50 for each college receiving your information. You don't have to submit the form, but you should if you want to get some of those big tuition discounts. Submitting the application is probably worth the $14.50.

CSS also publishes an excellent guidebook, updated every year, offering advice on how to figure the cost of your college. This guidebook includes explanations of financial aid programs. The book's title is *College Costs & Financial Aid Handbook.* Most neighborhood bookstores have copies of this publication in stock.

EFC

EFC stands for *Expected Family Contribution,* the amount you and your family are expected to pay for a year at college — any college, regardless of cost. (The difference between the college's cost and your EFC becomes your need. You can find more on all that in Chapter 11.)

The E in EFC — the expectation of what you should contribute — comes from a computer. This computer crunches the financial information you submit on your application through a formula devised by the federal government.

The result becomes your EFC for all federal aid programs. Some picky colleges want to calculate another EFC for giving away their own money in discounts, so they make you submit another form. (See CSS in this list.)

ETS

ETS is what people in the construction business call a subcontractor. ETS stands for *Educational Testing Service,* which is a company based in Princeton, New Jersey, that prepares, administers, and scores tests. ETS's best-known product is the SAT, which it operates under a contract with The College Board (the SAT owner). ETS also handles other items, like the National Assessment of Educational Progress and the Law School Admission Test which, at this point in your life, you don't care about.

When you took the SAT, your test booklet came from and was returned to ETS. The report of your SAT score came to you from ETS.

FAFSA

This term is pronounced just like it looks: FAF-Suh. FAFSA stands for *Free Application for Federal Student Aid.* The FAFSA is the application that every student submits to trigger eligibility for federal government financial aid programs and many private programs. Colleges often use information on the FAFSA to distribute their own aid money.

The word free in the title is important. For 20 years, every student had to pay to have an application processed for government aid. (The charge was made by the processing companies.) In the early '90s, Congress said those fees must end. Nobody should have to pay to get government aid. Part of the deal with contractors now processing the information is that they can't charge fees. To underscore that fact, free became part of the form's title.

FFEL

FFEL (pronounced *Fell,* or, if you feel really daring, *Feel*) stands for *Federal Family Education Loans.* FFEL a new term cooked up by the U.S. Education Department to distinguish between different kinds of student loans. FFELs come from banks. The other kind, Direct Loans, come from colleges. The difference isn't important to you because you get the same amount of money (with the same repayments).

You'll see the term FFEL a lot in financial aid literature, so you should know that it's just another name for a student loan. You'll also see — maybe in the same sentence — the words Stafford Loan. Don't let these two terms confuse you. Staffords are FFELs. The terms are used interchangeably. Bureaucrats decided to say FFEL instead of Stafford Loan because they had a heckuva time turning Stafford Loan into an acronym. How do you pronounce "SL" anyway?

FWS

Your parents probably knew this one as CWS in their college days. Then, this program was College Work-Study, a program that provided thousands of campus jobs to let students earn spending money. It still does. But a few years back, the U.S. Education Department's Bureau of Name Changes decided that CWS should be Federal Work-Study. So now it's FWS. Nothing else about it has changed.

In FWS, the government gives money to colleges to cover 75 percent of students' wages in jobs on campus or in the community. Students must be paid by the hour and earn at least minimum wage. Only students who have a financial need, as determined by the government's computer, are eligible.

PLUS

The first name considered for this program was Mothers In Need of Urgent Support. But that was scrapped because the name wasn't considered to be politically correct. It didn't include fathers. And some bureaucrat didn't like the acronym MINUS. So this program became *Parent Loans for Undergraduate Students*, or PLUS.

PLUS loans are a way for parents to borrow some or all of that Expected Family Contribution. These loans are also a way to cover a gap, if your college doesn't give you enough financial aid to meet your full need. PLUS loans are available only to parents. That's why P is in the title.

Parents can get a PLUS loan for the difference between the cost of their kid's college and the total financial aid package. Say Old Siwash costs $15,000 and offers you $7,000 in aid — your parents can get $8,000 in a PLUS loan. But they must start repaying the loan immediately. The interest rate, adjusted every year, can't go above 9 percent. The interest rate has been hovering around 8.4 percent.

SAR

SAR stands for *Student Aid Report*. The report is a light blue printout, usually about four pages long, from the computer that processes your Free Application for Federal Student Aid (FAFSA). The SAR contains many goodies:

- ✔ Your Expected Family Contribution for all government programs. With your EFC, you can figure your need.
- ✔ The size of your Pell Grant, if you're eligible for one.
- ✔ A list of colleges getting your information, and the opportunity to add more.
- ✔ A regurgitation of all the information you submitted on your FAFSA and the opportunity to correct any wrong estimates.

File your SAR in a safe place. The financial aid office at your college may want a copy for its records. And your SAR will be nice to have in the future — you can show your kids what financial aid reports were like in the old days.

SAT

For 60 years SAT stood for Scholastic Aptitude Test, the best-known admission exam required of students trying to enter college. SAT now stands for a family of 18 tests coming from the College Board under the SAT name and umbrella.

One of those 18 tests is called SAT I. The SAT I is what everyone used to know simply as the SAT. Designed to measure the aptitude of high school students to perform college work, the test is given to more than 1 million students every year. Almost all colleges require applicants to take the SAT I or its competitor, the ACT. Some colleges prefer one test over the other, but most accept either test.

A perfect score on SAT I is 1600. The lowest possible score is 400. For years, the national average hovered around 900, but that's changing as The College Board recalculates its scoring system. Now, the national average probably will be around 1000.

The other 17 SAT tests are called SAT II. The SAT IIs are tests of students' knowledge in specific subjects — English, math, chemistry, German, and so on — usually taken at the end of a high school course in each subject. For years, these tests were called Achievement Tests. Now, they're called SAT II.

A Bonus for Students from Abroad: TOEFL

You already have ten items in this list, so you don't have to read this one, particularly if English is your native language. TOEFL stands for *Test of English as a Foreign Language*. And the test is exactly what its name says. TOEFL comes in three parts, testing your ability to read and write English, plus understand spoken English. (More on TOEFL in Chapter 18.)

Most colleges require TOEFL for students — from the U.S. and other countries — whose principal language is not English. At some colleges, a minimum TOEFL score is required for admission. At others, a low score sends you to a class in English as a second language.

Chapter 22

Ten Big Mistakes in College Planning

*N*obody's perfect. Everyone makes mistakes now and then. But one of the reasons you're reading this book is to reduce the number of mistakes that you'll make in planning for college. Right? This chapter reminds you of some mistakes that many of your friends may make but that you'll know to avoid.

Some mistakes grow out of myths perpetrated by people who have heard something and believe it because a friend said that it's true. Some mistakes occur because people don't want to spend the time or energy to avoid them. Those people are, well, a little lazy.

I warn you about these mistakes at various other places in this book. Here, you get them all together in one handy list.

Applying to a College That You Haven't Visited

I like to compare going to college to getting married. Both actions require the same type of commitment, but going to college is not quite as permanent. When you apply to a college, you're asking to spend a portion of your life with it. Would you marry someone you never met?

You can find out a lot about a college by reading catalogs and brochures, and talking to people who have been there. But you can't find out all about a college that way. Some things you just have to experience for yourself.

Every college is a community where students learn from each other, as well as from professors. Visiting a campus, talking to students, and observing how they live give you a genuine feel for that college community. After you get a sense of the place, you, and only you, will be able to decide whether it's the kind of place where you would be comfortable. (Much more advice on campus visits appears in Chapter 6.)

I know several bright students, with outstanding high school records, who became so unhappy at college that they transferred after their freshman year. The common mistake among them was not checking out the campus before they applied. Transferring may not be as traumatic as getting a divorce. But to a college freshman transferring can seem pretty awful.

Visiting a Campus without an Appointment

Don't gamble when you visit a campus to see whether it's right for you. Don't take chances that you might get the information you need. In other words, don't show up unannounced. You'll be gambling that the people you need to see are there and have the time to talk with you.

The most important person to see on a campus visit is an admission officer. He's the expert at dealing with, and providing information to, potential applicants like yourself. You want to leave a favorable impression at the admission office, in case you apply. So call at least two weeks before you arrive to schedule an appointment at the admission office. Then build the rest of your visit around that appointment. (You can read more on campus visits in Chapter 6.)

You also should consider appointments at the financial aid office and, if you are leaning toward a certain major, with a professor in that area. Yes, a parent who's accompanying you can call for the appointment. But the people you visit will have a better impression of you if you make the call.

Ruling Out a College Because You Can't Afford It

This probably is Mistake Number One in terms of how often it's made. How many friends have told you that they won't even think about Colleges X, Y, and Z because they cost more than $20,000, and there's no way that they can afford the price? A lot, right? Have you shown them this book yet?

The number one fact to remember about money, despite what your friends say, is this: You probably won't pay the sticker price. How's that for calling the point to your attention? And I tell you all about paying less in Chapter 11.

As you read this book, keep in mind that two of every three students attending four-year colleges in the United States aren't paying the price advertised in directories. They're getting some kind of financial aid. Many are getting aid in the form of discounts off those five-figure prices.

Thinking That You Won't Get Financial Aid

This is part of the same can't afford it myth. Students know that financial aid is out there somewhere, but they don't think that they can get it. These students operate under the misconceptions that financial aid is

- ✔ Only for the poor.
- ✔ Unavailable to families making more than $50,000.
- ✔ Limited to families living in public housing.

You may be laughing, but it's true. I've heard otherwise intelligent students say those things. I've heard some parents say them, too.

Yes, some financial aid is designed to help the poor. Pell Grants, for one, go only to low-income students. But at the other end of the spectrum is the financial aid that goes only to very smart students, regardless of what size paycheck their parents bring home. They're the students who get aid as an enticement to enroll at certain colleges.

Between those two extremes are billions of dollars — yes billions — given away each year to average, ordinary students who are neither very poor nor very bright. And you can trigger the process of getting some of that aid by filling out a simple form and putting it in the mail. (Much, much more on financial aid can be found in Chapters 11 through 15.)

Making Up Information

Don't make up information! Don't even think about doing it. Not even on a simple little question on an application form that seems meaningless. And resist any temptation to embellish your record with a few colorful, but inaccurate, items.

Colleges are built on a foundation of honesty. If the admission office discovers you are less than truthful about any part of your application, you'll be dead in the water.

Missing Deadlines

This seems obvious, but some people — yes even intelligent high school students — allow deadlines to slip out of their minds and go unmet. Then they have to plead with whomever set the deadline to give them a break.

You have better things to do than plead for a break because you forgot a deadline. If a college wants your application by February 15, get it in by late January. You'll not only make sure that the application is on time, but you'll also beat the last-minute rush and get more attention in an unhurried admission office.

Submitting a Messy Application

If messy is your chosen lifestyle, that's fine. If dirty socks — and other assorted items — piled on a dormitory room floor is your kind of living quarters, fine, too. Go for it. But sometimes you must adjust your lifestyle to get what you want. And if you want to get into college, messy won't make it at the admission office.

Social scientists have empirical evidence (if they don't, they should) showing that 943 of every 1,000 college applicants are neat freaks. Their applications arrive neatly printed in the latest word-processor font with not a blemish in sight. If you don't have a word-processor, typing — or even printing — is fine, but keep your work neat. Don't use that goopy white stuff to correct errors. And don't cross things out. Get another form and start over, if you must.

Messiness in a college application sticks out like a weed in a flower garden. And such messy work creates a negative impression on the people who have to read the messy stuff. The last thing you need is a negative impression of you at the admission office.

Kissing Off Recommendations

Not providing recommendations is another mistake that's all too common and can be hazardous to the health of a college application. Some students won't give any thought to a college's request for recommendations by a teacher and counselor. They'll take the forms to school, leave them with someone, and forget them. And the teacher or counselor will fire off a boilerplate, cliché-filled letter that does nothing for the student's cause.

Letters from teachers and counselors often are vital to decisions made in college admission offices. Especially in marginal cases, where a student is teetering on the fence between a yes and a no, admission officers will look at the recommendations more closely to find out things about a student that they won't find anywhere else. Sometimes the things they find out help the student. Sometimes they don't.

In this situation, you have some control. You can pick the people — at least the teacher — to write your recommendations. You can tell them things about yourself and your accomplishments. And you can explain why you're interested in the college. Then they'll have the necessary information to write recommendations that will help you. (Read more about recommendations in Chapters 9 and 10.)

Choosing a College for Its Reputation

A college has a good reputation for one reason: A lot of people like it. But you're not a lot of other people. And what other people like may not be the same as what makes a college right for you.

I'm not suggesting that you ignore other people's opinions. Seek out opinions and listen to them, especially from people you respect. Give them serious consideration. But the final decision on where to spend a portion of your life must be yours.

Yes, a college's reputation can be helpful in finding a job after graduation. And that's one factor to consider — but just one. Selecting a college solely on its reputation, without mixing in all the other items important to you, is a good way to wind up transferring for your sophomore year. (I discuss how colleges get their reputations in Chapter 3.)

Putting Parents in Charge

In selecting the right college, your parents are your advisers. They undoubtedly are wise advisers. Their advice should be accepted graciously and considered seriously. But your parents cannot, and should not, make the decision for you.

When you go to college, your parents stay home. Your life is what's on the line. You're the one who must become part of a college community.

If your parents seem like they want to take control of your college search, show them this book. They'll be hurting you more than helping. When you arrive for a campus interview, an admission officer wants to see you bring your parents along — not the other way around. Face the fact, Mom and Dad, your baby's a big boy or girl now.

Chapter 23

Ten Questions to Ask about a College

· ·

In This Chapter

▶ Who are the students?

▶ Is four years enough?

▶ How's campus housing?

▶ Who gives advice?

▶ Who are the teachers?

▶ Do AP credits count?

▶ What is the class size?

▶ How close is it?

▶ What's the crime problem?

▶ Does merit get money?

· ·

*T*he things that you need to know about a college, to make your right decision, can be determined only by you. Only you know what's important to you. I suggest a lot of items to consider in Chapters 2 through 7. And these suggested items certainly need to be considered. But the emphasis you place on each factor is up to you.

Following is a list of some important items for handy reference. You can run these pages through a copier and stick them in a notebook or glove compartment for your campus visits. The pages will remind you of questions you want to ask. Some are questions that you will ask of other people. Some are questions that you will ask yourself.

Are These My Kind of Students?

Are you a computer nerd or a party animal? A neat freak or a mess? A liberal or a conservative? Do you like your music measured in megadecibels or soft and sweet? Is a campus dominated by fraternities and sororities appealing or a turn-off?

You probably fall somewhere between all of those extremes. But each college campus has its own personality. Some types of students are more prevalent on some campuses than others. The only way you can know how you fit in with the students is to visit the campus and spend some time with them. An overnight in a dorm is an ideal way to find out who these students really are and whether your lifestyles mesh.

Can I Get a Degree in Four Years?

Whether you want a degree in four years is up to you. If you're a cost-conscious person, you probably don't want to stretch it out to five or six years and spend more money. But if you want to do it in four years, can you?

Can the college guarantee that all the courses needed for your degree will be available when you need them? Or do they have overcrowding problems? Are students being shut out of courses, forced to wait until next year because classes are full? This factor could be important when your bank account dwindles, or your debt mounts, four years from now.

Can I Live on Campus? If Not, Where?

If you look forward to life in a dorm as part of your college experience, you'll want to know your chances of getting into one. What percentage of the freshmen can dorms handle? How — and when — must you sign up? How much money must you put down to hold a place? If all freshmen are not guaranteed dorm rooms, how do you improve your chances? Any competent admission officer can answer all of these questions.

If you're shut out of a dorm, what are your options? Does the college have a list of off-campus housing? Are facilities on a housing list inspected by college officials? Is any kind of approval required to get on a list?

If a college official shrugs off these questions or says she doesn't know the answers, ask for the name of a person who does. You're entitled to this information. If you can't get satisfactory answers, perhaps this is not the right college.

Do Faculty Advisers Really Advise?

Advising systems vary considerably from college to college. At some schools, the professor assigned to advise a freshman sits down with the student, discusses goals, and helps the student devise a schedule to meet those goals. On other campuses, students make out their own schedules and take them to an adviser for rubber-stamp approval.

The best answer you'll get to this question is from other students. Admission officers know how the system is supposed to work. They don't necessarily know how it really works.

Do Professors Teach Most of the Classes?

To sit down with 100 students in a large, required introductory course on principles of economics and find that the person in charge is a graduate student who's just a few years older than you can be frustrating. It's even more galling if you come into the class totally ignorant about economic principles, looking forward to learning something from professorial wisdom, and a professor is nowhere in sight.

Unfortunately, on many campuses, freshman-level introductory-type courses are turned over to teaching assistants, typically graduate students working for a Ph.D. in the field. Professors concentrate on upper-level courses — and their research.

On other campuses, I'm happy to report, full-fledged faculty teach every course enthusiastically. Graduate assistants, if they exist, do other things, like help professors with research.

 If it's important to you to have real professors in your classes, ask how it works at the college you're visiting. Ask the students, especially those majoring in the field that you're considering. The percentage of courses taught by graduate students is not a statistic the admission office usually publishes in its brochures. At colleges that have no graduate school, and award only bachelor's degrees, the problem doesn't exist. With no graduate students, there can be no graduate teaching assistants.

What About My AP Courses?

If you stayed up nights dealing with those Advanced Placement chemistry and history courses and prepared diligently for the AP exams, you naturally want credit for your work. At most colleges, you'll get it. But to be sure, ask.

The purpose of the Advanced Placement program in high schools is to earn college credit in advance and to be eligible to move on to tougher stuff when you get to college. A college typically will give you credit toward your degree for any AP exam in which you score a 4 or 5. (The scoring range is 1 to 5, with 5 being highest.) Some picky schools want only a 5. Others are more flexible and will accept a 3 or a 2. If the college literature doesn't spell out its AP policy, ask. An admission officer should know the answer.

Is there a limit on AP courses for credit? Can you score high on five AP exams in high school and enroll as a college sophomore? At some colleges, you can. Such a possibility can save you a year's tuition.

AP courses also help in the admission process itself. If your high school offers AP courses, an admission officer wants to see you taking some of them. The more, the better. That shows you're ready to accept the challenge of college-level work.

How Large (or Small) Are Classes?

Are freshmen required to take large introductory courses where a professor lectures from a stage and students are identified by number? Or are all classes small enough that teachers know students and you can get some individual attention? Ask this question of admission officers, professors, and students. Better yet, drop into a class or two and see for yourself. Be sure to sit in on a required introductory course.

How Often Can I Get Home?

How often do you want to go home? That's a question you should ask yourself early in the planning process. Do you need to be home every other weekend to see what the crowd is up to? Is once a month enough? Or can you tolerate returning to the nest only at Thanksgiving, Christmas, and spring break? Do you care, one way or the other? When you answer the question, you may be able to eliminate a lot of colleges because of their location.

How Safe Is the Campus?

Crime statistics is something colleges must tell you. Since 1991, federal law requires colleges to publish an annual report of campus crime statistics. The report also must describe security measures that are in place. And this report must be distributed to all students and applicants.

Some colleges go a step further than the law requires and give the crime report to all students who inquire about applying. If you haven't seen the report from a college, ask the admission office for a copy.

And then ask about what the report really says. Campus crime statistics can be misleading. If a campus is served by its own police force and the surrounding area is covered by local municipal police, the statistics could reflect only crime on the campus itself — and say nothing about the neighborhood.

Safety is another topic on which students' opinions are valuable. Ask those who live there how safe they feel. Ask about crime in the area. Ask about security in the dorms. A uniformed security guard may be standing at the dorm entrance, but does he check IDs of all who enter? When you get answers to these questions, toss them into the mixing bowl. If security is important to you, give them a high priority in your decision.

Is Merit Money Available?

If you read Chapter 14, you know that not all financial aid is distributed because of financial need. Even affluent students can get money because of who they are. In the jargon of the financial aid folks, it's called merit money. That's because this money is handed out for merit, not need. (Don't confuse colleges' merit money with Merit Scholarships, which is the name of a program rewarding outstanding high school students.)

Merit money has become more prevalent in recent years at high-priced private colleges competing with each other for the best students. The more attractive the student, the more likely that merit money will come his way. If you are a good student, ask either a financial aid officer or an admission officer if the college awards aid based on merit. Asking the question will impress them because it shows that you know what you're talking about.

Chapter 24

Ten Reasons Why a Two-Year College Is Worth a Look

. . . .

In This Chapter

▶ Convenience

▶ Cost

▶ Curriculum

▶ Faculty

▶ Attention

▶ Improvement

▶ Stepping stones

▶ Living

▶ Money

. . . .

*R*ight now, almost 6.5 million students are attending two-year colleges. Can 6.5 million students be wrong?

The two-year college — known in various places as a community college, junior college, or technical college — is the fastest growing segment of education at any level, kindergarten through Ph.D. Almost half of today's college students took their first college course on a two-year campus.

As you make your lists seeking your right colleges, the two-year option certainly is worth a glance. A two-year school may be your safety valve school. Such a school may turn out to be your college of choice. This chapter lists reasons you should think about attending a two-year college.

Convenience

Almost everyone in the United States (except in very rural areas) is within a 30-minute drive of a two-year college. Most people are even closer. Every state now operates some kind of community college system and tries to put a campus in every decently populated county.

Getting to a community college is like driving to a grocery store. You get in the car, go, park, attend classes for a couple hours, and drive home. Your expenses are a gallon of gas and, maybe, a buck to park. That's convenient.

Plus, almost all two-year colleges offer a large portion of their classes in the evening, which gives you the convenience of becoming a college student while keeping your full-time job.

Low, Low Cost

Forget $20,000. A $2,000 annual tab is too high at most two-year campuses. The average tuition at the nation's two-year colleges in 1995–96 was $1,387. And that's for full-time students. You usually have the option of paying by the course or by the credit hour so that you can work your way into life as a college student slowly and inexpensively.

After you pay the tuition, you'll encounter no other costs, except your books and that gallon of gas a day. No room and board. No fees to support the football team. No shipping and handling.

A two-year school education is a full-time education for maybe $1,500 a year. If you are a cost-conscious person, money is a big reason that a two-year college should be on your list.

Don't exclude Bigbucks U. because its annual cost is $26,000. You may get $24,500 in financial aid, and the cost to you would be $1,500. But if all else fails, Convenient Community College may be your low-cost backup.

Varied Curriculum

At a typical two-year college, the curriculum is varied and flexible. Course offerings are split roughly 50-50 between the traditional academic stuff (for students going on to four-year schools) and employable skills, such as computer repair, dental hygiene, and travel agentry (for students seeking a job or career change). The full course menu actually can be much larger than at four-year colleges.

The two-year colleges also can easily adjust their schedules to meet students' needs. If the demand arises for more word-processing classes, expert word processors can be hired from the community to teach them. If some students want to study Latin, a Latin teacher will be found.

Undistracted Faculty

Professors at two-year colleges have only one job — to teach. They're not distracted by more rewarding sidelines, such as research and writing journal articles, as are many of their four-year-college brethren. When a biology professor walks into a classroom at Convenient Community College, the students know that his complete professional attention that day will be focused on teaching biology.

Two-year colleges are not stuck in the tradition of four-year colleges that insists a Ph.D. is necessary to teach college courses. Many faculty members at two-year colleges are working experts in their field, holding full-time jobs in addition to teaching a course or two. Anyone who has knowledge — and the ability to share that knowledge — can become a two-year-college teacher.

A Way to Overcome the Bad Times

If you have a high school record that not even your mother can admire, a two-year college is the place to erase it. Just about all public two-year colleges (88 percent of them are public) use open admissions, which means anyone with a high school diploma or its equivalent can enroll. Those *C*s and *D*s on your transcript won't block your way.

When you earn all *A*s in your two years at a community college, you'll have an impressive record for an admission office on a four-year campus. If Flagship State sees you handling college-level work well, it will forget those bad times you had in high school.

Easy Access to Four-Year Colleges

The paths are well worn. Thousands of students make the trip each year. After earning an associate degree at a two-year college, they move on with little difficulty to work for a bachelor's degree on a four-year campus.

Four-year colleges look to their two-year siblings — especially neighbors in their area — as sources of good students. They're well aware what students can do if they complete the two-year curriculum. Transferring to a four-year college with a two-year degree can be the easiest way to get there.

In most cases, you still must fill out application forms to get into a four-year college. But even that task is disappearing. In some states, agreements between four-year and two-year schools allow students who pass prescribed courses to move on automatically. This transfer process is just like moving to another campus of the same college. These automatic-admission deals are known in the trade as *articulation agreements*. If you hear about one at your community college, you're in luck. If you don't, ask.

One Way to Enter a Step at a Time

If you're not sure that you're ready for the rigors of being a full-time college student, you can test the waters gradually, one toe at a time. Take one course at night and see how you do. The next semester, take two. Before you know it, you'll be earning *A*s and ready to charge into the student business full-time.

Financial Aid

Yes, even two-year college students are eligible for financial aid. All the rules are the same as for any other student. You can get a Pell Grant or a SEOG or a Perkins Loan to attend Convenient Community College just as you can at Bigbucks U.

The one big difference between Convenient Community and Bigbucks U. is simple: the cost. If you've read Chapter 12, you know that eligibility for most financial aid is determined by a magic number called your need. And your need is calculated by finding the cost of your college and subtracting the amount your family is expected to pay. If the cost of Convenient Community College is $1,100 a year, you'll need a pretty low Expected Family Contribution to have a need. And public two-year colleges don't give tuition discounts.

Glossary

Words You Should Know

. . . .

*A*s you search for a college and the money to pay for a college, you'll read and hear some words that people think you know. Maybe you do know them. Maybe you know them in other contexts, but not how they're used at college. So here's a list to help you understand the words you should know.

Articulation: An agreement between a two-year and four-year college in the same state. This type of agreement gives two-year college students who complete required courses automatic admission to a four-year college. This term is used as in, "You'll be happy to know we have an *articulation* agreement with Flagship State."

Coed: Serving both sexes, as in, "I'm living in a *coed* dorm." This term is used less frequently in its old, politically incorrect context to describe female students on a two-gender campus.

Degree: An award signifying successful completion of a course of study. An associate degree is earned in two years. A bachelor's degree takes four years or more. Master's and doctoral degrees are earned after the bachelor's degree.

Discipline: (1) A quality demanded by a football coach; (2) a penalty imposed for violation of a rule; (3) a field of academic study, such as history, psychology, chemistry, and math.

Environment: (1) A college's location, as in, "We offer you an idyllic rural *environment*"; (2) the student body, as in, "We pride ourselves on a diverse *environment.*"

FAF: (obsolete) A form once used extensively to qualify for financial aid. Some people still say FAF when they mean something else.

FAFSA: The form currently used to qualify for federal government financial aid. This term stands for Free Application for Federal Student Aid.

Gap: (1) A clothing store; (2) the difference between your parents' expectations and your grade-point average; (3) the difference between your financial need and your financial aid.

GRE: Graduate Record Examination. The SAT for graduate schools.

Institution: A college. Often used by a college to describe itself, as in, "This *institution* meets every student's financial need until our money runs out."

Interdisciplinary: An academic major that takes courses from several subject areas, such as English, history, sociology, and math.

Jock: A college student who receives a merit scholarship because of athletic merit.

Legacy: A student related to a graduate of the college (usually the student is a son or daughter).

Liberal arts/liberal studies: Other names for an interdisciplinary academic major.

List-padder: Usually a derogatory term used by college admission officers to describe a student who joins many organizations but contributes to none.

Merit: (1) An adjective identifying an excellent high school student, as in Merit Scholar; (2) the reason financial aid is awarded without regard to need, as in, "We have met your need, now here is some *merit* money."

Need: The difference between the cost of your college and the amount a computer determines you are able to pay.

Need-based: Refers to money you get because of your need, as in, "These grants are 100 percent *need-based.*"

Need-blind: The concept of admitting students to a college without considering their ability to pay, as in, "We're *need-blind* until our financial aid budget is spent."

NIP: An abbreviation for *Not In Profile.* This term identifies students who are not included when a college calculates its average SAT score. NIPs often are jocks and legacies.

Package: (1) Food from home; (2) a store that sells alcohol to go; (3) the total financial aid you are offered.

Pell: (1) A former U.S. senator from Rhode Island; (2) a no-strings grant to low-income students.

Post-graduate: Refers to courses taken after a bachelor's degree is earned.

Profile: (1) A publication by a high school describing the school's curriculum and grading system; (2) an extra form (PROFILE) that you must fill out to get financial aid from picky colleges.

Quarter: (1) One-fourth of a football game; (2) a coin that, when matched with three just like it, will start the laundry machine; (3) a period during which courses are offered, as in, "I'll wait to take zoology in the spring *quarter.*"

Rigor: The quality a college admission officer looks for in the high school courses an applicant has taken, as in, "There's no *rigor* here. Not an AP on the list."

ROTC: *Reserve Officers Training Corps.* A program operated at colleges by the Army, Navy, and Air Force to train students as potential officers.

SAT: (obsolete) A test once used extensively to measure a student's potential for doing college work.

SAT I: A test now used extensively to measure a student's potential for doing college work.

SAT II: The name given to 17 tests that measure a student's ability in specific subjects.

Solids: The courses that carry the most weight on a high school transcript. They are English, math, science, social studies, and foreign language.

Stretch: The act of applying rigor to a high school course schedule, as in, "We're looking for students who *stretch* themselves."

Undergraduate: A student trying to get a bachelor's or associate degree.

Underrepresented: Often used to describe minorities. The term usually includes all minorities except Asians.

Yecch: A word uttered by a college admission officer when reading an essay about a student's summer vacation.

Yield: The percentage of accepted students who enroll at a college.

Yourself: What you should be at all times during the college admission process.

Appendix

The Mull List

· ·

Questions to Ask Before Picking a College

1. **Where is the college?** Do you like life in small towns or big cities? Or in the suburbs? Or way out in idyllic rural environments? Colleges are everywhere. You have a choice.

2. **How large (or small) is the college?** Can you thrive on a giant campus with 20,000 or more students and many social and cultural opportunities? Or, would you feel better at a smaller school where everyone knows everyone?

3. **Do you want to leave home?** Do you look forward to college as a chance to cut the ties and flee the nest? Or do you want to start from the security of your home?

4. **How far do you want to go?** If you plan to leave, do you need to get home every weekend to check out the old crowd? Or can you tolerate returning to the nest only at Thanksgiving, Christmas, and spring break?

5. **Do you like the opposite sex?** Would you be more comfortable on a campus where your sex is dominant, or where you're in a minority? Or would you prefer an even balance between the genders? All three kinds are out there.

6. **Can you get in?** Do you have a reasonable shot at meeting the college's minimum academic criteria. Is your grade-point average in the range that the school considers acceptable? Are your test scores at least in the school's middle-level range?

7. **How much do you have to pay?** Forget the published sticker prices. Two-thirds of today's students are not paying the prices listed in directories. How much will a college expect you to pay to be a student? How much financial aid will you get?

8. **Does the college teach what you want to learn?** How strong are the courses in your field of study? What kind of vibes do you get from the professors who teach those courses? Go there and find out.

9. **Can you live with these people?** Does your personality mesh with the college's personality? Are the students the kind of people you'll be comfortable living with for four years or longer? Does the campus have your kind of social life? Check out the school in person.

10. **Can you get a degree in four years?** Will a college guarantee that you can get all the required courses in four years? Or is there a chance that you could get shut out due to overcrowding and be forced to pay for an extra year?

11. **Can you live on campus?** Do all freshmen get a room in a dorm? If not, what are your chances of getting one? And if you can't, what other living accommodations are available?

12. **How safe is the campus?** Read the college's report, required by law, on campus crime statistics and campus security measures. Then, when you visit the campus, ask students how safe they feel.

13. **How large (or small) are classes?** Are freshmen required to take large courses where a professor lectures from a stage and students are identified by number? Or are all classes small enough that teachers know students and you can get individual attention?

14. **Do professors teach?** At some colleges, freshman introductory courses are turned over to graduate students not much older or wiser than you. Ask professors and students. See whether they give you the same answer.

15. **Do advisers advise?** Do faculty advisers talk with new students and about courses needed to meet their goals? Or do they just rubber-stamp a student's class schedule? Students will give you the best answer to this one, too.

16. **Can you get credit in advance?** Will a college give you credit for AP courses that you take in high school? What score do you need on an AP test to get credit? Is there a limit on AP courses that count?

17. **Are special talents rewarded?** Will your talent as a musician or actor or newspaper editor score points when a college considers your application? Could a special talent mean a special break in financial aid?

18. **Does the college consider finaical need while reviewing applications?** Is a student's ability to pay the bills a factor in deciding who gets in? Or are all applications considered without regard to financial need?

19. **Is merit money available?** Does the college give financial aid based on a student's academic ability? Do the best students get the best aid packages?

20. **Are you ready to borrow?** You'll probably take a loan to buy a car and a house. Is a college degree just as important to you? If you're a typical student, you'll have to borrow to pay part of your bills. Are you ready?

Index

(continued)

(continued)

WHY APPLY!?

Apply! is a unique CD-ROM that eases the arduous college search and application process by enabling students to use their personal computers to find, apply to, and pay for college. As typewriters become obsolete and harder to find, *Apply!* provides a stress-free solution. Students simply fill in applications onscreen, print out completed forms, and submit them to colleges.

Apply! helps ease the tension of the application and admissions processes by giving students the tools they need to easily and effectively find the right colleges for them and then complete the applications. Features of the software include:

- A college search database with information on more than 1,500 colleges.
- Exact duplicates of the applications to more than 500 colleges with the ability to fill in basic information just once!
- Information on more than 180,000 scholarships, loans, and grants.
- A financial aid area with an estimated financial need calculator and a student loan application.
- 30 days of FREE Internet access and a free copy of Internet Explorer.

Best of all, this truly innovative software is available **FREE of CHARGE** thanks to the generosity of national sponsors and the participating colleges. Do not miss the opportunity to order your free copy today!

EDUCATION TRUST
A SallieMae LENDER

The **APPLY! Education Trust** is the answer to the question, *"Now that I've been accepted, how am I going to pay for college?"* A partnership with Sallie Mae allows Apply Technology to provide the most comprehensive borrower benefits available with the most flexible, lowest cost, education loans you can find anywhere. For more information or a loan application, please call 888-888-3469.

**Visit *Apply!* on the web
www.weapply.com
or call 203.740.3504 to order.**

Please clip and mail to:
Apply! '98, P.O. Box 8406, New Milford, CT 06776-9848

YES... I want to order the free *Apply!* CD-ROM!

Name _____
Address _____
City _____
State _____ Zip _____
School _____ Grad Year _____

☐ **Windows**   ☐ **Macintosh**

IDGW
CPFD

Orders begin shipping in September, 1997.
Orders received after 3/1/98 will be considered pre-orders for *Apply!* '99.